Introduction

By Jerry D. Vickery

Retired Owner and Publisher of *The Easley Progress*

The purpose of this book is to share a literary treasure trove with acquaintances, friends, and admirers of Dr. Lloyd E. Batson. These published works, which appeared in *The Easley Progress* from 1999 to 2004, will also inspire and entertain thousands of readers who have not had the opportunity to read the works of this dedicated Christian servant.

Dr. Batson has a unique way of writing about ordinary daily experiences. Through his Christian insight, Dr. Batson turns these experiences into extraordinary inspirational, sometimes humorous, masterpieces for us to enjoy and relate to.

It was my fortunate fate to have served as Advertising Director, Publisher, and Owner of *The Easley Progress* for over three decades. During this time I became acquainted with Dr. Batson. Serving Pickens First Baptist Church as Pastor for thirty-three years, his realm of influence far exceeded the geographical area of the City of Pickens. Along with his jovial personality and benevolent attitude, he has been an inspiration to me along with thousands of others over the decades.

As I began writing this introduction for our book, I pondered on how I could describe this remarkable man and his life in a brief, concise, and accurate way. Shortly into an interview with Dr. Batson and his lovely wife, Joy, the answer came. In describing her husband, Joy emphatically exclaimed, "He loves people. He was always available if anybody needed him for any reason. This was a love. Nothing he did as a pastor was a chore. In fact, I don't know of anything he does that is a chore. He loves life."

What a wonderful tribute. There is no way I can say anything that would reach this descriptive pinnacle from the person who knows him best.

Lloyd Ellis Batson was born in Greenwood, South Carolina on June 22, 1924. He was the second son of Paul Otis and Eva Lyons Batson. A year after Lloyd was born, Mr. Batson, a Baptist minister, moved the family to Sumter County where he took the pastorate of Graham Baptist Church and served this congregation for the next thirty-four years. This church was eight miles out into the country from the city of Sumter, right alongside the Pocataligo River swamp. Lloyd, along with his older brother and four younger brothers, grew up exploring the swamps of Sumter and Clarendon Counties.

In addition to the general ministries of a loving church to Lloyd in his growing years, two major events in his life were administered by the Graham

Dr. Batson and his lovely wife, Joy.

Baptist Church. He was baptized in 1932 and ordained to the gospel ministry in 1947. He was one of the first in that area to have a woman sit on the ordaining council. She was a foreign missionary who had grown up in and was a member of the Graham Baptist Church.

Continuing to serve Graham Baptist Church as pastor, Lloyd's dad moved the family six miles down the road, still along the swamp of Pocataligo River, to Alcolu. Here, in Alcolu, Lloyd's dad took on a second pastorate at the Clarendon Memorial Baptist Church. Mr. Batson continued to preach at Graham Baptist Church in the Sunday morning worship service, and preached at Clarendon Memorial Baptist Church in the Sunday evening service. Although Alcolu is where Lloyd spent most of his young years he did not change his membership from Graham Baptist Church until he became pastor of Pickens First Baptist Church years later. Alcolu was a small sawmill town near Manning. D.W. Alderman and Sons' Co owned the sawmill. According to Lloyd, they were wonderful people, and not just because most of them were members of his Dad's church, Clarendon Memorial Baptist Church.

Being an enterprising young fellow, Lloyd started a paper route in the Alcolu community from scratch at the age of ten. He had an agreement from the afternoon *Columbia Record* that if he could sell ten subscriptions to begin with he could have the route. Obtaining that goal, Lloyd set out delivering the paper six days a week for the price of fifteen cents a week per subscription. He would earn five cents a week per paying customer.

Continuing the paper route for several years, he also worked full time during the summer at the Alderman and Sons' company store. Sometimes the workweek would stretch into seventy-two hours, but Lloyd didn't care. He was young and loved to be around people. Many of the store customers would let only Lloyd wait on them when they came to shop.

He vividly remembers that at this time there existed a starkly segregated society. That was the way it was, but Lloyd didn't actually realize it until later in life. He loved everybody regardless of race or economic status. With a big smile on his face, he told me, "I probably was the only person in that village that apparently was welcome in every home, black or white. They were all my friends."

Lloyd went on to say, "On one occasion I was invited to a wedding for two of my black friends. I was the only white person invited and the only white that attended. I rode my bicycle out to the home where the wedding took place out in the yard. Upon arriving, I found the yard was jam packed with guests. I took my place in the back, but the crowd politely opened up a small alley so I could see the ceremony. In fact, I had the best view of anyone except those sitting on the front row. I was the first one down after the ceremony to congratulate the couple and shared big hugs with both the bride and groom."

Lloyd attended Manning High School, four miles from Alcolu, and it was during this time period that he actually began what would become his lifelong career. It wasn't something he had planned, but happened by accident. His Dad was scheduled to preach a funeral in a nearby community, but became ill and didn't have time to get a replacement. He asked Lloyd to do the service and explain to the family and bereaved friends why he was there. At fifteen years old, this would give Lloyd the opportunity to take the family's Chevrolet sedan out alone for the first time so he eagerly agreed. He didn't know the name of the family but knew he could do the service. He had already been speaking on numerous occasions in church. He had also been with his Dad enough to know how a funeral was supposed to be conducted. In recalling the event Lloyd said, "The people had never seen me, but I told them I was there to represent my father; he had gotten sick and he had asked me to come in his place. I asked them if it would be all right for me to do the service and they opened up their arms. I, fifteen years old, conducted that funeral for somebody I didn't know and they sure didn't know me, but I never got a better reception in my life. My Dad was so well respected in that area they would have accepted anybody he had sent. It would be some time before I knew I was called to be a minister, but I got my feet wet."

Lloyd graduated in 1941 from Manning High School. Entering the then North Greenville Junior College that fall, he graduated Valedictorian in 1943 with an Associate of Arts Degree. North Greenville Junior College was an easy choice for Lloyd mainly because it was affordable, according to him, and his Dad was an alumnus.

After graduating from North Greenville in the middle of World War II, Lloyd volunteered for duty in the army. He reported to the assignment center at Fort Jackson in Columbia. He was sent for basic training to Camp Wallace, Texas, near the coast between Galveston and Houston. This was a fairly new facility built in the marshes where they got rid of everything, according to Lloyd, except the mosquitoes.

It was here at Camp Wallace that Lloyd's life was going to change drastically. Lloyd had always gone to church wherever he found himself. It was not at all out of character for him to be hunting a church or a place to worship the first chance he had after arriving at Camp Wallace. The first Sunday he found a chapel on base and went in and joined the worship service. At one place in the service, the Chaplain prayed. The prayer seemed to go on and on for a very long time. Trying to be reverent, but getting a little restless, Lloyd opened his eyes and began to look around at the group that had assembled. Almost immediately, his eyes met the eyes of a beautiful sixteen-year-old young lady who was also looking around. This beautiful young lady, Joy, from New Mexico, who, seven years later, would become his wife, was also the daughter of the Chaplain! Lloyd says that if Chaplain Barrick had known what his long prayer would lead to he probably would have shortened it considerably.

Lloyd served his military war duty in Europe with the 87th Infantry Division. After the war, and after receiving his Bachelor of Arts Degree from Furman University in 1947, and the Bachelor of Divinity Degree from the Southern Baptist Theological Seminary in Louisville, Kentucky, in 1950, Lloyd married Joy Louise Barrick on July 2, 1950, in Albuquerque, New Mexico. Lloyd began to work on his Doctor of Theology degree at the seminary, and teaching there as he did so. While at the seminary he served as pastor of two churches, Commiskey Baptist Church in Commiskey, Indiana, and Bear Creek Baptist Church near Scipio, Indiana. In 1956, he answered the call from Pickens First Baptist Church here in South Carolina to be their pastor. Early in his Pastorate at Pickens First Baptist Church, Lloyd, in 1957, received his Doctor of Theology degree from the Southern Baptist Theological Seminary. In 1987 Furman University honored Lloyd with the Honorary Doctor of Divinity Degree. He continued to serve as pastor of Pickens First Baptist Church for thirty-three years, retiring in 1989, and moved to Easley, South Carolina, where he and Joy still live.

I could fill several pages with all the honors bestowed on Lloyd along with all the activities he has been involved in and those he is still involved in. However, I think his example of a Christian life, his wonderful relationship with his lovely wife, Joy, for over fifty-nine years and the achievements of their two fine sons say it all.

I also think that as you read through these wonderful experiences you will better understand just how dynamic Lloyd Batson's influence has been on many of our lives. I am truly thankful for the opportunity to know him and work with him all those years at *The Easley Progress*. More than one time I had to call on him for help in restoring my faith, and he always came through. One column in particular was the column I asked him to write after the 9-11 attacks on our nation. This column can be found on page 34.

Dr. Batson's advice of "seeking identity with known strengths" was exactly what I needed to hear and led me to immediately seek out those strengths. I still use this advice and will be ever grateful for it.

Dr. Batson, thank you so much for your inspirational gifts. You provided encouragement for our many readers and myself each week in years past. Now, with the publication of this book, you will provide inspiration for many generations to come.

Jerry D. Vickery

Cover
Photo of
Table Rock
taken by
Jerry D. Vickery

Joseph can fix it!
A Christmas Meditation

She was not yet four, one of my granddaughters. We were spending the Christmas in her home. On Christmas Eve she was carrying out a ritual of childhood, putting out food for Santa and his reindeer, arranging fruit, carrots, and cake in precise order. Her father, noting all this, asked her, "Aren't you going to give Jesus anything?"

Without hesitating, she replied, "Yes, I am. I'll give him my broken flashlight."

"That's what you are going to give Jesus, something broken?" her father, with evident disappointment, queried.

"Yes, Joseph can fix it," the little lady, more discerning than many adults, declared to her father and went to get the broken flashlight.

Whatever Christmas is, it is a powerful drama affirming and celebrating that the angel had it right that long ago night as he, in the midst of the bright glory of the Lord, startled shepherds with the announcement, "I bring you tidings of great joy which shall be to all people." A baby had been born, unto them and to all people, a baby who is, and forever will be, Christ the Lord. Peace and good will among people, the angels declared. Impossible, no! Possible, yes! God had acted in favor of darkened humanity with the glory of his son come to earth!

A drama whose central and enabling character was, and is, Jesus, a drama still being played out as the new millennium is so near at hand! Look at this magnificent drama. There is the central character but there is the supporting cast. Who is the supporting cast? All who have received the true joy of Christmas!

Years and centuries have come and gone, but true Christmas never has gone and never will! The central figure is still alive, and so are the renewable supporting cast members, those who have received glad tidings, who celebrate joy, those who find the peace of a true encounter with the real Christmas.

That true Christmas, the Christ child, the Savior, the Lord, has enlisted his supporting cast to herald to a broken world filled with broken lives, families, values and dreams that glad tidings are still to be heard and to be had!

There are millions who are involved in God's great drama of joy and gladness, set in motion that first Christmas, and unfolding today. Can't we who are supporting cast members in God's great drama of true Christmas take seriously our role and deal honestly with the vast brokenness around us, and do it with gladness and great joy?

Yes, Kelsey, keep on believing there are Josephs all around who are identified with Jesus and can deal with broken things and fix them, in the name and power and love of that true Christmas, the one the angel declared to be Christ the Lord!

Written by Lloyd E. Batson
Published Christmas 1999

Behind a Door

Many doors I have opened in my time, in a thousand and one places, and circumstances. While doors work generally the same way, all designed for a person to get from one side of a wall or barrier to the other side, I seldom find opening a door purely a mechanical or routine move on my part.

Opening a door, wherever it is, regularly sets loose some sort of excitement, some run of my imagination, some "guessing game" as to what I will find on the other side. Could doing so ordinary a thing as opening a door be ordinary to me? It seldom is.

I have no idea how many doors I opened yesterday, but let me use one to illustrate my door opening adventures. I had taken my younger son to the airport so he could return to Union College in Schenectady, New York where he is a professor. I had told him I planned to stop on my way back to visit a person in the hospital. So, when I did stand at the hospital door I was already anticipating how I would find my friend that I had not seen in a good while. His health had been bad for a long time and many difficult things apparently had been happening to him recently.

For a moment, I stood before the door, my door opening "excitement" off and running. Hearing no answer to my knock, I gently (though my wife says I don't do anything gently!) opened the door. There my friend was, surrounded by imposing machines of varying sorts with their tentacles known as tubes affixed to the pale person in the bed. The restless sleeping was not easy to watch.

I stood for a bit at the foot of his bed, hurt by the trouble he must be having. I breathed a quiet prayer, "Please, God, don't let things be so hard on him."

Then, in a kind of jerk, he waked with wide, staring eyes. Suddenly, those eyes came alive with brightness. The broadest smile I think I ever saw creped across his face and he called me by name. What a welcome!

Well, many things happened. I stayed a couple of hours, by his desire and mine. Nurses came in. An evening meal was brought, and he ate as we talked, ate surprisingly heartily. Two pleasant folk came to visit. They had not come to see me but I, too, received the goodness of their caring.

Am I writing something ordinary? Well, I open many doors but what is beyond them is not ordinary for me. Beyond this door was the surprise of a welcoming smile from a very ill person. There was the warmth of obvious gladness that I had come. The conversation was simple in that neither of us needed to "put on airs" with the other. We talked of many things - even grandchildren! The talk of the difficult journey finally leading to the hospital bed was not morbid or burdensome, only informative.

We could talk of what might lie ahead as two friends might, easily, without fanfare, with no need to gloss over anything.

The physical door had opened. Then naturally and beautifully another kind of door opened, the door to the mind, the heart, and the soul. I could hear, among voiced feelings and concerns, my friend speak of a simple, certain faith in the Lord, a faith that had the force of pushing way down the list the importance of unknowns and uncertainties. I could hear a voiced faith that rose higher than opinions and feelings of others, or even the two of us.

My prayer on departing was for my friend, yes, but just as much for myself. It was for me almost as if I had two voices, one speaking to God about my friend, the other silently thanking God for what I had found beyond the door I had opened two hours before.

So, is opening a door mechanical or routine for me! Not this one. And not many others.

Written by Lloyd E. Batson
Published January 26, 2000

"My gravy got loose"

Ah, what a meal! Turkey and all the fixings! Carefully prepared festive dishes. Excitement of the family being together, feasting at the holiday gathering! Every space at the table taken, with family members trying to be patient while everybody got a chance at every dish.

Suddenly, a wail from my four-year old grandson! "My gravy got loose," he cried. Every turned eye saw the calamity. He had loaded his plate, carefully shaped a mound of mashed potatoes, made a hole in the middle of the mound and poured gravy therein. The thinnest side of the potato mound gave way and the gravy rushed out to spill over all his food. He was heartbroken. His gravy had gotten loose! Spontaneous laughter from around the table did not help.

Our nation is currently in the throes of the normal practices and processes of election of a president gone awry and many are confused and wailing. I do not pretend to know how we should handle this mess, or what ultimately will be the impact of it. It is a bit naive, I know, but I have been thinking about the parallel of my grandson's problem with our infinitely more serious national problem. Our gravy has gotten loose and made a mess! What do we do now?

For one thing, we must know we cannot put it back like it was, or pretend the mess did not happen. We have to make the best of it and learn from it if we can. Charges and counter charges as to who, or what, was responsible will not solve the "loose gravy" problem. I watched my grandson get upset, survey the situation, look aghast at beans, beets, and corn floating around in gravy, and after making some momentary attempt to undo the mess, finally decide that good gravy is still pretty good with about anything. He then, with gusto, set about enjoying his dinner. He apparently had decided he would get nowhere holding a grudge against a potato mound that gave way. He would learn from whatever went wrong and plan a better way to shape the mound for the next feast. In the meantime, he would be glad he still had the gravy.

Our nation is not perfect, and never will be, because imperfect people make it up. But, it still is the best there is! To use Miles' "loose gravy" problem, we have made an untidy mess but the "gravy" is still good. Let us learn from this mess and make preparation for doing better next time.

Written by Lloyd E. Batson
Published December 4, 2000

Camped out in my mind

It was Sunday afternoon, December 7, 1941. I, seventeen years old, had been a college student just three months, having gone to North Greenville Junior College in Tigerville, South Carolina in September from Alcolu, South Carolina. College had been a new experience, moving away from home, adjusting to an entirely new environment of learning, work, meeting new friends, and enjoying every moment! Nothing seemed intimidating to me.

While I was not a ministerial student, I had found a challenging and enjoyable activity. On Sunday afternoons, after eating our something less than exciting meal in the college dining room, some of us often would go up into the hills above school to some home in what was sometimes called the Dark Corner of South Carolina to conduct a worship service or give some kind of program. We walked, of course, none of us having an automobile (and besides the roads weren't very good).

Sunday afternoon, December 7, 1941! We had walked four miles up into the hills (we usually said "mountains"). It was an exceptionally exciting experience. The folk of the home in which we held the service welcomed us warmly and had invited numbers of neighbors to join us. We sang, prayed, I made a stumbling attempt at preaching (My, I wish I could hear now what I said!). I have preached many thousands of times since then but my memory has held that attempt at sharing the Word of God as a blessed and treasured experience.

We stayed with the wonderful folk some considerable time, simply enjoying their warmth and receptivity. Reluctantly we left to go down the winding road of the "mountain." The four miles back seemed so much shorter than going up. Our walking sometimes turned to skipping. We laughed and sang (my voice sounds so much better reverberating through the woods and hills than it does in church!).

As we got near to the campus, up the road starting near Woods Store (the one and only shopping center in Tigerville - meaning the one general store there!) we saw three excited students running to meet us. We thought that they might be wanting to hear about the service up in the hills. Instead, we heard the shouting of "The Japanese have bombed Pearl Harbor! The Japanese have bombed Pearl Harbor!"

Ecstasy turned to somberness! As far as I knew, I had not the foggiest notion of what and where Pearl Harbor was. The students had heard the news on the radio. By the way, in 1941 radios were scarce on the North Greenville campus. As we walked from down near the Woods Store up the road to the college campus we talked about the startling development. Intuitively we knew that war was at hand! We did not know what to make of it but we knew our lives had suddenly changed!

Up into the hills we had gone, joyfully, to share Good News. Now I knew, with no capacity to take in the magnitude of that infamous day and happening out yonder somewhere in the Pacific, that I would be involved in something I knew nothing about, something dealing not with Good News but with the ugliness of human nature, something evil called war!

I would indeed serve two and a half years in active military service, plus one year of enlistment in a reserve corps prior to active service. My war field would be in Europe with the 87th Infantry Division.

Strange what you remember, but it is indelibly fixed in my mind. As I neared the campus, carrying the somber word I had heard a few minutes before, a thought camped out in my mind, "That Good News you spoke about up yonder to those mountain folk, will it be true to you in war and see you through?"

December 7, 1941, a day to remember - as long as I live. And, by the way, the answer to that question that came and camped out in my mind is "Yes!"

Written by Lloyd E. Batson for his grandchildren
Published December 7, 2000

Singing, just do it

During World War II, I served with the 87th Infantry Division in Europe, with the artillery of that division. At one point, sometime early in 1945, Chaplain Ben Erickson, a Swedish Evangelical, a delightful and committed minister, needed somebody to play the portable organ for the worship services he conducted.

After searching and finding nobody, Chaplain Erickson found me, I who had had a few piano lessons earlier in my life. So, I began to go with the chaplain on his rounds, driving a jeep stenciled with the words Sky Pilot across the front. I had a great time. The chaplain and I became good friends. I helped find and set up meeting places, encourage attendance at the services, carry needed equipment, etc.

A part of my responsibility was to play for the services that black, folding, Estey organ we hauled around. One Sunday morning we had set up in a barn, a part of which had been destroyed with artillery fire. Our big guns were firing not far away. Some German shells were coming in nearby. A lot of noise was in the air. But we were having church in the barn. Sitting on a funny shaped bale of hay, I was furiously pumping away on that organ and singing with all my heart the announced hymn in that thin red book we were using.

I can feel it now. How he got there without my seeing him I do not know, but the chaplain, who had been to my right as I faced the gathered men, laid a hand on my left shoulder. As I turned toward him, Chaplain Erickson, with less than religious exasperation, said to me, "Batson, either play what you are singing or sing what you are playing!'

For good or bad, mine or others around me, across the years I have not let the Chaplain Ericksons in their various forms deprive me of the joy of sharing in the worship and praise of God. Singing, while my skills and talents in music have been terribly short, has always been of great importance to me. Congregational singing is one way I have to express my feelings about God and what he means to me. So, whenever singing is going on in church, I sing. Skill and beauty of voice is not as important as participating. I hope for you, whether you have a lovely singing voice or not, the special joy that comes only from singing your faith - Please, please, don't let the lovely voice of somebody standing by or near you intimidate you. That lovely voice is no more important to God than yours as you raise it in praise.

Just the melody, or something approximating melody, of singing is good for the believer, but how much more meaningful can our singing be when we pay attention to the words we voice and allow them to express, with understanding, what we feel. I've started noticing the words I use in singing more than I ever did, and it has been good for me. I recommend such a practice to you.

Something akin to a miracle happens in congregational singing. I sing, you sing, others sing, and somehow a beautiful spirit of fellowship steals across the singers, making me a part of all others. Singing, good, bad, or in between, draws folk together. It's great!

Chaplain Erickson, I wasn't much, but I was all you had. And we had fun and served the Lord together, didn't we? And I am still singing - the best way I can!

Written by Lloyd E. Batson
Published January 24, 2001

Church in the Grocery Store

Where have you been?" my wife asked when I got back from an errand on which she had sent me (I guess I actually had been gone longer than my errand should normally take).

"I have been to church," I answered.

"Church? I thought you went to the grocery store," she more than slightly chastised

"I went to church at the grocery store," I replied, smilingly, I think. Of course, I was jesting, but not totally.

Well, there was some more conversation I won't include here.

A question to her led to further conversation, the question being, "Why can't you go to church in the grocery store?"

At the grocery store, or store of any kind, or for that matter nearly everywhere I go, I meet and enjoy people I have known for years, and I meet strangers, and often get acquainted with them. I do that at church. Why should anybody be any different away from church? Isn't he or she the same person whether in church or in "you name it?"

In church one enjoys seeing his or her fellow worshippers. That shouldn't change wherever one is. In church a person normally tries to be nice to strangers who may be there. Why shouldn't that be so in a grocery story? In church, a person tries to portray basic values important to him or her. Why would that be different in a store? In church a person is pleasant to people who are nearby -unless it happens that person is a neighbor or another member with whom she or he has had a run in! That for sure is one-way church and public places are alike -bitterness and alienation are the same in church and out! In all candor, I have on occasion been witness to some unpleasantness in church that made me wish I was in a store or just somewhere else.

Can't the beautiful warmness of friendship and love be experienced in a store as in church? The "et ceteras" of this simple thought could go on and on. Don't mistake me; I don't suggest a store is a church! I do suggest, however, as I believe, that church doesn't mean much if a person can't take church to the grocery store, or at least be the same person there as he or she is at church, expressing the same love for God and respect for people God loves (and that is everybody!).

I like "to go to church" in the grocery store! I hope I see you there sometime.

Written by Lloyd E. Batson
For *The Easley Progress' Friday Edition*
Published February 16, 2001

Is there something else you need to know?

She was a wonderful lady, one of those elegant Southern ladies of culture, well educated, a musician, and a Presbyterian. She lived across the street, and actually had the same house number on her doorpost that I, her neighbor, had on mine (in Pickens at that time the numbers mattered nothing - the postman delivered mail to the person, not the house number!). Though I was a Baptist minister, she considered me her pastor, and I did help conduct her funeral at her departure.

This sophisticated, intelligent and delightful person finally got old and had to go to the local nursing home. I always visited her when I went there. In time she began on occasion to be less than fully aware of reality.

One day I stopped to see her. She was sitting in her wheelchair, sad looking, in something of a trance. Her roommate, in the other wheelchair, was sitting as glumly. Not liking anybody to be sad, I bounced into the room, stood by her wheelchair and inquired, "Well, (here I called her name), how are you today?"

She drew back, looked at me whom she had known for years, and asked, "And who are you?"

My answer was, "I am Lloyd Batson. Did you ever hear of him?"

"Oh, yes," she replied.

"What did you hear about him?" I asked, a dangerous question, by the way.

"Oh, I have heard so many wonderful things about him that it makes me want to fall in love with him."

That other elderly lady, who had not spoken, now proclaimed, loudly and clearly, "That's not what you told me!"

That exchange, though hilariously funny to me, is reflective of a serious factor in human relationships. There nearly always is another side to what we hear, or at least some important insight that could help us in our reaction and interpretation. We rarely know or hear the whole story about anything, even though we tend to react as if we had.

So many reactions and actions are based on one side of a story, which story is often a prejudiced one, even inaccurate or wrong. I have seen many complications arise when a person does not know about other facts of a given situation and does not bother to try to learn and understand them. This kind of stuff creates problems in organizations, in work situations, in individual relationships, even in churches.

Regularly I have to tell myself that before I form opinions or take actions about something I hear, or think I discover, I had better make sure that I understand there may be some other things I need to know. There often are some mitigating factors that if I knew them might influence my reaction and understanding.

Thank you, two elderly ladies, now in glory. Many times you still bless me! And instruct me!

Written by Lloyd E. Batson
Published February 23, 2001

Learning to live with things that have died

I drive a 15-year-old car, and am proud to be able to do so.

Many things have died on my car. Like the thing that hollers when the lights are left on or the keys are left in the switch. Like the radio, and the tape player. Like the cruise control, and a few other "little" things. My wife doesn't like to drive my car because she likes, and wants, the kind of things that have died.

The fact is I like my car. I have adjusted to every one of the missing things. Besides, my car's motor is powerful and runs smoothly, and the ride is great. Any new car fever has died, in part because my capacity to buy a new car is dead. Besides, I like the "almost nothing" car taxes on a car this old, and the lower cost of car insurance.

I have learned, pertaining to my car and a lot of things, to live with the things that have died because I have found so many things that still work wonderfully.

I think one of the chief things any person in his or her life has to do is to learn to live with things that have died, and I am not now talking about things on an automobile. Here I mention, as examples, only a few of many, many things that "die" and require learning how to deal with such.

I never learned to type, and my desire to learn has died. A mistake! And what a nuisance! My wife has agreed to type my handwritten things (she says I never learned to write legibly either!). In this case, I have learned to try to be just nice enough to keep her in good enough humor to type what I hand her! Major adjustment!

Many a person has missed an opportunity to do something helpful for somebody and lives to regret it. That opportunity has "died." But what do you do? Worry yourself silly about it? You just try harder to be alert not to miss another opportunity - even to seek one out.

An opportunity for a better job is lost? Giving up and staying miserable isn't good or productive. Do your crying and be done with it; then try to enjoy and to benefit from the job you do have until you do get a better one.

Miss a friend who moved away? Or died? You can't replace that one, but you can enjoy the memory you have. And you can make a new friend.

One of the hardest areas of learning to live with something gone is when a mate dies. Hurt, sorrow, loneliness are there every time you turn around. But one can, and must, discover his or her own life needs to go on. Adjustments have to be made sometimes with difficulty, but a lot of living can, and must be, discovered.

Self-respect can die when a person has committed a terrible sin. How do you adjust to that? Seek forgiveness, even if such seeking hurts, and be sure to do the necessary self-forgiveness (that's often terribly hard to do).

You can discover a good life, believe it or not, if you want to.

The list goes on.

Back to my car. I have learned to live with things that have died because the rest of the car is in such good shape. The motor is unbelievably smooth and dependable and the ride is good (and the horn is loud!). I have learned (as my wife has not!) not to major on the things that are wrong with it, but on the things that are right and still functioning.

In things more important than an old car, you can learn to live with things that have died, and you can best do it by majoring on what still works.

Written by Lloyd E. Batson
Published March 14, 2001

Blessed by a silhouette

The other day I walked, at some distance, by a window in a building I enter frequently. Through that window I saw the silhouette of a person whose friendship I have enjoyed a long time. While I actually saw only a silhouette, in my mind I saw the full person.

And that is the point of this reflection. Silhouettes can be special blessings! When one has had a pleasant and warm relationship or encounter with a person it takes only a partial glimpse of that person, a word from somebody about the individual, or even a thought to evoke a renewed pleasantry in recall of that person.

Memories, too, are silhouettes, with the capacity to bring alive again the fullness of people, events and things once experienced, to be treasured all over again. How blessed the person who has a large portfolio of memories!

Silhouettes come in all kinds of packages. Ideas are silhouettes, of things not fully seen, but are portrayals of what might be. A lot of the discoveries and inventions that have blessed so many appeared first to the seeker only in silhouette. Without the silhouette they might never have come to pass.

Involvement in the beginning stages of some effort to make a community a better place is a silhouette of what can be. Working with needy people in some kind of assistance program is a silhouette. One sees the distress of the needy folk and envisions a person taking new courage and hope because of what is being done.

School teachers do their best teaching when there are silhouettes before them. The shadowy beginnings in learning offer a glimpse of the joy and excitement of those who may truly learn and blossom under their guidance.

Parents, often frustrated by the hectic demands of meeting the needs of their children, may seem to be in over their heads; but let the silhouettes of the persons the children are - and will become - be regularly noticed and the picture changes to fullness and excitement.

Faith itself is a silhouette. As the Bible says, "Faith is the ... evidence of things not seen." Over and over again, while we do not see enough, or know enough, to understand how life will unfold, presently and in the after life, one can see the silhouette of faith not filled out, but assuring us of the fullness and victory already at work to be revealed later.

Multiplied are the silhouettes that have major roles to play in shaping the meaning of life for us.

The blessings of silhouettes are endless!

The more silhouettes you have in your life the more blessed you are.

Start looking!

Written by Lloyd E. Batson
For *The Easley Progress' Friday Edition*
Published February 16, 2001

A street corner praying

What caused me to notice the woman in the car I don't know. She was sitting in a car in front of the Pickens County Courthouse, facing the building. As I approached, walking on the sidewalk between her car and the courthouse, I saw her staring straight ahead, her facial expression depicting some kind of agony. She made no attempt to wipe away the tears streaming down her face. I don't think she ever saw me.

I didn't know the lady. I didn't know her problem. Instinctively I wanted to stop, to sit beside that lady, to share whatever it was that disturbed her, to comfort her if I could. I knew better than to intrude, I, a stranger. However, I confess I cried a bit inside myself as I walked on by to the street corner, breathing a prayer for that distraught person.

My prayer kept getting touched with a bit of curiosity. A few passing thoughts became barriers to my praying. Was she about to go into the courthouse to be involved in some kind of trial going on? Was she going to family court because of a domestic problem or going through a divorce procedure? Did she have a son or daughter being charged with something?

I stood on the corner, beyond the car, for a time, not looking back now but reflecting upon what I had seen and my reaction. Pretty soon I was praying for myself. My prayer for myself came out of my reflection upon what I already knew - that I didn't need to know what it was that troubled the lady. It was not right for me to speculate on what was wrong with her, especially to toy with the idea that she might have done something bad.

She may indeed have done something bad. She may indeed have grievous domestic problems. She may indeed have a heavy heartache about her children. But why should I even speculate about it? Isn't this the stuff that gossip is made of? I knew, what I had already known, that I could carry a person, whatever the problem, to the Father. He knows everything! And has not one bit of idle or speculative curiosity - only love and caring!

How easy it is for us, without evil intention, to sit in judgment on people we know and people we don't know. Before I react to somebody I need to remember there usually are reasons for a person doing or being what he or she does or is. Realizing that may make me kinder and more understanding. I do know, too, that curiosity, speculation and looking for "juicy information" can make mockery of the stance of caring or praying.

I went back to praying for that lady, appreciating the privilege that is mine to say, "Father, here is a person troubled about something. You know what it is, and you love her. Please, God, help her."

And you know what? I hope that when I am carrying a burden somebody will be more interested in loving me and praying for me than in speculating, with some curiosity, about what kind of mess I'm in.

It takes some doing sometimes truly to care or to pray!

Written by Lloyd E. Batson
Published March 30, 2001

You don't see many mules anymore.

A Pre-Easter Reflection

You don't see many mules anymore.

I grew up with mules. They plowed the fields and the gardens. They pulled the wagons. They were riding animals. They were barnyard friends. Mules were as important members of most families as the folk in the house. Mules, you couldn't do without them.

Funny what things you remember from more than sixty-five plus years that are as vivid as if they happened yesterday. When I was about ten, I was visiting my Grandpap Lyons, who had two skinny mules with which he farmed. One day, Edwin, my uncle only a little older than I, and I "saddled" the mules (if you can call use of a burlap bag a saddle) and took off on a cross-country ride. I couldn't sit comfortably thereafter for days. I would stand, hanging on to the mantelpiece, while mother kept putting salve on the raw undersides of a skinny boy too long in contact with a skinny-back mule.

I do not now know a single mule. Do you? The last one I knew belonged to one of the families of our church, who, after the mule got past usefulness on the farm, put the old mule in charge of the pasture and tended him lovingly in the barn until he died.

Now let me tell you about Miss Rosa Keith. In 1952, in the Commiskey Baptist Church, Commiskey, Indiana, where I was pastor while in the seminary, I decided one Sunday to find out what the congregation remembered of my preaching. So, in the morning service, I quizzed the congregation. What did I preach on last Sunday night? A whole host of hands went up. Last Sunday morning? Sunday night a week ago? Sunday morning before last? Etc. I was shocked and delighted that the congregation could go back an entire month. Then everybody got stuck on the Sunday before Easter. I kept prodding. Then, down to my left and three rows back, the elderly Miss Rosa Keith began to get excited. Miss Rosa, in the gray coat, could hardly contain herself while she struggled for the title of a sermon she obviously remembered. Then suddenly she stood up and called out loudly, "Don't forget the mule!"

Indeed, on that Sunday, Palm Sunday, I had preached a sermon entitled, "Overlooking the Colt!" In it I observed that people then, in their excitement about the appearance of Jesus, seemed not to notice he was riding a donkey, and thus they seemed to miss a declaration Jesus was making about who he was.

Don't forget the mule! The crowd seemed to be welcoming a king. But look what he was riding, a mule! No conquering hero on a white horse! A mule!

The lowly donkey was a servant animal. One will never fully understand who Jesus is until he or she notices the mule. Jesus came not to be the bread king they wanted and welcomed, one able to satisfy all the materialistic and nationalistic hopes, but to be a servant.

He was, and is, the Suffering Servant, bearing the hurts and ills of a broken folk, people alienated in their sins from God.

There, sitting upon a work animal, comes the Savior! This is who he is, a servant! It is only a servant that can minister to earth's real needs.

Don't forget the mule!

Nearly two thousand years have passed since Jesus rode on that servant animal. Christianity has enrolled myriads of followers. It is still easy for the world to be confused about what Christianity is all about. Unless it can see the servant nature of faith it cannot know who and what the Savior is.

Many followers of Christ are enamored of the conquering white horse syndrome. But the Christ rides a mule! And so must his followers!

You don't see many mules anymore.

Written by Lloyd E. Batson
Published April 4, 2001

Surgery I wish I could do

A few days ago I did drastic surgery! I had bought a new shirt I liked very much, put it on, and carefully tried to coordinate everything else I was wearing with it. I wanted to look nice at a special function where I was to be the guest speaker.

It was hard for me to enjoy the occasion because the label in that shirt collar kept irritating me with a rough corner on it. I am certain my speech was affected by the constant irritation (I don't always have such an easy explanation when I strike out in a speech or sermon!).

I came straight home, took the shirt off and cut out the label. That irritating label reminded me of two other shirts that had "scratching" labels I had tolerated too long and so I did surgery on those shirts, too!

I only wish I could do such surgery on other labels that bother me! In general, our society seems to be a "labeling" people. Has it occurred to you how easily we put labels on others? Or how many "labels" you might have had put on you?

We tend to look at people, programs, institutions, activities, and immediately "label" them whether we have adequate or justifying information or not.

No area is free from "labeling." Politics, religion, economic or social levels are fertile fields for labeling. The way one looks, dresses, speaks, behaves, or even walks invites "labeling." Churches get labels. Clubs do. Houses do. Restaurants do. Et cetera.

Clothing labels aside, labels in general irritate me, in part because they often are unfair. They are so freely stuck on people by others who may not know enough to be "judges." Labels applied to others often stem from one's own position or prejudice without any effort to understand or appreciate the integrity of others.

A problem with labels that you and I put on others is that generally those labels are barriers to any further understanding, communication, or possibly profitable relationships. Usually when we decide, for example, that a person is "so and so" we make that stance permanent, whether or not it is valid.

Often when we ourselves are wearing "labels" people put on us (and they do, you know), we aren't even aware of it and wonder about the coolness or rejection that is apparent.

I know I can't do much about labels people put on me, but I surely can try harder to avoid the easy practice of putting on folk or things some kind of label that may not even be right to begin with.

Labels! I wish I could be a label surgeon!

Written by Lloyd E. Batson
Published April 18, 2001

Life shouldn't have to be wasted

Thinking to stir a little life into what appeared to be a dreary day for her, I brightly asked the elderly lady sitting in her wheelchair in the nursing home, "Well, what worthwhile things have you done today?"

Before the elderly lady could reply, her roommate, one I thought was totally "out of it," spoke up, "Nothing! And I'll tell you something else. Tomorrow it'll still be nothing!"

After I laughed I nearly cried. It is sad for any person to believe that the sum total of the worth of living is "nothing." Can you imagine going to bed feeling that the day has been worth absolutely nothing and that when you get up in the morning it will be a repeat of the day before? Can you imagine the emptiness that is in the life of the person who feels that he or she can contribute absolutely nothing worthwhile to a twenty-four hour period?

Older people who for various reasons feel sidetracked into a routine, empty life can easily get to feeling they are now useless, useless to anybody, useless to themselves. Getting old is something everybody who still lives inevitably will do. Getting old should never be a cause of shame, though I know some who seem by word or demeanor always to be apologizing for getting old. What a ministry of great value nearly anybody who cares about people can perform by helping older folk keep a sense of self-respect and worth! I have come to appreciate greatly people who spend quality time with older people, who often feel worthless, and help them then get a little joy out of living.

It is not only in nursing homes, skilled care facilities, et cetera, where there are older people for whom life has become difficult and dreary. Every community has many elderly citizens living lonely lives, folk who either have been generally overlooked or who have allowed themselves to feel nobody cares much about them.

It's not, however, just the older person, sidetracked from life, that has trouble doing worthwhile things. Pathetic is the case of the person, young or old, who makes no effort whatsoever to contribute something worthwhile to life. Sad is the situation where one is hectically busy at many things but who has no inner sense of worthwhileness in much of it!

Back to older folk whose lives are hugely empty. Wouldn't it add some sense of worthwhileness to active people if at least part of their energy and involvement would include helping "isolated" folk, old or young, discover some sense of self-esteem, some personal joy, some personal sense of worth?

Take a good look around. There are a lot of older people everywhere. One day we, too, will be old. I think everyone is of worth! I hope when I get "old" somebody will help me focus on and act upon that!

"Tomorrow it'll still be nothing." Life shouldn't have to be wasted like that!

Written by Lloyd E. Batson
Published May 9, 2001

A reaching hand

A mother with a precious child recently sat directly in front of me in church. I had spoken with them before I took my seat. Early in the service the pretty little girl, about four or five years old, sitting on the end of the pew, turned and smiled enchantingly and I was warmed through and through.

A bit later she slipped her hand around the end of the pew and, without looking back, gropingly felt for my hand. I touched gently that beautiful little hand and felt somehow that a gift from God had just come to me.

A hand groping for mine! Unspoken joy and goodness as our hands touched! No exchanged words were needed, and none could have spoken more eloquently.

Time after time in my life I have needed, sometimes not even aware of how great was my need, somebody just to reach for me and touch me. I have had burdens made easier, repressed joy set loose, hope restored, an inner warmness of the soul kindled anew, a refreshing anointing of love, just by somebody who reached a hand to me. I have had, often just as I needed it, a kind of healing of an aching spirit as somebody reached toward me to touch me with some kind of gentleness, of caring, of simple blessing.

So, what is on my mind? That I think every person has a gift to give to others, the simple gesture, either literally or figuratively, of reaching a hand toward others. There are an infinite number of ways to bless and help others but there may not be one easier to do or more needed than to reach out a hand, in fact or deed, to touch people.

That night, in church, I am sure I heard the pastor's sermon, but my whole being, blessed by the groping hand of a child, moved to an awareness that there is another hand that always is reaching for me, the hand of God. Time after time the reaching hand of God has found my hand, and me, and done for me exactly what I have needed, and when I have needed it.

There is blessing and there is power in a gift every person has to give, a caring hand reaching to touch others.

Thank you, precious little girl. May all your life you use the gift you already have to give joy and help to others. And may all the rest of us, perhaps hardened and calloused by many years, discover we, too, have such a gift!

Written by Lloyd E. Batson
Published May 16, 2001

Don't put your ashes...

The scene is indelibly etched in my mind, a difficult Fourth of July moment.

I had gone, as I often have across the years, to stand in front of the Pickens County Courthouse to read again the words of the monument there honoring the four citizens of Pickens County who have been given the highest award for bravery our country has to give, the Congressional Medal of Honor. There may not be another county in the country with that many recipients of the Congressional Medal of Honor!

The names of the four men, two from World War II, one from the Korean Conflict, and one from the war in VietNam, are inscribed on flat stones in front of a standing monument which reads:

In Honor of All Men Who Paid the Supreme Sacrifice for Freedom in War

"Greater Love Hath No Man Than This That a Man Lay Down His Life for His Friends"

As I neared the monument I noticed three men standing in front of it, pointing to the inscription and speaking among themselves.

I stood back a bit, waiting for a moment to be there alone. The three men then walked away. As the last man passed the monument, he flipped the cigarette he had been smoking onto the flat surface where the names are inscribed. I confess I was strangely hurt. Somehow I wanted to believe the man meant nothing disrespectful as he carelessly tossed his cigarette. That probably is a part of the hurt I suddenly felt, the man just didn't think. So many people show disrespect unintentionally simply because they don't think!

In the hurt which I felt, and for which I was not prepared, I sensed that I had seen a very disturbing thing, that a person, and by extension a growing number of folk in our land, could see a reminder of courage and sacrifice for something important and walk away unmoved, even in apparent disdain.

I do not champion blind and irrational patriotism. I do not encourage extreme emotionalism. Still, I am disturbed whenever I see disdain for our country or hear a derogatory put-down of our land. I fear the day when folk cannot get sentimental about heroes and acts of bravery and evidences of selfless acts in behalf of the good of the country. We need desperately for people of intelligence and understanding who, with whatever it takes, even their lives, will try to make our country and our world what they ought to be, and could be, if enough people cared about the way things are going and tried courageously to do what is right.

I guess what is on my mind, as a citizen who appreciates the privilege given him to live and work in this land, is that I don't like to see anybody "flip a cigarette" on my country, and what it stands for!

Written by Lloyd E. Batson
Published May 25, 2001

Bad math

I was going down the street, bouncing along, enjoying the gorgeous day, trying to take in all I could see. Suddenly, to my dismay, I saw one of the leading men in our church standing in front of the liquor store, his right hand clasped around the neck of a brown paper bag. "No, not that man! Surely not him!," I muttered to myself. Disappointment and embarrassment shot through me.

What should I do? I toyed with the thought of crossing the street in a hurry, or turning around with the hope that he hadn't seen me. Apprehensively, though, I decided to go ahead and speak to him as naturally as I could, though I, his pastor, surely didn't know what I would say. The exchanged greetings were awkward on my part, but not his. Then he quickly opened the paper sack and handed its contents to me to look at as he proudly announced, "I've been looking for one like this for a long time and I just now found it." It was a paint brush he had bought in the hardware store next to the liquor store!!

What I had done before I got to the man was the kind of math that is so easy to use and so regularly practiced, the "two plus two makes five" kind. Jumping to conclusions is what it is called! The problem with this kind of math is not only that it is wrong, but it usually is counterproductive.

Had I crossed the street without talking to the man I would have been cheated, by my own doing, out of my good opinion of him and my warm relationship with him. This because I had jumped to a conclusion that was wrong. The man himself, without his awareness of it, would have been wronged. I don't consider myself a "gossiper" but would I have been tempted to tell others what I had seen in his hand in front of a liquor store?

Even though it is a popular kind, "two and two makes five" math is bad stuff!

There are myriads of kinds of "paint brushes in brown paper bags" that confuse human relationships because it is so easy to practice bad math, the kind that is called jumping to conclusions.

How is your math these days?

Written by Lloyd E. Batson
Published May 30, 2001

On to something great

Two great-grandchildren of a friend of mine are on to something great!

Recently these two precocious youngsters were in a car passing near the church. The boy remarked, "There's Grandpa's church. It's the one with the big steeple. I can see it from the playground at East End, too."

The girl replied, "I know that. I have a secret place on the playground I go to when I feel lonely. And I can see Grandpa's steeple from there and it makes me feel close to Grandpa. Then I don't feel so lonely."

Most people I know need sources of strength and goodness in their lives. How fortunate are those who both have and can identify some of those sources which unwaveringly give to them what they need.

Here are two great-grandchildren who have Grandpa! They don't have to be physically present with him to be blessed by him. In this case the steeple on Grandpa's church has become a symbol to them of who and what Grandpa is. To see the steeple is to experience a closeness to the one they love and from whom they draw so much help and love.

That church steeple is impressive in its size and beauty but its connection with somebody who attends the church there is what makes it so special to those children. Yes, I know that a steeple and a church building should always be a testimony to God. Still, a steeple and a church building with no people connected thereto wouldn't say much to either an adult community or to children therein.

There is a basic fact that God who is real can't be seen but people who worship God certainly can be, and are! Isn't it so that God is most often seen reflected in the lives and characters of those who worship in a particular place?

Wouldn't it be great that every time somebody in a community passes a church he or she can warmly say, "That's (_____)'s church!"? How blessed is the person who can identify a given church not alone with God but with somebody who has been strength and goodness to him or her. In my head and heart I know a steeple and a church are in a community to bear witness to God. I also know, as those great grandchildren do, that if I see a steeple or a church and can immediately think warmly of some who worship there, I am blessed!

For myself I want a steeple or a church to call my attention to God, but I, like those great-grandchildren, need the joy and peace of being reminded of somebody that goes there who has helped me!

Written by Lloyd E. Batson
Published June 6, 2001

I can smell them

A few weeks ago I was visiting a very ill man in the Greenville Memorial Hospital. How terribly demanding illness can be! And how hard on attending loved ones!

In the other bed was a very sick elderly man who apparently could lie only on one side, a man totally blind as well. I went over to talk with the waiting daughter who, when I commented on the lovely flowers on the side away from her father, told me she had brought them from her yard. As I began a conversation with the blind and ill man I began to feel that I was talking with a person I wished I had been privileged to know in his well days.

At one point I began to talk about the flowers on the side away from him, describing them and saying, "I wish you could see these beautiful flowers your daughter brought you."

His response was not what I expected but was one that still blesses me. Without any trace of bitterness or regret, the elderly gentleman said simply, "I can smell them."

Paul the apostle, in writing about his own needs, said, "I have learned, in whatsoever state I am, therewith to be content." I think that elderly man had joined Paul in the discovery of a beautiful formula for living. The blind man couldn't see but he could smell! Paul had learned to make the most of whatever the situation was with him.

No good that I know about comes from feeling sorry for one's self, or from dwelling on that which is wrong. Isn't there good to come from the attitude of "if I can't see the flowers I am glad I can smell them?" I'm not talking altogether about what some call the "power of positive thinking," though many difficult things are made easier by that power. I do not believe a person who is feeling terribly bad can make himself or herself feel good by pretending and saying, "My, how good I feel!" I do believe, however, one must not be blinded to possible good things because something is bad.

Across the years I have dealt with folk who seem to dwell only on what is wrong with them and apparently never upon what is right. As a minister I have sometimes had to bite my tongue to keep from responding to complaining folk who seem to see only bad things. For example, I have wanted, and I must confess I have sometimes done it, to tell somebody who has complained of the way the family or neighbors have been treating him or her, "Hey, I happen to know another side. I have seen much care and love expressed in ways you seem not to have noticed."

To me, it is sad to settle for seeing only what is wrong and not noticing what is right.Thank you, elderly man, now sick and blind. Your life will always have meaning if while you will never see flowers you are grateful that you can say, "I can smell them!"

Written by Lloyd E. Batson
Published June 13, 2001

Trip through Georgia reminds me to appreciate beauty

On the way to a church in Georgia on a recent Sunday morning, my wife and I stopped at a station, both to get directions to the town to which we had never been and for "refreshment." A cup of coffee helped, too (can you believe that the coffee was excellent!).

While I was paying for the coffee and thanking the lady for her pleasantries, I noticed the thick and high-priced Sunday edition of The Atlanta Constitution-Journal in the rack. I was struck with the question, in large print, a sub-title to the lead story on the front page, "What if you waked early one morning and the songbirds were gone from your backyard-forever?"

I wish now I had bought the paper so I could have read the whole story. I did read the statement at the beginning of the story that "if things go like they are, your children and grandchildren might not get to hear birds sing."

From that chance stop to the church to which we were going, with the taste of a truly good cup of coffee still lingering in my mouth, that question haunted me. Bird songs gone! No way! But suppose it did happen? The apparent implication in that newspaper story was that if such happened, people would have caused it, with their poor environmental stewardship.

I got to thinking, not so much about birds and their songs but about the place and value of beautiful things in our lives. Do we truly need beauty in our lives? For enrichment? Perhaps to balance the ugly? Is a human life ever truly good without beauty in people, things, events?

I think somebody is supposed to have said, "Beauty is in the eye of the beholder." All I know is beauty comes in a great variety of packaging. For me, while I have no gifts at making or doing beautiful things, I know I need greatly to see beauty, to receive it as healing ointment on my mind and soul, to feast upon its ministry of grace to me.

I simply cannot imagine a world, and my limited part of it, without beautiful things, people, experiences. I cannot sing with beauty. I cannot paint strikingly beautiful scenes. I cannot do the things of fine art that many can. Must I then be impoverished? No! I can notice - and appreciate - what is all around. I must receive the blessing from things, big and small, still in abundance all around, that are beautiful. If I don't, I am cheating myself of a basic human enrichment. I need the presence of beauty, and appreciation of it, in my life simply to be a decent human being!

Am I responsible in any way for the keeping of songbirds in my life? Of course, I am. Am I responsible in any way to help keep beautiful things available for my children and grandchildren and all others around me? Of course, I am.

Indeed, can you imagine a world without songbirds? I hope not. Can you imagine a life without some beauty to nourish that life? I hope not.

So, I guess what is weighing heavily upon me is that I can and must have something, however small, to do with making sure beauty, in its many forms, never disappears from around me.

Beauty? Who needs it?

I do! And I think you do!

Written by Lloyd E. Batson
Published June 20, 2001

"One Nation, Under God"

The tiny Bible School youngster, giving the pledge of allegiance to the flag of the United States of America, reared back and said it loudly and clearly, "One nation, under God..."

I thought, as I watched him, "How fine that he has already learned that!" But then I realized that, while he could say it, he did not comprehend what it meant. He had memorized it but he had not yet learned it.

To my mind came other recollections. At an outdoor gathering of adults the pledge to the flag was being said. The man in front of me mumbled some words while he read his newspaper. He knew the words, but couldn't care less. He knew the words, but he really had not learned the meaning. Then there was the convention and the pledge was being said with pageantry. All around me the words were sounded forth - and forgotten before the "... and justice for all" echo had died. Had they learned it, or did they just know how to say it?

"One nation, under God ...." Who really has learned that? Only those people who, with conviction born of a faith in a living God, understand that nations, too, like individuals, are known by the Creator and Divine Governor and find their destiny under his sovereign control. Only those who, believing thusly, live out the conviction in daily, personal lives. Only those who demonstrate a continued and profound gratitude for past blessings and sincerely believe that the God of the past is still alive-and relevant! Only those who go beyond the griping about trends and troubles to some kind of effort at remedying them! Only those whose sense of values allow for spiritual values to be greater than material ones-in private and personal lives as well as in the nation. Only those in whose lives the principles of liberty and justice have neither died nor withered.

Who has learned to say, "One nation, under God...?" Perhaps all of us who know how to say it have some learning to do. It takes only a few minutes to memorize "... one nation, under God . . ." but it takes a lifetime of practice to learn it.

Written by Lloyd E. Batson
Published June 27, 2001

Home can come home to you

The mail finally caught up with us, after a rather long dry spell of nothing. It was sometime in March, I think, of 1945, somewhere in an accelerating march into Germany. We were beginning to see some white sheets hanging out of windows, indicating that the local people, if they were still in their houses, would be no problem to the advancing Americans. Mail arrival had been unpredictable. What a celebration to get a batch of letters, and sometimes packages! It was also sad to see some men not get any.

In my mail was a package from home, a can of cooked quail. Sometime in the fall my father had gone bird hunting (to say bird hunting back then meant only bobwhite quail). Mother had fried some of that great delicacy and used some home canning equipment she had gotten just before the war. On a chance that the tin can of quail would get through to me and still be good, she had mailed it. Two or three months later it did!

Excited, I invited a friend to help me find some way to heat or cook it, whatever was necessary after I opened the can. In a small village largely damaged by artillery fire, we found a partly blown out house that still had a chimney standing and a small iron stove attached, on the second floor as I recall. A search in the basement had uncovered two rather large potatoes. With pieces of splintered wood we got a fire going and there with some badly botched potatoes and some South Carolina quail, heated in the can it came in, we had a glorious feast. It is now one of treasured memories from a gruesome war!

What a meal! It was great! But greater was the touch of home! Home had come to some unidentified place in the midst of the ravages of war. The quail was wonderful (the poorly cooked and scorched potatoes didn't add much!) but it was home coming to me where I was that made that stop in a blownout house somewhere in Germany a precious experience.

Many times, in many places, in many circumstances, good and bad, across the years, home has found me and given me the peace, the joy, the encouragement I have needed.

Home is not a house! It is at its best an experience, a receiving of love, an implantation of strengths and values, an intermingling of relationships that can seek out and come again and again to folk who have truly known what home is about - no matter what is happening and where.

People who have ever really had a home never have to lose its presence or need be long separated from it!

Home! Yes, one of its great blessings is that it can keep coming to you!

It helps, too, to keep looking for it to show up!

Written by Lloyd E. Batson
Published July 4, 2001

About telling the truth

We were at my son's house, in a community just out from Louisville, Kentucky. The street where he lives has a lot of children, many of whom I know. Since my grandchildren call me Granddad some of the neighborhood children do so, too.

I was out in the backyard, enjoying the collection of youngsters, when suddenly a loud thundering started. I gathered the youngsters around me to allay some of their fears. One of the kids present was Jamie, six years old, who lived next door, and just about the politest youngster I ever saw. I told them all to stand still and listen, that the clouds were throwing bowling balls at each other and were having great fun making noise.

Jamie, slightly behind me, put his hand on my elbow and said to me, "Excuse me, Mr. Granddad, but you are not telling the truth." Then, to my astonishment, he began giving me the scientific explanations of thunder and lightning.

My, my! They are making today's children smarter than they used to! I am constantly amazed at the learning capacity, and experiences thereof, of children today.

It is not what Jamie, so young, knew and could explain that I have thought about a lot. It is the openness and truthfulness on the part of adults that must be established with children. It is the great need to tell truth, consistently, so that children who know us can trust us and respect us. It is the need for children, and grownups around us for that matter, to be able to believe us when we speak.

Children whose nature generally is to believe what adults say can also spot phoniness and hypocrisy easier than we think. Parents have many things to convey to their children that have lifelong implications. A chief one is the reliability of their always telling the truth. How can any parent reasonably expect his or her children to be truthful if those children see lies, half-truths, and hypocrisies in the daily lives of their parents and other adults around them?

It would do all of us good to see politeness in children, yes, but it would do us, and them, greater good to see us being honest with people.

Polite little fellow, you were blunt, but you were right. Truth is the way to go!

Written by Lloyd E. Batson
Published July 11, 2001

The sound of chains

I can still hear them! Chains clanging, hauntingly so.

For several years, in my earliest days in Pickens County, I went regularly to the county stockade, an old stone building on the right going into Pickens from Easley. There I conducted worship services for the prisoners, who were required at that time to attend.

I can hear them now! As I sat at the front and the prisoners were marched in, the leg chains they wore made the eerie sounds of clanging and dragging mixed in unholy alliance. How long will those sounds last in my head? Until I hear heaven's golden bells ringing!

To be sure, the prisoners were there because they had in some way broken the law, or laws. But chains? In a place of worship? I know nobody has ever learned the best way to deal with law breakers, nor will anybody ever so do. I, for myself, am glad chains are gone. But what do I do with the sounds I still hear?

I will tell you that there is another sound related to that stockade that is stronger, and certainly more pleasing, than the dragging and clanking leg chains. When I hear in my mind the sounds of chains I get relief by tuning in loud and clear the voice of a nineteen-year-old prisoner as he told me, after I had preached, that a changing faith had come into his life as he listened to me and he faced a God who, while he was guilty of breaking the law, loved him and forgave him.

That nineteen-year-old on his way out still clanged and dragged his chains the way he had done when he had entered, but his exit was of love and hope. How do I know? At some point that young man was released from the stockade. To my surprise, and great pleasure, for years he drove once a year from the Rock Hill area to visit me in Pickens.

What I now hear, louder than the sound of chains, is the happy voice of a prisoner, truly set free, as he reported on his work, his family, and yes, his church! Though I saw him only about once a year, his happy sounds of a good life stayed with me all year long. They still do! I suspect that to him the sounds of his own leg chains were diminished, or removed, by the new joy and goodness that had come to him.

Sounds occur, of all kinds. Many of them remain in the background of our lives. Many of them are raucous, unnerving, haunting. How do we deal with them?

How fortunate and blessed is the person who does indeed, in the midst of "chain" sounds, have happy sounds and can hear them over and over again. In general, I think, for example, that good memories last longer than bad ones.

I can still hear the sound of chains, but over and over again I have stored up joyful sounds to be heard many times. These mean more to me than the ugly sounds of life.

Thank God for the happy sounds! They simply make life better!

Written by Lloyd E. Batson
Published July 25, 2001

Hope

The Intensive Care Unit waiting room in the large city hospital was full of anxious people, some very distraught. All were heavily affected by what was going on back in the unit. Some had been there so long, carrying such heavy burdens. It was hard for them to know it was Monday.

The family I was with had a beloved member in the process of dying. I had moved around the waiting room, sitting with the other people, none of whom I had previously known, quietly asking about their family members so ill, sharing with them as best I could.

At what seemed to me an appropriate time I spoke out loud to all the folk, saying to them that I knew it was a big and busy place and not a chapel, but I wondered if it would be all right if we had a prayer time. Nodding assent came from all over the place. I then asked the other minister in the room to pray and I would conclude with a prayer of my own. Such a beautiful, moving, and helpful prayer the man prayed.

When the minister ended his prayer, I prayed, in the prayer calling by name the loved one of every person in the room, for I had quietly learned, and remembered, each person's name. To be in the presence of so much anxiety, to be acutely aware that some folk back in the unit were gravely ill and one, at least, was in the process of dying, and to be asking for Holy Presence and help was, as it always is, an awesome experience. When I opened my eyes at the end of my prayer I found I was looking straight at a beautiful baby, only a few weeks old. His little eyes seemed focused on me. For a moment I was transfixed. I felt God was revealing himself to me.

A little baby in the presence of anxiety about death!

One couple who had come in while we were praying excitedly told me that they had just come from their very sick child who had just pitched a tantrum! Wonderful tantrum! Their child better enough to pitch a tantrum, and they were rejoicing!

I looked into the eyes of that baby and felt again the grace of God. One may die, but life keeps coming. Hope! A loved one may die, but life for the living goes on.

For a brief moment, when as a man so acutely conscious of suffering all around me, I looked into the face of a small baby and saw not the little tyke before me. My heart's eye saw another baby, the Babe of Bethlehem, held in the arms of an adoring mother, a baby who would come to walk among suffering folk, and would himself die a horrible death. Death would not hold him. He was raised to a new life. Forever the word goes out that death is not victor. Hope!

I looked at my friends. They were hurting, and hurting terribly. I wouldn't for anything in the world want one in the process of loosing a loved one not to hurt, and to hurt deeply. My friends would lose a precious one to human death, but they could know death for him would issue in a life with no end. Somewhere along the way, and soon I hope, they will discover that they themselves have a lot of living to do yet, until their own time comes for exit to eternal life. They will get on, spurred by hope, with a living that yet can be good. Different, yes, but still good!

May it always be that in the desperate hours of one's life he or she can see a baby!

Hope! By it life is made good and by it death loses its sting!

Written by Lloyd E. Batson
Published August 1, 2001

A smile

Across the years I have worked hard to get ready for every sermon, and have attempted to deliver it in a way the congregation would be attentive and acceptive. Still, I have learned that there is one thing that will always "outdraw" me (and you know what? I will always gladly yield!). That moment is when a group or choir of young children sing!

Recently I watched a choir of very young boys and girls line up at the front of the church to sing. What a mixture of excitement and uncertainty in their faces. Then their singing, glorious to me, with exuberance on the part of some, with others their lips just barely moving! I was in position to watch both the children and some of the parents that I knew.

One little girl, with head bowed slightly, in the several songs the group sang, never opened her mouth. It is likely some insensitive person in the congregation was wondering what was wrong with that little girl. Hadn't she learned the songs? What was she doing up there if she wasn't going to sing?

What was I thinking? The fact is, I watched her with joy, more than any other child, and I watched her parents. I was receiving from her a huge blessing, a major contribution to the singing and to me. She stood there, not singing but smiling sweetly, angelically it seemed to me. Her smile sang to me! I watched her, at the end of the singing, go back to her parents who hugged and kissed her. I wanted to do so myself!

I am sure that precious little girl will learn to sing, even exuberantly, but she was using a great talent she already had, her smile! I don't now recall what songs the group sang but I am still warmed by the memory of her smile.

What a ministry to others a smile is! And how available it is! Some folk I have known have worried that they seem not to be talented in any way. Not so! Everybody has the talent, whether it is used or not, to bless other folk with a smile. All around us, in every day, are folk who need their lives brightened by something so simple, and yet so beautiful, as a smile.

Smiles communicate without the need for words. A much beloved spiritual is, "There is a Balm in Gilead," dealing with the need for a healing balm for the soul. Balms of many kind we need, but I am convinced that in every person there is a balm that can so easily and generously be given to others. It is called a smile!

Precious little girl, I hope you will learn to sing words, even exuberantly, but please keep on using the great talent for blessing you already have, that of smiling.

And may it so be with all of us!

Written by Lloyd E. Batson
Published August 8, 2001

Singing those good old Baptist hymns

What a gorgeous place to conduct a worship service! In Table Rock State Park under Five Oaks picnic shelter on a brilliant Sunday morning. And early, at that, for I had to get back to conduct a service in our church.

At the end of the service, one of the large crowd of campers attending the service came up to thank me for the service and sermon. Then he, from out of state somewhere, and from what church affiliation I had no idea, exuberantly declared, "It was great singing those good old Baptist hymns again!"

I smiled (more like grinning it was), thanked him, and told him I was glad he had enjoyed the service. I didn't have the heart to tell him that we were singing out of a Methodist songbook that the Methodists had provided!

Yes, I am a Baptist, but faith belongs as well to anybody who will receive it. No denomination I know holds a corner on the way faith is to be expressed. Singing is a beautiful meeting ground for people of faith. I am sure there are hymns Baptists like, as there are songs Methodists like, as there are for Presbyterians, Lutherans, Church of God folk, Catholics and many other groups of believers.

There are many differences among people of faith, I know; but there are so many things we share. There are many differences, yes; but there are many commonly held understandings. Every group, rightfully, has matters important to that group that differ from others; but we have so much we could celebrate with others, and so much we could learn from them.

Let me shift to something that may seem to be unrelated to my "good old Baptist hymns" story. The area all around us is rapidly changing, with people from all over moving to live here. They come from a great variety of backgrounds and cultures. There are no longtime citizens of our area who have not in some way benefited from those who have come to our area from elsewhere.

Many of the "newcomers" (some "old-timers" tend to think of some who have been here many years as "newcomers"!) have so much to offer us, and, I think, we to them. A community it seems to me is at its best when every person, having the right to be and to do according to his own desires and needs, discovers what others have to offer to the good of all and is glad for it! It would be a drab sort of place if everybody was just like everybody else. A community that encourages, and allows, its citizens to contribute to the welfare of the whole is going to be a great place to live.

I am not now speaking of religion or hymns when I say that in a community we can discover in one another some "songs" we can sing together. It probably comes down to this, that we who would like everybody else to sing our "songs" could discover some "songs" that others like and we could sing them together!

A community able to respect one another's "songs" and find some "songs" to sing together with others has got to be a great community!

Written by Lloyd E. Batson
Published August 15, 2001

Angels in Black Trash Bags

Angels come in all kinds of packaging, including black trash bags!

Doting grandparents had their nine-year-old granddaughter and five-year-old grandson from Kentucky, by themselves, for ten hyperactive and hyper-happy days A long checklist of possible things to do had been sent ahead of time to them for choosing and to be returned before they got here. One activity checked by both youngsters was a day up in the mountains at a place wonderful in memory and in fact to both the grandparents and the children's father.

A lovely old house at the end of the road, right alongside a small mountain river, the rushing waters of which offer a continuous serenade day and night. Picnic style meals on the back porch and out back. Multiple mountain things, including crawfish, snails, and bugs, for curious youngsters to enjoy. Cold river water, but not too cold for adventurous youngsters who use up their "wearing up there" clothes as swimming attire. That left only the one extra set taken along to be worn on the late afternoon hike through the hills, a hike that forced not so young and hypocritical grandparents to pretend they were getting along all right. Collectively the now not so doting grandparents breathed thanksgiving when the hike was interrupted by the discovery of a high red clay bank that offered the challenge of climbing, sliding, grabbing roots, etc. Quickly, clothes, skin and hair become the same red wet dirt of the bank. An hour later happy, hilarious youngsters and wearied oldsters, too grateful for the hike interruption to complain, at near dark, head back down to the river to wash off at least some of the red dirt.

No clothes now to wear on the ride back home! The grandmother tells the children the ancient tale of "The Emperor's New Clothes," while the grandfather finds two black trash bags in his car trunk, and cuts holes for the head and arms. Now there are clothes to wear all the way home! The children think it is hilarious (and the youngsters joyfully get out for a visit on the way home with the gracious lady who had provided the key to her mountain place, and they frolic in their designer clothes on her front lawn!).

The point of all this? The grandfather kept looking at the two youngsters, so precious to him, recalling the happy events of the day and the pure joy of time with them, and could laugh and be warmed through and through because what he saw were angels in black trash bags!

If angels are messengers from God, and that's what angels are, then can't a granddaughter and grandson who had nothing but black trash bags to wear be angels reflecting joy and unfeigned love? Mine were!!

God has so many ways to give blessings to earthbound folk. Isn't it our joy to recognize them, however they come, and be grateful and glad, even, and perhaps especially, if they are wearing black trash bags?

Written by Lloyd E. Batson
Published August 29, 2001

Precious Memories

I have recurring and treasured memory.

Granddaddy Batson was a special person, gentle and kind, a man of simple and unswerving ideals about things that counted. He loved children, even rowdy and exuberant grandchildren like me.

A trip to visit him sometimes involved a ride with him to the corn mill. What a treat! While I now know I was more hindrance than help, Granddaddy would allow me to feel important by "helping" shell the corn that down the line would be cornbread. Alternately I could shuck an ear, stick the ear in the sheller, or turn the handle. Corn was shelled one ear at a time. When the burlap sack had enough corn in it, Granddaddy and I would load it on the one-horse wagon. In fact, he was lifting the sack and me onto the wagon, while I thought I was doing it.

When the mule was hitched to the wagon, off we went, he on the plank laid across the front of the wagon, I on the sack of corn. What a triumphant ride, down the hill, around and across, until the mill on the creek came in view.

Excitement galore. The mill. The babbling waters of the creek. The huge water wheel being turned by the water pouring on it from the trough routing the creek water to the wheel. Noise of mysterious grindstones largely out of sight under the floor. The mill operator measuring corn from our sack, corn which would be his pay for grinding.

Wonderful feelings! A boy's hand with spread fingers allowed to intrude into warm meal pouring out of the wooden chute, worn slick from years of service. A boy in his glory leaving the falling veil of ground corn to explore the bank of the creek, aware all the time of watching eyes of a mustached grandfather.

But the trip home! That was the best of all. Toward dark now. The grandfather, reins in hand, clucking to the mule from his seat on the plank. The boy, basking in unparalleled happiness of a shared adventure with the grandfather, warmed in spirit by the ecstasy of the moment and warmed in his bottom by meal in the sack on which he sat, meal still warm from the grinding.

The creaking wagon being pulled up the long hill toward home by an old, thin mule. Without comprehending why, the euphoric boy on the sack noticing the quickening pace of the mule heading home. Heading home and arriving almost on the run. Home. For the mule. For the grandfather. For the boy. Home! Tired, from the exertion and excitement of the trip, but home!

What a joyful sense of belonging I had! What an awareness of well-being because I knew I was loved. Family. Home. A part of others' lives. Secure in the strength of family.

How many times I have had a longing to go back to a ride to the mill with my grandfather! You can't do that anymore, you say? Yes, you can! Once you have sat on a sack of warm meal as an important part of a family, once you have shared the goodness of unfeigned love and caring, once you have been warmed by family security, you can go again to it any time you need to!

Family! Home! Thank God!

Written by Lloyd E. Batson
Published September 5, 2001

Chuckling, an antidote

She was one of those folk nearly every community has, an elderly recluse, living away from close neighbors, with no way to get anywhere but to walk. Her less than desirable small trailer house was stuck away in the woods.

This reclusive individual hardly ever spoke. In her long walk from her home to go up town she sometimes stopped at our house and came in at our invitation. She seldom talked as she sat on the couch, leaning forward. My wife or I would do all the talking (no conversation, for that requires exchange!), sometimes awkwardly scrambling to find something to say. Then she would leave without a word until she either came again or I would visit her, which I occasionally did, with the same scenario of "conversation" at her place.

Once she was in the hospital and I went to see her there. What her ailment was I do not know because again she didn't talk. I tried the best I could to do something meaningful, including praying. I said good-bye and was leaving. As I put my hand on the door, to my astonishment I heard a remarkably strong and clear voice call out with the only thing she had said, "Old age sure is a job!"

Of course I laughed and turned to see that she, too, was chuckling. I said good-bye again and left, with considerable delight at what had happened.

"Old age sure is a job!" she declared in assessment of her predicament. She did understand how demanding and difficult advanced years can be for some. The latter end of our earthly journey, especially if it is a prolonged one, can bring many kinds of problems difficult to handle.

This "old age is a job" stuff I won't elaborate on, because I am there! She did reveal, though, what I think is a key to handling the problems that can arise in later life. As she made her assessment of her problem she chuckled!

A sense of humor is a great antidote to burdensome matters. Trouble, of course, is not a laughing matter, but the capacity to "chuckle" surely takes some of the sting out of trouble. There are those who seem to feel unable to "chuckle" when things are tough. My personal conclusion is that that is probably a matter of choice. To be sure, one sometimes has to think about the necessity for finding something a little lighter than what is happening, and may even have to work hard to get past the present burden's demands.

But look at the gain! That "age sure is a job" lady knew she had pulled a "funny" and suddenly she felt a little better. And I did!

I suggest a little practice at "chuckling," meaning finding something on purpose to chuckle at to make things a little easier. I think that the practicing will develop into a valuable resource. And you might like it! And need it badly some day!

A "chuckle a day" might not, like an apple, as it is said, keep the doctor away; but it will certainly make the doctor's job easier!

Written by Lloyd E. Batson
Published September 12, 2001

Publisher's Note: This column was already printed when *The Easley Progress* **reached the newsstands earlier on Tuesday morning before the tragic events of September 11, 2001.**

September 11, 2001

A horrible image, fixed indelibly in the mind and spirit of every person who saw it pictured! The twin towers of one of the world's greatest and most important buildings aflame at the top and then slowly and relentlessly collapsing amidst billowing smoke until emptiness was where powerful hugeness had been!

Unbelievably, the greatest nation on the earth had been attacked! The forces of hate and terror had found a way to reach for the soul of our beloved nation.

September 11, 2001, a defining day for America! In one brief span our present and future took on a radical new look.

It will be long before we know all we need and want to know, long before we can understand what now has to be done in response to such a dastardly attack against who and what we are. We do know, though, one thing that absolutely we as individuals and as a nation must do. We must not allow that image of the burning and collapsing towers to become a symbol for the victory of hate and terror over our people and nation, and freedom loving people of the earth.

As I write this I have just come in from a prayer vigil at our church, one of countless such prayer vigils across our land. As I joined the many others in agonizing prayer I was stirringly aware that, while hate and evil had struck hard against us, our God had not collapsed in a heap. I could join the hundreds present around me and the innumerable others elsewhere in waiting in Holy Presence beseeching his help and direction for this horrible moment thrust upon us and for the days ahead. I could believe that we had not become a great nation without his blessing and that he would not cease his care for us if we will receive it.

In the middle of the afternoon of this horrifying day I pecked out a quick e-mail word to my two sons, one in Kentucky and one at the moment in Europe, the brief word here quoted, "What a crazy world! All this seems so much like fantasy, but the problem is that it is real! All I wanted to do is not to talk about all the ramifications of this, but to reach out and touch two people I wanted identity with, my sons. I love you! Dad."

Where do we go in the days ahead? How do we keep the horrible picture of hate and terror from being a symbol of victory for such evil? I think it lies in our seeking identity with known strengths. Let me suggest a few. Faith in God, of which I have already spoken. Love for people dear to us (and letting them know it). Faith in the basic principles on which our country was built and has thrived. Confidence in the capacity of our citizenry to get together to do what is right. Courage to face hard times. And somehow discovering afresh that as we reach out to touch one another with caring and love we do gain strength for whatever is needed.

As individuals and as a nation, which I happen to think with all of its problems is indeed a great nation, we must, and we can, deny hate and terror its dastardly, sought-after victory. In the language of the saw mill village in which I grew up, "May God see after us!"

Written by Lloyd E. Batson
Published September 19, 2001

Sanctuary

A shocking sight for a 5- or 6-year-old!

In 1929 or '30 in rural Sumter County an excited passerby told me a big crowd was gathering up the road in front of Uncle Joel's house (Uncle Joel Davis was not related to us, but everybody in the community called him Uncle Joel). It was just after dark and I, either 5 or 6 years old, took off running up the road to see what it was all about.

When I got up there, about a half a mile away, folk were gathering along a ditch. A variety of lights, including torches, made dancing shadows of the crowd, folk talking animatedly. Because I was little I could pick my way through the line of folk right to the ditchbank.

In the flickering light, to my horror, I saw a man lying in the ditch, disemboweled! With a mixture of morbid curiosity and horrifying disgust I watched that man who apparently had been knifed to death in a fight and slit open. The first death from violence I ever saw, and the 5- or 6-year-old boy didn't know how to handle his emotions!

This time I shoved a path away from the ditch and ran back down the road, faster than I had come. Where did I run? Not to my house, but past it, through the trees between our house and the church. Through the trees I could see the silhouette of the white framed church building. I kept running until at full speed with outstretched hands I bounced off the side of the church.

For a long time, still with churning emotions, I stood touching the church. Slowly my fright diminished and, with outstretched hands on the side of the church, in the darkness peace came to me. Then I could go to my home and tell my parents what I had seen.

Why did I run to the church? I'm sure I didn't know the word "sanctuary" or one of its basic meanings, a place of refuge and protection. I just knew I needed security and the church was that to a little boy who was frightened beyond his comprehension.

Many times in the more than 70 years since that frightening night I have slipped into a church somewhere, because I needed a sense of sanctuary, of refuge, of protection, of peace. In times when I have needed something bigger or stronger than myself I have sought sanctuary and blessedly received it.

In addition to a church, sanctuary can be found in many other places and relationships. I happen to believe that a church can offer to me the most visible and available experience with God who offers the peace and security troubled folk so often need. Still, sanctuary is an experience more than a place. I know, and have discovered so for myself, that sanctuary comes in many forms. I know also that I have never known a single person who has never needed a sense of sanctuary at some time, usually many times.

Like that youngster who had a horrifying experience and ran to the church that was already established in his mind as a place of refuge and help, it is best for every person to identify ahead of time where sanctuary can be had.

Sanctuary? Who needs it? Everybody!

Written by Lloyd E. Batson
Published September 26, 2001

Recognizing personhood

The sudden and loud crying that came from the back of the chapel was startling, the sounds penetrating a very solemn occasion.

I was guest speaker at a beautiful and meaningful memorial service conducted by an area funeral home, one honoring those that had died during the year and for whom the funeral home had handled the farewell procedures. Additionally, tragic events of the terrorists' attacks on our country called for somber reflection. One by one the names of the deceased were called and family members came to light candles in memory of their loved one. One woman was in the process of lighting a candle when the loud crying erupted.

From the rear of the chapel a small child, crying, started running toward the front. Beautifully, the woman, apparently the mother of the child, left the candlelighting table, went to meet the brokenhearted youngster, picked her up in her arms, took her back to the candles, helped her light one and together quietly they returned to the back.

It was precious to me! The child apparently had felt left out of something very important and wanted to be a part of it. I interrupted the lighting procedures to say something like, "Isn't it great that little children both give and receive love, too? It's beautiful."

I know it is hard sometimes to be as wise as we would like to be, but I have concluded that children don't have to be sheltered always from sadness and sorrow, from hurtful times. Children have feelings. They can hurt deeply for they can love greatly, and they need to express both.

Death, though often a mysterious thing to them, as it often is to adults, calls forth in them, too, a grief that needs expression and love to be given. I have come to the point in my life, after having been involved for many, many years in grief experiences, my own and others, that I encourage families to let children, as much as possible, in on what's going on, let them share in their own way. Help them, yes; but don't take away their right and need to be involved and to
express their feelings.

Though immature, children are persons! One of the greatest difficulties of parents, about many things, is recognizing and dealing with the personhood of their children, whatever the age may be. Parents handling themselves properly is one key to helping children, of any age, with problems and needs of many kinds. For that matter, inattention to, disrespect for, and belittlement of the personhood of another regularly creates problems in nearly all human relationships!

The music, the solemn calling of names, the lighting of candles, the sense of Holy Presence, the electricity of sorrow, the privilege of honoring loved ones, all the special features of the memorial service made the moment special and good.

So did the brokenhearted crying of a child!

Written by Lloyd E. Batson
Published October 3, 2001

Tire marks and behavior

Out on the highway near where we live there is a place in the road where there are tire marks at an angle on the pavement, marks made by police and patrol cars coming out of a secluded place off the road. Every time I go out on the road I notice these tire marks, and the bare places in the grass and under the trees off the road caused by the patrol vehicles using that spot.

Speeding and reckless driving have long been problems from cars both entering and leaving Easley. Several bad wrecks, even fatal ones, have occurred along this stretch. Such problems do seem to have been considerably alleviated lately.

While I try to monitor my speed to fit posted signs I am probably more careful on this stretch than anywhere. Why? Is it because posted signs indicate the legal limits or because I have seen patrol cars many times in that well-chosen place? Do the tire marks remind me that an officer may be watching me?

Plainly put, for me the question is, "Do I try to drive at or less than the posted limits because I am afraid of getting caught, or because it is right so to do?"

This question has many important spin-offs. For example, do I sometimes do good things because it is right to do good things, or do I do them because I feel required to do them even if I wouldn't otherwise choose so to do? Do I try to "look religious" at times because I feel it is expected of me or somebody is watching me? My wife sometimes tells people who comment upon my politeness in opening the car door for her that I only do that when I think somebody is watching.

Back to those tire marks in the pavement. Laws requiring certain behavior are necessary for the welfare of the populace, as a whole. No society could last long without laws and regulations. And laws have to be enforced or they would cease to have any effect. Except for the existence of divine laws, and some general concept of moral laws, all laws are made by imperfect people for imperfect people, but they are designed for the welfare of the whole. Our society suffers, and sometimes terribly so, from the results of laws being ignored or deliberately broken.

Isn't a posted speed limit a law designed both for my own welfare and all others? Should obeying such a law ever be a problem for me? Wouldn't it be great if I could live my life all the time without needing any laws and their enforcement to make me do the proper things? Human nature usually doesn't work that way. Back again to the tire marks coming from an obscured place. Yes, because I notice them and become more alert, I am glad they are there.

Furthermore, it may not sound like proper prayer language but I think perhaps I should ask God regularly concerning many things to put a lot of "tire marks" in my life. And give me the good sense to notice them!

Just for the record, I haven't been one who caused the tire marks to be made - yet!

Written by Lloyd E. Batson
Published October 10, 2001

When love and messes get together

Several children were playing in that huge and lovely lobby of St. Francis Hospital in Greenville. I hadn't noticed anything out of the way. I just went over, as I often do, to speak to the children.

As I approached, one boy ran, plopped himself down in one of the big chairs, and announced loudly, "I didn't do it!"

Then I noticed a pot of flowers scattered on the floor.

Another of the children quickly said to me, "My little sister did it. But she didn't mean to. I'm going to clean it up."

A verse from the Bible, which interestingly, I had just read that morning, flashed through my mind. "Above all, love each other deeply, because love covers a multitude of sins" (1 Peter 4:8). Whatever that verse means, I think it surely touches upon a beautiful human relationship, that of the supportive, helping ministry of caring, loving folk. A community is perhaps at its best when it offers assistance to those who at a given moment have some trouble in their lives. In this sense love covers a multitude of needy matters.

Look at that boy who ran, sat and proclaimed, "I didn't do it." It was a defensive mechanism, one we use so quickly and easily. As a matter of fact, though he didn't actually knock the flowers over, he had been playing and by his running around had kept the tempo stirred up. It was almost irrelevant that somebody else actually knocked over the flowers. Aren't we quick to see no fault in what we do as long as we don't get caught? Don't we, generally, help set the tone for what goes on around us? Isn't the moral climate of a community pretty much what its citizens allow it to be? Don't we contribute, for good or bad, to much of the activity around us? Sometimes we may say, "I didn't do it," but the truth is that often we have had much to do with it. And don't most of us make messes of some kind? Also, doesn't it sometimes seem to be much easier to criticize than to help?

I watched that terrified little girl as she viewed the mess she had made. Then I saw the terror go from her face as she looked at the bigger brother act in her behalf. Terror became peace when love covered her misdeeds by reaching out to her. It did something good to me to see that brother down in the mess his sister made, cleaning it up because he loved and understood. I could almost forget that other boy sitting, self-righteously, in his corner!

Love in action, isn't it beautiful?

What a mess love can clean up!

Written by Lloyd E. Batson
Published October 17, 2001

When you feel trapped

Once, while I lived in Pickens, somebody in the office at Easley Baptist Hospital called me to ask if I knew a certain person and, if so, where he and his wife lived. I said, "Yes, I know him, but I don't know where he lives and I surely didn't know he has a wife."

The lady went on to tell me that the man was a patient in the hospital and had been supposed to go home the day before, but the wife didn't come to get him. She asked me if there was some way I could find the lady and tell her please to come get her husband. I agreed to try, but it took some time before I located where they lived, or where they were thought to live.

Out west of town I went, 12 miles or so, past a beer joint landmark given to me, to one house, the wrong one. A huge, black, mangy dog stopped a charge with gaping jaws exactly three inches from me! I breathed a sigh of relief at escape and went further in search.

At the next place I stopped, I walked through a clean, freshly swept dirt yard, walked up on a little porch and knocked. Getting no response I almost made a tragic mistake by going around to the back and up on a cluttered porch. I nearly jumped out of my skin when a huge, Amazon type, yelling woman, with tobacco juice on each side of her mouth, came suddenly around the house. I met her in the yard and before I could tell her why I came she informed me that it was a good thing she suddenly remembered I was some kind of preacher she had seen at a funeral or something. She said that behind a window she had her buckshot-loaded gun trained on me and started to let me have it when I walked up on the back porch.

When I told her why I had come she verbally blasted me and blamed me for all sorts of things, including some slights she felt she had received in the hospital. As I stood there, only occasionally getting in a soft word, she circled me several times, spitting tobacco juice at my feet as she circled, all the time yelling at me.

At the high point of her vehemence I almost laughed out loud (and that could have been another mistake!). It dawned on me at how ridiculous I must look, being circled by a towering, angry woman and trapped in a ring of tobacco juice showing markedly on the freshly swept yard. Perhaps sometime I will finish this story, but what is on my mind is not the humorous entrapment in a circle of tobacco juice, but some of those serious things in which we find ourselves trapped, feeling helpless and confused about what to do.

Sometimes we find ourselves in utterly confounding situations from which there seems no escape. What in the world are we going to do? I have so few easy answers to those things in which I myself feel trapped and I often agonize at not having answers for many who confide in me. Yet, I think I find some help in that ridiculous encircling I told about. It's important not to panic. It's important to remember that you honestly have tried to do right. It is good to remember that there usually is some explanation, whether it is right or not, for the bad experience happening. Trying to discover what it is helps some. Too, I think it really helps not to allow even bad times to strip us of the capacity to laugh occasionally or to smile, or to enjoy some things that are good even while we are severely trapped and tested. Then, it is most important to remember that in some way, often unexplainable but very real, God shares in our difficult times.

I still wish I could have been an outside spectator to that encircling episode!

Written by Lloyd E. Batson
Published October 24, 2001

A terrible disease

As I walked up to the elderly lady sitting in a wheelchair in the corridor I asked, "Well, how are you feeling today?"

With precise and clear speech she responded slowly, "I am disappointed to have to tell you I am feeling better."

How do you reply to something like that?

That elderly lady, whatever she had in mind, reflected, in her statement at least, the attitude that some people allow to be normal in their lives, that of pessimism. In the same vein as this dear lady's statement is the word which I have heard in a variety of forms, "I feel pretty good today, but I know I'm going to feel bad tomorrow."

All of us know some people who seem to "enjoy" poor health, or imagined poor health. What is on my mind, however, is not the poor health that some seem to enjoy, but the attitude of looking for the worst in everything. Some folk, for example, have difficulty enjoying what good times they do have for worrying about the bad times they think are coming. Some folk have difficulty enjoying the good qualities in people because they allow something they have heard or imagined to block out the good. I have long felt that one of the most common and most harmful diseases that runs through society is the "but" ailment.

It is the "but" that counters good in people and things. It is the "but" that keeps the mind soured. It is the "but" that keeps barriers raised long after they should have come down. It is the "but" that poisons relationships. It is the "but" that plants suspicion and encourages distrust.

To illustrate, here is one person impressed with and helped by an act, or work, or example of another person and so expresses that to a third person. The third person relies, "Yes, but ..." and proceeds to tell something he or she knows, or thinks he or she knows, about the other person that isn't pleasant or commendatory. The "but" disease has not only soured and warped the third party, but now is thrown at another person who probably will be affected and infected by it.

Gossip is a direct product of the "but" disease. Good people, well-meaning people often feed gossip machines with the infection of the "but" disease.

Even church folk sometimes infect the lives of other church folk and non-church folk with the "but" disease by refusing to allow something good to be said about the church, a Sunday School teacher, a program, the pastor, a deacon, a leader in an organization, the denomination, etc. without throwing in the "but."

I think it is true that some folk live more unhappily than they really need to. And the "but" disease is sometimes responsible.

All of us ought to be careful. The "but" disease is easy to catch!

Written by Lloyd E. Batson
Published October 31, 2001

The Good Earth

I don't know if one, a "one horse farm," exists anymore, in our area at least. Just a few days ago a person was telling me that his parents had raised their family on a 15 acre farm, feeding them, providing the basic necessities of life, educating them, all in a strong environment of love.

The good earth!

To be with our two youngest grandchildren, a first grader and a forth grader, during their fall break from school, we went in October to Kentucky. In the midst of the week we took them to a huge farm in Indiana, operated by a couple for whom I had performed their wedding ceremony 45 or so years ago. Harvesting was in high gear! Huge combines and massive trucks, moving through large fields of corn and soybeans, never stopped.

The good earth!

What pleasure to watch two youngsters having the time of their lives feeling a part of the good earth and hard working folk!

Granddad, who had seen it all across the years, seeing it afresh through the unbridled happiness of two youngsters!

At the end of the day what was best of all for the youngsters? Running hands through grains of corn only a short time from the fields? Riding the many little roads through multiple fields? Eagerly searching in the pastures of herds of cattle looking for a small calf tagged No. 177 separated from mother cow No. 177 and finding it? Walking on rocks across a creek and looking down the flowing waters to the deep hole where nearly 50 years ago their granddad had many times baptized folk? Getting the driver host to stop in the fields so they could get some "fuzzies" they had spotted, "fuzzies" being the caterpillar looking ends of a certain kind of weed? Excitedly feeding newly born calves with milk bottles (until one eager calf missed the nipple and slobbered all over the six-year-olds hand)? Standing on the wooden fence, watching in awe the Texas longhorn cattle and two buffaloes? Et cetera.

The good earth!

That was it! At the end of the day an unidentified but real sense of appreciation of the good earth as supplier of some of mankind's basic needs!

The good earth!

We must never take it for granted. Without it we cannot do! And without the commitment of the hard-working farmers, in the great variety of kinds, large and small, we cannot do!

The good earth!

Thank God for it!

Written by Lloyd E. Batson
Published November 7, 2001

DUM SPIRO SPERO

Many times I have been with folk worried greatly about some personal problems or anxious about a difficult illness, of themselves or family members. Sometimes, to break the tension and to make a point, I have asked, "Do you know what is on the official seal of the State of South Carolina?"

Nearly always the answer is, "No, I do not."

"Well," I say, "it is in Latin. Do you read Latin?"

The answer to that is usually "I certainly do not!"

When I tell them "DUM SPIRO SPERO" is on the front of the state seal; folk usually want to know what it means.

First, let me tell you briefly about the state seal. The Provincial Congress of South Carolina on March 26, 1776, set up an independent government and elected John Rutledge president. Quickly the General Assembly authorized the President and the Privy Council to "design and cause to be made a Great Seal of South Carolina."

After the Declaration of Independence a design by William Henry Drayton, a member of the Privy Council, was accepted. This seal, with the reverse side designed, as it is generally thought, by Arthur Middleton, was engraved as a great seal in Charles Town and used by President Rutledge for the first time on May 22, 1777. The two sides of the seal symbolize the battle fought on June 26, 1776, between the then unnamed fort at Sullivan's Island (now known as Fort Moultrie) and the British fleet.

The design details on both sides of the Great Seal (pretty small, actually only four inches in diameter and four-tenths of an inch thick) reflect events I won't relate here but I focus on DUM SPIRO SPERO. Translated, the Latin says, "While I breathe I hope." The fledgling state of South Carolina faced great unknowns and many struggles but chose to affirm faith and courage for times present and yet to be that as long as breath remains there is hope! As long as there is breath one can bring to bear all the strengths and resources available. By the way, on the port side of the state seal there is another Latin phrase, "ANIMIS OPIBUSQUE PARATI." That phrase means "prepared in mind and resources."

Long ago, our South Carolina forefathers chose to put on the Great Seal of the state words (Latin was an important educational language then!) that are important to human welfare and development today, to times of crisis and opportunity, to challenge and privilege, to well-being and achievement.

DUM SPIRO SPERO! It is not important, many people apparently feel today, to be able to read Latin. However, doing away with the study of Latin does not invalidate the continuing need in our lives to draw strength and courage from an understanding that "While I breathe I hope!"

DUM SPIRO SPERO!

Pretty good stuff to know and to practice!

Written by Lloyd E. Batson
Published November 14, 2001

The 'Pilgrims' of our lives

It was nowhere near Thanksgiving, but I was giving the gathering I was leading opportunity to express something they were thankful for. One delightful youngster burst out excitedly, "I am thankful for the pilgrims."

When I asked him why, he replied, "Because if it weren't for the pilgrims we wouldn't be here!"

His childish logic makes great sense! I am convinced that we owe a great debt to those that have gone before us. Officially, Thursday is Thanksgiving. I think it is great that our nation sets aside a day every year for national thanksgiving. With all the stress upon our nation and our people at this present difficult time it is all the more important that we turn our thoughts to many things that are right and good. A sensitive person knows that every day there are multiple reasons for being thankful. Having reason for thanksgiving and giving thanks, however, are not necessarily one and the same.

Some will say that true thanks is spontaneous and should not need an official day called Thanksgiving. There is indeed an element of spontaneity in giving thanks, but thanksgiving often needs the prodding of reflection, the stimulus of evaluation.

So, what are some of the "pilgrims" in your life, for example? What factors and people have gone into making for you the life that you now live?

Have you thought lately about the contribution your parents made, such contribution often taken for granted and hence unappreciated? What about the pioneer citizens of Pickens County who helped mold the basic character of our area?

Have you lately reflected upon those who established churches, built schools, devised systems of law, developed systems of medical care? What teachers, secular and religious, have played a role in your life?

Are you aware of the stalwarts of faith and those in every generation with foresight in so many areas that history has recorded them as having major determinative roles in the affairs of people before us? What about the ones who, unsung either by their peers or history, quietly went on with the kind of living that influenced others around them!

Thanksgiving by its nature involves God and many of the direct blessings and ministries of God, but there are also many "pilgrims" of ancient and near times who have played major roles in our being here.

Like that little fellow aware of the pilgrims, and his very existence here because of them, I am determined this Thanksgiving to be grateful to, and give thanks for, not only those who landed at Plymouth but those many others to whom I am indebted.

Amidst the feasting and festivities of this Thursday, Thanksgiving Day, do you suppose all of us could identify and give thanks for the "pilgrims" of our lives?

Written by Lloyd E. Batson
Published November 21, 2001

The colors of God

I saw something both very difficult and very beautiful just recently.

Often I am in the local hospital and frequently I go by the chapel to deal with some of my own needs or to share with somebody seeking help there. A few days ago as I started to enter the open door of the chapel I saw that a lady I did not know was seated at the end of the bench very close to the stained glass window.

I started to leave but I couldn't. I was drawn to the agony of hurt and intense thought on her face as she stared at the window. Should I approach her or quietly leave? She wasn't aware I was there, so I waited and prayed.

After a bit, as quietly as I could, I spoke, "Lady, you do not know me but I am a minister and a volunteer chaplain here and I want to tell you before you speak to me what I have just seen. By the look on your face I know you must be carrying a heavy burden. You don't have to tell me about it, but I want to tell you that I watched the colors of the stained glass window carried to your troubled face by the bright sun outside. I assume you have been trying to present your hurt to God. I just want to tell you that I think God has already bathed you with his presence."

As a hint of a smile began to mix with her troubled expression she turned slightly to me, yet retaining the transplanted aura of mixed colors from the chapel window. Now she began to speak softly of her burden, as uninhibited as if she had known me all of her life. Out came her trouble, her sorrow, her anxieties, her confusions, her hurts. In her wavering faith and hurt she had entered the open door of the chapel, she told me, not really knowing why but hoping for some kind of peace, some kind of indication of hope. At intervals I spoke softly of some words I had learned from God's Word for difficult times. Mostly I listened.

How long I was there I do not know, but I watched as it happened, the transferred beautiful colors from the chapel window being mixed with the warm and beautiful colors of a peace within stealing into her face. Yes, as she quietly related, she now knew God's presence had come to her. Things would be better.

In tones so soft that I had to listen carefully to understand her, she said, still mostly looking at the window, that she knew God had sent me, a total stranger, to call her to see the presence of God.

Her thanks to me was nothing compared to the thanks I offered to God for once again being able to witness the miracle of seeing God's presence come with peace to a troubled soul When I left, I felt that the colors of God's presence had come to me, too!

Written by Lloyd E. Batson
Published November 28, 2001

—

Sadness and happiness
Death's strange mixture

It was a little thing, about an inch and a half long. Who can say how big happiness has to be?

It was a fun night, when my 6-year-old granddaughter, Kelsey, took us, her grandparents, along with her mother, daddy, and small brother, to the Fall Festival at her school. Crowds of people. Happy boys and girls. Games. Contests. Prizes tried for. Some won. Most missed.

Kelsey, unlucky at some of the games, but always getting a piece of candy, or something as a consolation prize, finally hit the jackpot! A little ball fell into a cup. Wow! A prize. What a prize! A small goldfish, dipped from a tank and carried proudly home in a plastic bag. A goldfish that brought instant joy and happiness!

Ah, the pleasure of hunting a bowl, getting a favorite aunt to make a trip to find fish food. Then the name Little Swimmer!

Grownups have difficulty recalling the pure joy of owning a pet, a pet that becomes a friend!

Days passed. Feeding. Watching. Changing water. Noticing movement around the bowl. Watching small bubbles form. Imagining the moving lips were making talking words. Pride showing in faces pressed against a bowl. Bonding with an inch and a half of shimmering gold Happiness!

Then, on a Friday night, just a few minutes ago, while a friend was on the phone inviting Kelsey to an outing in the park on Saturday, the 6-year-old saw a shattering thing. The once shimmering gold was still, lying askew! Death had come to a friend! Devastating, horrible feeling! Sadness. Weeping. Hurting.

Can healing come? Yes, and sometimes surprisingly quickly. This time it came in the quick desire to write a poem, a tribute, and to do it sitting on the lap of a grandfather who has never learned adequately how to bring comfort either to grieving adults or suddenly sad youngsters. So, Kelsey wrote, and then illustrated, a tribute to her friend. Little Swimmer. In her words and in her way! And, because it was deep feeling honestly expressed, a kind of peace moved through her and the tears changed to slight dampness reflecting the joy of having had, even for a short time, a special friend, a serendipity that will continue in remembering!

Death of a goldfish? A little matter? Not on your life! Not with a 6-year-old. Death! Is it all bad? No! Remembering happiness lasts longer than grief.

Little Swimmer! This old grandfather, a veteran at sharing death on many levels, watched the miracle of a child and a goldfish unfold in life, and in death. Little Swimmer! An inch and a half of happiness that was the opportunity of getting bigger and bigger yet.

Written by Lloyd E. Batson
Published December 5, 2001

Publisher's Note: Written immediately after watching a 6-year-old granddaughter grieving deeply about the sudden death of her goldfish friend, Little Swimmer.

Back roads have a story!

The back roads of Pickens County can be a parable for its citizens about who we are and what we are about.

A few days ago, needing to go to a certain place in the county, and having several possible ways of going, I chose to go on one of the back roads. I was driving slowly so I could enjoy the ride. I had not gone far until I saw, in a driveway to a house, a young woman standing by her car in the process of handing a very young child to an older woman. An older man stood nearby.

Everybody was smiling as the young child stretched out hands to the older woman. What was happening? Perhaps the child being delivered for the older folk to care for while the mother went to work? Or perhaps a child about to spend the day with grandparents? What I do know is that children need the care and love of older people in myriads of ways.

A bit farther down the road, still driving slowly, I noticed that coming down a rather steep drive was an old lady, on her way to the mail box, carefully pushing ahead of her a four-legged walker. Did this lady live by herself and have to struggle to do ordinary things? What I do know is that for many elderly folk life is very difficult. Is there some way to make life a bit easier for the many for whom life is very hard?

Then I came to a small church, just off the back road, where some folk were repairing the church yard. A young lady had some kind of flat metal strapped on her feet and she was stomping some uneven places to level them. A church on a back road important to some folk, including a young lady arduously stomping uneven places to make them smooth! Is worship important enough to sweat for (she was wiping her brow as she stomped)?

Next I noticed in a cleared place in a thin patch of woods a man and a woman, about 25 years of age I would guess, standing close together, the woman with her left arm on the man's shoulder as the man pointed to some stakes connected with string. Was this young couple proudly anticipating what would be their new house, perhaps their first home? Were they joyfully dreaming of a home and a family so important to them and to society?

Not much farther down the road I passed an ugly mess close to the road, an ill-kept house with a yard filled with a cluttering array of trash and junk. In Pickens County? Can people get used to ugliness as a way of life?

Other things I noticed, and pondered about on a relatively short ride on a back road in Pickens County last week, but what was I delighting in when I pulled into the main road near where I was going? The waving to me of a man I didn't know, one leaning on a fence around a small field! Was that wave on a back road telling me something important about basic ties between people that can flavor life for good?

Back roads in our area abound. A ride on one of them some time might be a welcome change to the hurried pace of lives. Paying attention to what can be seen on one of them might result in discovery that back roads have a story to tell.

Written by Lloyd E. Batson
Published December 12, 2001

Christmas is...

It is one of my "tears of Christmas" gifts that still blesses me.

The large group of precious boys and girls, who through no fault of their own were in varying stages of physical and mental deprivation, some severely so, was giving their Christmas program, one titled "Christmas Is...."

At one point the group was singing a Christmas song that called for every child to have a bell of some sort to ring. One big boy, strapped at an awkward angle in a wheelchair, with almost no mobility in his outstretched arms, had no bell. I saw a teacher lovingly find one on a strap, go to him and put it in his hand. Barely could he move it, but he had a bell and his bell was as important as any bell there! What joy bathed his face as his bell became his voice!

Christmas, I suddenly felt, is putting a bell in somebody's hand! That's what the first Christmas announcement was all about. "I bring you good news of great joy that will be for all the people," proclaimed the angel to the shepherds who had no bell. People deprived of hope, people wearied and hurting, people alienated and separated from God and man, people walking in a thousand kinds of darkness, have had placed in their hands a bell! God has brought good news of great joy! The bell brings a new voice, one of hope, of liberation, of victory. It is Jesus who is, if you please, the bell of God which becomes a priceless voice of joy.

Christmas is not only what God has done. In the symbolism of that simple act by a loving teacher, Christmas is putting a bell in somebody's hand by everybody who knows what Christmas is all about.

God's love becomes a love translated through the caring acts of those who themselves can ring the joyful bell of Christmas. All around us are people who need a bell in their hands! God's people have a bell to give!

There is such hunger and such need in this earth for a bit of love, a bit of hope, a bit of joy. Everybody needs a bell to ring! Not everybody, however, has one or can reach one, or can even hold one by himself; but isn't this what Christmas is all about, putting a bell, a new voice, a new joy, in somebody's hand?

Let not a one of us think it is too small a thing to do, to notice who doesn't have a bell and to try to help that person get one. It just might be the greatest thing you will ever do!

Written by Lloyd E. Batson
Published December 19, 2001

Christmas---Gone Yet?

A few days after a Christmas he was in one line, I was in another. He called to me, "Did you have a good Christmas?"

"I'm still having one," I replied, above the chatter all around.

A simple exchange? Yes, it would seem. But it must not have been, because when I came out of the building that man was waiting for me to say, "I've been thinking about what you said. I reckon I already let Christmas go. That's a shame, isn't it, to let something so good go so soon."

I just let the man talk without saying a word.

"Besides, if Christmas means anything on one day, it's bound to be good for every day," he went on. "No, I guess I really didn't have a good Christmas, though I thought I did, if it's gone already. You see that fellow across the street, the one in the blue hat? I just blasted him awhile ago. No, I guess Christmas didn't last long with me. Wonder what he'd think if I went over there and apologized?"

At this point I said my first words, "Why don't you find out if you can still have Christmas? Go see that guy."

I know we can't have the festivity of Christmas every day, with all of its holiday celebration, gift giving, and frenzied activity; but before there were any of these there was the word, "Glory to God in the highest, and on earth peace, good will to men." Surely the return to normalcy shouldn't squelch that word!

Unbelievably, 2002 is right at hand. Will we have to wait three hundred and sixty or so days to have Christmas again? The celebration, yes, but not the meaning of it. If it's true for one day, it's got to be true for every day or it belies itself. The year 2002 will be formidable in many diverse ways but the Central One of Christmas, and the meaning of life he gives, is for every day.

Much of the experience of letting Christmas slip away so soon has to do with relationships with people. Can the warm glow of December 25 stand the test of a personal encounter on January 1? If it can't, Christmas has gone away too soon! Will 2002 be a year of living the good news of Christmas? When the worst is besieging, will the best have a chance? Will the difficulties sure to come be made easier with the glow of the real Christmas still fresh?

Why don't you find out if you can still have Christmas?

Written by Lloyd E. Batson
Published December 26, 2001

An alternative to resolutions

`The delightful, bubbling, intelligent first-grader, for whose parents I had the privilege of performing their wedding ceremony, keeps a journal, even bringing it to church to record things happening there. Recently, with her father's guiding grin and glance, I enjoyed getting to see how she had begun her entry for that day.

"My life is OK" was the introductory sentence. With this I had seen enough to delight and excite me. This alert youngster has unwittingly encouraged me to take a different approach to the New Year. It is traditional to talk about making New Year's resolutions, as finally ineffective as these usually are. Instead, I am letting that bright youngster set my course at this New Year's beginning.

Whether that six year old has articulated it or not, "My life is OK" amounts to identification and affirmation of important things, things that can, and do, make for a good life, things already at work in her experience.

So, this year, instead of resolutions easily made and poorly kept, I am letting that astute teacher, the six year old, turn my attention to the affirmation of what is in my life that I know is good for me and, with attention and diligence, can help make for a good life, yes, an "OK" life.

Most people I know, certainly including the one I know best, myself, need to make improvement in numerous ways. Wouldn't the identifying and affirming of basic truths and blessings already in existence be a start of a new response to them? Wouldn't a new awareness of what one has going for him or her, and consciously affirming them as being valid and good, introduce the possibility that 2002 AD will be a "My life is OK" year? By the way, to affirm the "AD" would be one good thing to do! AD stands for anno Domini, which means "in the year of the Lord!" To decide to begin the new year with affirmation instead of resolutions would require an honest look at what matters to you, what matters in fact not just fancy! Affirmation requires deliberate identity of what you know to be good and true. The end result? Most likely a better year than one based on resolutions that usually expend themselves in the making.

To be sure, I have intentions of doing a whole lot better about many things in 2002 anno Domini than I did in 2001. Still, I am already identifying and affirming afresh basic matters involving faith, family, community, work, and a host of areas that affect me.

Thanks, little lady, for prompting me to affirmation this year rather than resolutions! I think I have identified and affirmed enough to let me, if I were to keep a journal, begin an entry by writing, "My life is OK."

Anybody join me?

Written by Lloyd E. Batson
Published January 2, 2002

Two boxes

Two boxes are sitting side by side on my desk in front of me. Two small boxes, but much larger than their size!

One box is empty. The other is full. Both boxes speak to me about how, in part, I will live my life in 2002 AD.

The empty box, once full, held the envelopes I used to share, financially, in the ministry of our church locally and around the world, it having had an envelope for every week plus some extra ones for special causes. The full box has an envelope for every week of 2002 AD plus ones for additional opportunities. I used all of the ones for 2001 AD, but, at this writing, have not used one for 2002 AD. No one required me to use the ones for last year and no one will this year.

Why do I find myself starring at both boxes? Both boxes have an appeal to which I will respond during the year. Both boxes represent how I may relate to the challenge of human need all around me. The two boxes on my desk happen to be church offering envelope boxes, but the fact is that, in some form, other empty and full boxes abound in my life, "boxes" representing varying opportunities to be involved in helping in human need, both physical and spiritual.

I stare at the empty box. A box could be empty because I "dumped" the contents, feeling I had no time, interest, or resources to use them. It could be empty because I did use them, with full or limited response.

Assuming I used the opportunities as they appeared, what do I let the empty box cause me to say now? A common reaction to the "empty boxes" of one's life is to feel "I have done my part. Let somebody else do what needs to be done now." As a pastor, for example, over and over I heard, in one form or another, "I have had my turn. Get somebody else." To put it bluntly, will I allow myself to bask in what I have done in the past to the point I am not available to share in the opportunities and needs at hand now?

I stare at the full box. Human needs, spiritual and physical, abound all around me. How do I feel about my role in trying to help in meeting them? The box is full but nobody can require me to use the opportunities reflected in the "box." If I do start using the box, will it be because I feel some kind of obligation which I will meet, however reluctantly or meagerly? Or, will it be because I am grateful I have the privilege to be involved?

I stare at the two boxes, one empty and one full.

I know that my choice as to the role of those "boxes" in my life will have no major impact in dealing with the massive human needs, physically and spiritually, in my world. I know that I am not equipped with resources and talents enough to make a major difference in my world. Yet, that full box appeals to me more than the empty one! That box represents what I can do! And I can do something!

I know I cannot respond to everything that needs to be done or to everything somebody wants me to do. Yet, as a human being and as a child of God I know I have the privilege of trying to be of some help in my world.

Two boxes! What my track record in 2002 AD will be is yet to be determined but I am tossing the empty one and will work on emptying the full one! And be grateful for the privilege!

Do you see any boxes in front of you?

Written by Lloyd E. Batson
Published January 9, 2002

Oh-oh

In a corner, away from the crowds who passed by the casket to speak with the family, I stood with a man who had lived in this area in his early life, but for many years had lived in another part of the country, only rarely coming back to visit. I more observed to him than asked, "I suppose you have some difficulty knowing who all these people are."

"That's right," said he, "but, look, I know that gray-headed man, and that other one back yonder near the door." He proceeded then to identify about five people in the huge room.

"I really don't know many of the people my own age, they've all changed so," he continued, "but those older people, like that gray-headed man, I remember well. They were the grown-ups who were nice and helpful to me when I was a youngster." He went on to recount some of the specific things that made him remember that gray-headed man, and the others.

Then I heard this man, in a low whisper, mutter, "Oh, oh! There's one coming in I wish I didn't remember." I'm rather glad he didn't elaborate, because I recognized the man, too.

I was struck again, as I have been many times in my life, with the impact, for good or bad, that older people have on young lives. Older people who care about younger people make lasting impressions upon them. Older people who don't care about younger people also make lasting impressions upon them.

Sometimes I sense an anxiety on the part of folk about not having much talent or opportunity to do great things. What a major ministry available to all people in the very thing represented here! For one older person to influence for good a younger person is a great thing. To do something helpful for a younger person is a continuing possibility and opportunity that all people have. And what a needed ministry!

The contrary is true, too. Careless or indifferent attitudes and behavior of older folk directly to, or in the presence of younger folk, make a detrimental impression that goes on and on.

Grown-ups affecting the lives of young people! Yes, that is the way it is, for good or bad!

Would it matter to you if some day some person standing in a corner watching you go by said to one standing near, "Hey, there's a person who was nice and helpful to me when I was a youngster!"? Or,"Oh, oh! There's one I wish I didn't remember!"?

I hope it would.

Written by Lloyd E. Batson
Published January 16, 2002

Here comes the doting grandfather again!

A friend

My older son just sent me a copy of something his 6-year-old son, a first-grader, typed on the computer at school. I am repeating it here exactly as my grandson wrote it. It had to do with his first sleepover at a friend's house. He wrote: "Sam was sleeping I had a hard time sleeping I was at my friends house it was fine in the morning but not at night their was scary noyses and I couldn't say a thang in not to long I shut my eyes and went to sleep. Not to long it was morning time and Sam as me if I had a good night I said first I had a hard time sleeping in thin I got use to it as if it were magic I should of bin brave not scaird After breckfist I went home my dad askt me if I had fun? I said yes he askt me what I did? I said first we played outside thin we played with his legos my dad said you must have had fun I said I lirnd I should never be afrade at a friends house."

My grandson along the way will learn to spell correctly, to do the proper things with punctuation, etc., but he has already learned a fundamental truth that is basic to happiness and well-being. A friend offers, without constant need for articulating it, pleasure, strength, and fulfillment.

Most people have many acquaintances but among them are those that are "friends." There are no set formulas as to what makes a friend. In a sense, friends just happen, they just are, because they turn relationships into a sharing of interests, experiences and comforting identity.

"Be there with you" is a common term nowadays to express relationships, and that certainly helps define friendship. A friend will "be there with you," in the good and the bad.

Many of us have had "scary noyses" make us appreciate friends who are "there with us." When I read Miles' essay I quickly thought of some very special people who have been my friends, folk who make my life better, giving me a sense of well-being. I thank God for them.

And you know what? I thank God, but I think I need to thank them!

Written by Lloyd E. Batson
Published January 23, 2002

Wants do vary

I am now into my 13th year of being old, having "retired" over 12 years ago! During these years, to borrow a descriptive phrase from early Methodist history, I have been a "circuit riding minister," preaching, speaking and teaching in many churches and places where I am invited and having a great time!

Recently I was to preach on Sunday in a church in the absence of the pastor. I taught a Sunday School class here in Easley, drove to that church, and got there a bit before the morning service was to begin. In the sanctuary I went to sit in a pew near the front to wait. Directly in front of me was a boy, about 12 years of age. I told him that I noticed in the printed order of worship that the pastor was absent and a guest minister would speak. I asked if he knew the visiting minister, the Dr. Batson indicated. When he said he didn't, I told him, "Well, I surely hope he is a good preacher because I want to hear a good sermon." Quickly the boy replied, "Well, I want to get out early!"

I am not certain that I accommodated that young fellow. I recall once that I wanted one of my sons, then 8 years of age, to come upstairs from the basement where he was. At the head of the stairwell I called down to him, "Son, I wish you would come up here." From the basement the reply came, "Well, your wish does not correspond with my want!" Plain spoken!

By the way, I have been invited back to that church and if that boy is on the front row again I plan to accommodate to his "want," even if I don't get mine. I wish there were some way I could confess to that boy that I, too, have had times in church, and elsewhere, when I wish I could have gotten out early or earlier than I did!

Across many years, however, I have believed that when I go to a public meeting it is important, particularly when it is in church, to ready myself ahead of time to profit from being there, without depending on the eloquence of the sermon, speech or talk (or even the length of it), to impress or persuade me to believe it was worthwhile to be there. One does not have to go into neutral to survive a meeting. The mind, and the heart, doesn't have to go dead even with the dullest of the dull speeches, presentations, or sermons. I have learned that the more I put of my attention, thought, intellectual and emotional search into the activity going on the more I get out of it. In the case of a sermon, as important as it is, it is but one part of the reason I have gone, which reason is to worship, and worship is my responsibility. I am aware that largely what I get out of "church," or anything I attend, depends upon me, and my readiness to receive, and not upon what somebody does for me. I confess, though, that it surely helps if the speech, program, or sermon is interesting, good, and well presented.

Young fellow, I am not sure I can remember what the "guest minister" that day preached about, but you made my visit there memorable.

Written by Lloyd E. Batson
Published January 30, 2002

Everybody needs an Uncle Clarence

Everybody needs a favorite uncle in his life. I had one. His name was, to me, Uncle Clarence. Once when I was about 10 years old, we went from downstate to visit Grandpap and Grandmother Lyons on their farm upstate in Laurens County (they were always tenant farmers, never owning any land; wonderful, wonderful people they were!). So many exciting experiences were to be had while visiting there!

Uncle Clarence, about 10 or 11 years older than I, was still living at home with Grandpap and Grandmother. Uncle Clarence smoked cigarettes which he rolled from tobacco bought in cloth sacks with draw strings. He kept two or three sacks of the smoking tobacco, his brand being, I think, Golden Grain – anyway it had a blue label on it – over the mantel piece in the front room.

One day, when nobody was in sight, and for what reason I do not know, I went to the mantel, took one of the tobacco sacks and slipped it under my black sweater into a shirt pocket. I am sure I didn't know what I would do with it. Perhaps to try to make a cigarette and smoke it? I don't know. Anyway, I went out behind the barn and was standing there when I heard from behind me Uncle Clarence call my name. I nearly died! He had, unknowingly to me, seen me and followed me out to the barn.

Uncle Clarence asked me why I had taken his tobacco. I said I hadn't. He asked me what that bulge under my sweater was. I was caught!

Quietly and gently, Uncle Clarence talked to me about what I had done and how it was wrong to take what belonged to somebody else. Then he, with unbelievable kindness in his eyes and a gentle smile, told me that if I handed to him his tobacco and promised I would never do such a thing again he would not tell Eva (his sister and my mother) what I had done. Then he told me he loved me and forgave me.

Wow! What an awesome moment behind that barn! I loved him and he loved me until he died! I never did such a thing again in my life. Forgiving love had touched me!

Uncle Clarence! Everybody needs an Uncle Clarence in his life!

And everybody needs to be an "Uncle Clarence!"

Written by Lloyd E. Batson
Published February 6, 2002

Lost your honeymoon?

Slumgullion Pass! An unusual name – when compared to the commonplace names of Pickens County like Oolenoy, Pumpkintown, Sassafras Mountain, Terrapin Crossing, Nine Times, Sugar Likker Lake, Rocky Bottom, etc.! But Slumgullion Pass was important to us because it was the only name we could remember from our honeymoon trip into Colorado in 1950, after being married in Albuquerque, N.M.

Can you ever lose a honeymoon? Well, we did. Somewhere, probably in the move from Louisville, Ky. to Pickens County in 1956, we lost all the pictures we took and the travel brochures related to our honeymoon trip to Colorado.

For many years we had been unable to recall where it was we spent those interesting and exciting days. We could remember we were on a beautiful lake, surrounded by towering mountains, near a small town, and that we stayed in a cement block cabin, sparsely furnished, but only one name remained, Slumgullion Pass. I could remember taking a picture of my bride standing by the sign marking Slumgullion Pass, giving the elevation as over 11,000 feet.

After many years we found Slumgullion Pass on a Colorado map. Following a work session at Glorietta Baptist Conference Center in New Mexico, we headed out in search of our honeymoon! Would you believe we found it? Not far from Slumgullion Pass, at Lake San Cristobal near Lake City, Colo.! The cement block motel unit, for which we paid, I think, four dollars a day, is now a storage shed. But Lake San Cristobal is still there, more beautiful even than we remembered.

Would you believe we had as good a time this visit as we did those many years ago, maybe better?

Can you ever lose a honeymoon? We've laughed about losing ours and we delighted in finding it again.

On a much more serious level I see so many people who seem to have lost theirs and seem never to have found it again. I'm not talking about a place, a trip, or even an initial exciting experience. I'm talking about one definition of "honeymoon" the dictionary carries, "a period of harmony immediately following a marriage."

A lot of jokes are made about honeymoons, such as, "Well the honeymoon must be over." Why should that ever be? Of course, relationships must change and develop, must take on growth and meaning. It's serious business, being married. Marriages must mature beyond those beginning hours and days, but please tell me, why should the honeymoon ever get over, particularly the concept of "harmony immediately following a marriage?"

Honeymoons get lost for many reasons, many of them in the areas of neglect, indifference and selfishness. Some get lost and are never found again. Most people who have lost their honeymoons could find them again, if they want to, and if they are willing to go in diligent search.

Any of you lost your honeymoon? You are the poorer for it if you have.

Feb. 14 is Valentine's Day. Wouldn't it be a good time to start looking again for important things that may have been lost?

Written by Lloyd E. Batson
Published February 13, 2002

The magic of colored rings

What a difference those little rings have made, for about 20 years now! Blue ones, yellow ones, white ones, red ones ^ plastic rings, about the size of a half dollar, with teeth protruding inwardly. Some very wise person once gave them to us for Christmas, simple plastic rings that have contributed lastingly to the family well-being.

For years it had been a constant source of irritation, this hunting for socks that match, this trying to find socks that had gotten mixed with another family member's socks, this collection of single socks that once upon a time had had mates. After the advent of the rings, each male of the family had color-coded rings through which to push his pair of socks when taken off. That particular brand of a family irritation went away, and how sweet it was! When they came out of the washer and dryer all one had to do to have matched socks that were his own was to remember his ring color! And the washing machine seemed to quit swallowing up single socks any more!

Why didn't I find those rings earlier in life, or come up with some similar arrangement like pinning them or something? Well, I don't know. I just didn't and that is the point. Most of us perpetuate a lot of unnecessary irritations, when a little thought or planning or effort could do something constructive about them. Many people work hard at solving major problems in their lives while allowing a lot of little things to go on untended.

Wouldn't it be great if families would learn that a lot of the bickering over little things, sometimes allowed to go on for a long time, could be eliminated by recognizing what is happening and working at a solution? Wouldn't people, in general, get along better if the little irritating things between them were improved with a little attention to them.

Common sense, applied to dealing with the repetitive little irritations in the household with things and people, could deal with most of them and surely make life more pleasant.

There is even spiritual help in dealing with recurring irritations.

There is a little phrase in a well-known section of the Bible that means a lot to me, "Give us this day our daily bread." Whatever else this part of the Lord's Prayer means, it says to me that God invites us to bring in prayer to him the daily things that bother us. The Creator knows that physical things have to do with a lot of a person's daily concern, and these things, too, can be presented to the Father. Our lives are usually affected by an accumulation of little things more than they are by big things. These little things include irritations, alienations, petty jealousies, etc. We can seek help in these very human things!

Thanks again, friend, for some colored plastic rings! For many years they have made family life a bit more pleasant! And they have helped with seeing that other "irritations" don't have to keep on being irritations!

Written by Lloyd E. Batson
Published February 20, 2002

A ministry of oohing and ahing

I saw them meet, and heard their greetings to each other. I saw the faces of two of them light up when the third asked about the couple's family. Then I saw the scrambling through the lady's purse as she hunted what I knew had to be pictures. Then such pride glowing from the couple's faces as the pictures were handed to the other!

I wish that was all I had seen. What I saw next was what I have seen many times, a quick shuffling of the pictures with hardly a glance at them and a murmured "nice," followed immediately with some question about politics in the area where the couple live. The glow on the couple's faces faded. Their moment of joy had been snatched from them by the careless and thoughtless inattention of one with whom they wished to share something important.

I know all the stuff people say about grandparents boring others to death with pictures and stories about grandchildren, for example. By the way, I'm glad that I happen to be one who likes to look at others pictures! In many situations I know that what others have to say or show may not always be interesting. But, still, I know the disappointment, even hurt, that comes when it is obvious the other person doesn't care enough to listen or watch while one tries to share something important to him or her.

What I'm actually campaigning for at this moment is the development of a ministry of attentiveness! Most people really don't intend to offend by inattention. It just happens. One needs to develop the awareness that paying attention to what is important to another, whether or not the subject is interesting, is one of the best gifts one can give to another. It is terribly deflating to have somebody treat indifferently the thing that is of great significance to that person.

There is a ministry everybody can do. I call it the ministry of "oohing and ahing," responding with full attention to whatever it is somebody takes joy in and wishes to share. It's a simple ministry, but it finally is a beautiful one. And besides, the one who makes sure he or she is attentive to others will probably discover some new pleasure.

Thoughtlessness, carelessness, and inattentiveness, at certain times, can have about the same effect as a slap in the face.

Maybe we ought to pay attention to whether we pay attention! It's a small thing to do. It's a big thing not to do!

Written by Lloyd E. Batson
Published February 27, 2002

A waving bye place

Many times across the years I went to the stately old two-story white frame house up beyond Ambler School on Highway 8. The house sat back from the highway and had a bending road going in front of and then alongside the house.

The hospitality was always warm and the food great, but one thing I always looked forward to was standing in front of a certain window there. A first-timer there without awareness of its name and use would simply see it as an ordinary window. To the family it was a very special window, a place precious to them. They called it the "Waving Bye Place."

As a family member, or members, left, or as a guest who had been in the home departed, the one or ones left would stand at the window, follow with gazing eyes the bending approach to the highway, all the while waving goodbye. Often both smiles and tears brightened the faces above the waving hands.

The waving goodbye told a story. It was a way to express the joy and goodness found in family and friends. It spoke to ties that bind even in separation. The waving was a form of a blessing upon the departing by those that stayed, a kind of well wishing that needed no words. The waving was a kind of prayer to the Father God for the welfare of those leaving.

The waving from the "Waving Bye Window" had another precious dimension to it. Even as the waving took place there was a sense of anticipated joy in the return at some point, soon or at some distant time, of the one or ones leaving. The very window offering an expression of farewell would become a welcoming place! The window, though called a "Waving Bye Place," was in essence also a place of hope.

Every household, with or without a specific, available window, needs a "waving bye place," a ritual of some sort, a way of expressing ties of love and appreciation for family or friends. We, in our own family, discovered that we, too, without naming it, had a "waving bye place," ours being at the back door at the top of our steep driveway. It is a different place where we live now, but the ritual is the same.

There is another greatly important moment that at some point inevitably comes to every family that, too, is a "waving bye" experience. That moment is when a loved one dies and a final farewell takes place. The earthly goodbye has to be expressed, with all the mixture of emotions that moment brings. But look at what becomes priceless, the last element of the "Waving Bye Place," hope! The hope of seeing the loved one again!

How eternally important to make sure through all the "coming and going" years that the final earthly farewell will be blessed with the full assurance of seeing the departed again!

A "waving bye place!" An important place and experience!

Written by Lloyd E. Batson
Published March 6, 2002

One could be wrong sometimes!

I have the world's worst filing system, I know. At the bottom of a drawer I found a note I once made about an exchange between my older son, then 8 years old, and me, his father. Apparently I had made to him some kind of statement, pronouncement or ultimatum, the validity of which he disputed. Here's what followed:

"Son," I declared, "you know I don't lie to you."

"I know you don't lie to me," he retorted, "but you could be wrong."

There is wisdom for all ages, right there!

It is right at this point that many of the problems between people are caused, with good, and often sincere people, making assertions, issuing statements, taking stands, voicing categorical evaluations without realizing there may be another side to the question at hand. We see it nearly every day, somebody expressing an opinion, making a judgment on the basis of an incomplete or even erroneous information.

Neighbors get at odds with one another, friends get crossed up, and divisions come between people because assertions, judgments, and declarations are made without the awareness that one could be wrong.

Many homes have been hurt when the husband or wife, or both, lose recognition of, or respect for, the intelligence and understanding of the other and assume an authoritarian, know-it-all, "I'm never wrong" attitude.

Many churches across the centuries have suffered because of strong-minded persons who have a sense of infallibility about themselves and their opinions and ideas.

Often an individual has shut off the counsel and wisdom of others by feeling he or she already knows all that needs to be known. Often a person has been hurt by another who proclaims something to him or her as if such an assertion comes from God himself.

Certainly there are times when decisions have to be made, stands must be taken, and positions established. These should be done on the basis of honest understanding based on as much information as can be obtained. These should be done with an openness for further light, if it comes, and with a respect for others who, equally as honestly, may hold other viewpoints. But whatever is done, a person needs to avoid developing an aura of infallibility.

As much as it may be deflating to us, sometimes, sincere or not, we just may be wrong!

Written by Lloyd E. Batson
Published March 13, 2002

The magic of small umbrellas

During one of the recent greatly welcomed heavy rains I went to a department store to purchase a single item. From the parking lot I followed to the store a couple, huddled closely under a very small umbrella. As they kept bumping one another, with the overspill of each of them getting wet, they laughed heartily and kept turning to one another with a warming smile that said, "Hey, this is fun!"

From behind them I said out loud, "What I think this world needs is more small umbrellas!" Inside the store I had a delightful conversation with the two pleasant people, strangers to me. I was still enjoying remembering that couple when I found what I wanted in the electronics section and went to the counter to pay. When the checkout man finally came I remarked to him that I hoped his day had been good. Gruffly he declared, "My wife and I have had a big fight'" Still in the euphoria of the "small umbrella" incident I replied, "Well, think how sweet the making up will be."

"I want her to pack her bag and go," he spat out.

Conversation ended!

As I walked sadly away I confess I said a prayer for the man and woman with such alienation, and asked God to find a way to get them both under a very small umbrella of some kind. I had seen the magic of a small umbrella in a rain a number of times before but when I got back to my car I sat for a time thinking about other "umbrellas" that can work a special kind of magic at bringing folk together.

A primary "small umbrella" for married folk is a fresh look at the wedding covenant, a covenant of two differing personalities and varying interests brought together in the oneness of marriage. An open and honest consideration of the good things they have going can serve as a catalyst for renewed closeness. Just a simple attempt, in the midst of problems, to be nice, or at least courteous, to one another can reduce the distance between them. Married folk have more "small umbrellas" than they may think if they would look for them and use them "when it rains."

It isn't just married folk who could benefit from a "small umbrella." Neighbors, fellow workers, students in school, folk of different races and cultures, even people in church could learn to enjoy one another by seeking out and discovering the goodness of sharing common experiences a bit closer to one another.

Is it too far fetched to think that even nations could benefit from some kind of "small umbrella?"

I think I am right. The world does need more small umbrellas!

Written by Lloyd E. Batson
Published March 20, 2002

Easter's story

The yearly observance of Easter in today's world has come to involve varied practices that are enjoyable and exciting to many. Yet, at its base, Easter celebrates the resurrection of Jesus Christ from the dead.

I thought it well to quote some of what the New Testament of the Bible, the basic textbook about the resurrection, has to say of such a monumental event. Here are some selected statements of what the Bible says about the resurrection (Scriptures from the NIV):

"After the Sabbath, at dawn on the first day of the week, Mary Magdalene and the other Mary went to look at the tomb." Matthew 28:1

"...Do not be afraid, for I know that you are looking for Jesus, who was crucified. He is not here; he has risen, just as he said. Come and see the place where he lay." Matthew 28:5,6

"...go quickly and tell his disciples: 'He has risen from the dead....'" Matthew 28:7

"Jesus said to her, 'I am the resurrection and the life. He who believes in me will live, even though he dies; and whoever lives and believes in me will never die. Do you believe this?'" John 11:25,26

"After his suffering, he showed himself to these men and gave many convincing proofs that he was alive. He appeared to them over a period of forty days and spoke about the kingdom of God." Acts 1:3

"Why should any of you consider it incredible that God raises the dead?" Acts 26:8

"...was declared with power to be the Son of God by his resurrection from the dead: Jesus Christ our Lord." Romans 1:4

"We are therefore buried with him through baptism into death in order that, just as Christ was raised from the dead through the glory of the Father, we too may live a new life." Romans 6:4

"If we have been united with him in his death, we will certainly also be united with him in his resurrection." Romans 6:5

"And if the Spirit of him who raised Jesus from the dead is living in you, he who raised Christ from the dead will also give life to your mortal bodies through his Spirit, who lives in you." Romans 8:11

"By his power God raised the Lord from the dead, and he will raise us also." 1 Corinthians 6:14

"But Christ has indeed been raised from the dead, the firstfruits of those who have fallen asleep." 1 Corinthians 15:20

"...because we know that the one who raised the Lord Jesus from the dead will also raise us with Jesus and present us with you in his presence." 2 Corinthians 4:14

"I want to know Christ and the power of his resurrection and the fellowship of sharing in his sufferings, becoming like him in his death, and so, somehow, to attain to the resurrection from the dead." Philippians 3:10,11

"Since then, you have been raised with Christ, set your hearts on things above, not on earthly things." Colossians 3:1

"...through the appearing of our Savior, Christ Jesus, who has destroyed death and has brought life and immortality to light through the gospel." 2 Timothy 1:10

"Praise be to the God and Father of our Lord Jesus Christ! In his great mercy he has given us new birth into a living hope through the resurrection of Jesus Christ from the dead...." 1 Peter 1:3

HAPPY RESURRECTION CELEBRATION!!

Written by Lloyd E. Batson
Published March 27, 2002

Where is a holy place?

Ever get sent home because you were not properly dressed? Well, I was. Just recently, at a Madhatters Luncheon, a benefit "performance" for two facets of our local hospital!

I had been "volunteered" to help serve the luncheon. When I got there I was told I needed a hat (I didn't know what "Madhatters" were all about!) and I was sent home to get one. I don't own any dress hats so I grabbed my ancient fishing cap off the garage wall, a cap dirty, misshapen and splattered with paint - pretty sorry, I know; but it is mine, and I wouldn't trade it for a brand new one. Back I went to carry out my assignment, wearing that "hat," serving that wonderful array of folk, predominantly women, most of whom had designed and were wearing the most elaborate hats I ever saw.

The shocker? When the parade started and the judging of the hats took place I won the prize, a really nice one, a quality knife - for the "tackiest" hat!

Fun!

Afterwards I had the privilege of telling some folk about my ancient cap. After we retired and moved to Easley I decided our house needed painting and, while I never had painted a thing, I wanted to paint our house all by myself. And I did!

The day I started, and wearing my cap, I was aware of a particular person with a special need. As I started painting across that first board, with no semblance of artistry, I found myself praying for that troubled person. As I started across the next board another person appeared in my mind and heart and I, with eyes wide open, and smearing paint as I did so, prayed for that individual. By the time I had painted a few more boards with similar praying I knew what I would do!

The result? The paint job wouldn't get expert approval, but every board, on all sides of our house, had somebody prayed for as it was painted!

Somewhere in the length of time it took me to complete the job I was guest minister in the church where I had been pastor for 33 years. Before I began the sermon, I told the congregation about what I was doing and that I had prayed for some of them. After the service one lady came to me and asked, "Have you gotten to my board yet?"

I responded, "Lady, I have painted your board twice!"

Some people told me that when I got to them please make it a long board.

My cap is a special one to me, not alone because it is my fishing and working hat, but because it also reminds me of something I need to remember and can experience regularly. Many times I need a holy place, a place I can think, or pray, or express my deepest feeling, and a place I can feel I can meet God about anything important to me.

A church is easily recognized as a holy place, but what my dilapidated and paint-spattered old cap reminds me of is that a holy place can be anywhere I need one! I can meet with God on a ladder while spreading paint with my eyes wide open! Anywhere I am and need a holy place, when I talk with God that "anywhere" is a holy place.

If I get to stay around a little longer I probably am going to try to paint my house one more time. Anybody need your name on one of my boards?

Yes, a holy place is anywhere you need it to be - and will make it so!

Written by Lloyd E. Batson
Published April 3, 2002

Watching a bird smile

Did you ever see a bird smile? I think I did.

I was standing at the back window in our dining area, simply enjoying looking at the world outside. I became aware of movement just below me in the edge of the azalea bushes along the wall. There was a bird, a medium sized one, one that in my growing up days we called a brown thrasher. I do not know if that is a correct name.

The bird was furiously striking with its beak at something small and round, possibly a nut of some kind it had unearthed. I was enthralled. Whatever it was apparently was very hard. Over and over again the bird struck at the round thing, for what seemed an interminable time.

Occasionally the bird would stop briefly and seem to take a deep breath. Then the steady striking would start over.

I was transfixed. Then the round thing parted, but the bird started immediately in on one half until it was in several yellowish pieces. After the bird seemed to rest a bit, it started on the other half until it, also, was a cluster of tiny pieces.

What happened next I will recall with pleasure for a long time. The bird lifted its head and smiled! I don't know if ornithologists would admit a bird can smile, but on this one I saw a smile! Then with an air of delight, as I saw it, the thrasher started eating the tiny yellowish specks of whatever it was.

When all was gone, I saw that bird cock its head sideways and look up - for a long time - and, as I interpreted it, seemed to be offering thanks to its heavenly Father.

The smile seemed to come back as the bird bowed its head, and then walked away. What I had seen also in that tiny creature was full commitment to what it took to get done what needed to be done. Wouldn't it be great if that were always the case with all of us humans? And wouldn't it be great if we could regularly be thankful, and express it, for the life we have and the provisions available.

The Bible pictures God as knowing and caring about every bird! And about every one of us!

Do you think a thrasher can know about God? I surely am not one to say it can't! I only know that I saw a bird smile and raise its head in thanks!

Written by Lloyd E. Batson
Published April 10, 2002

The motor done suck up a sock

I suppose that had there been someone watching a few days ago he or she might have thought some "loosely put together in the mind" old man had escaped the care of the hospital. As I left Palmetto Health Baptist Easley, after visiting some sick folk, I decided to take a meandering walk to my car just to look around. Out near the road I burst into laughing, a laughing that took a while to simmer down into a chuckle.

There, in my mind, I saw it again, after many years. I had been in my car leaving the hospital. Out in the road, in front of the hospital, a car was stopped with the hood up. Standing around the car were several people, one a woman with a screwdriver in her hand with which she was punching and twisting at something under the raised hood. I stopped to offer a set of battery jumper cables which I always carry in my car and often use to help people stranded by a dead battery. Said a man in the group to me, "No, thank you, but that's not our problem." From under the raised hood, the woman with the screwdriver said, with some agitation, "The motor done suck up a sock!"

Struggling to maintain my composure, I saw what had happened. The oil filter cap on the top of the motor on that car, an old one, had been lost and somebody had stuck a sock into the opening to serve as a cap. The sock had disappeared into the motor! Trouble indeed! "The motor done suck up a sock!" It is pretty bad to have that happen to a motor. Can't your imagination take you under the valve cover of the motor and show you that sock getting tangled up in all kinds of important stuff?

When those folk discovered the oil filler cap was missing, instead of getting a proper replacement they simply substituted something more convenient but inferior. I have witnessed many more serious problems than that in the lives of some people whose "motor done suck up a sock."

People who have a serious problem and refuse to deal directly with it, but go on substituting one thing after another for what is actually needed, will finally get into trouble. Most of us can recognize many situations in our lives that could have been better handled if we had just done the right thing to start with, as inconvenient or difficult as the right thing might have been. The human life, like a motor, has to be maintained with dependable and proven strengths and values. All of us have social, economic and religious needs for which substituting "socks" will invite trouble. As one example, let a person refuse to deal directly with some destructive habit and that person ultimately will suffer.

In my involvement with people as a minister, I have shared the hurts of many people who need God in their lives but go on trying to find something else instead. These folk finally have trouble indeed!

Individuals, communities, society in general, and even churches will get into trouble if real needs are ignored or handled carelessly.

At a given moment it may be demanding, or even difficult, to do the right thing; but to substitute inferior solutions is to invite a discovery down the way that the "motor done suck up a sock."

Written by Lloyd E. Batson
Published April 25, 2002

Somebody needs you

The young man's mother had died. I knew how close they had been across the years, this son and his mother. I more observed than asked, "You and your mother had a good thing going, didn't you?"

While we stood in the yard, in no hurry to go anywhere, he began to speak of his feelings for his dear mother, with a beautiful sense of delight showing through grief. After he had shared at some length his admiration and gratitude for his mother, he ended the whole discussion with four words, "She was my encourager."

"She was my encourager." Isn't that a lovely thing to be said about a person? I have heard, and appreciated, many beautiful things said about people, but this must surely be one of the highest tributes I have ever heard offered.

Many people can do great and outstanding things to help and to impress people around them. But who, truly, has done more for a person than to be his or her encourager? Furthermore, while talents and opportunity influence many of the measurable standards for recognition and achievement, there is nobody that cannot be somebody's encourager.

The world is full of people who need encouraging. I am one of these. You are one of these. Everybody I know is one of these. So, for those who sincerely would like to find a meaningful ministry, it is not difficult to discover one. People who need encouragement are everywhere.

There are no special skills needed to be an encourager. An encourager, though, does have to be a "noticer." The selfish person, whose world is largely his or her own circle of interests and concerns, cannot do much encouraging of others because he or she doesn't pay much attention to the fact that another may be perplexed, confused, disturbed, uncertain, down and out, or just simply "in neutral." An encourager does have to be a loving person, or certainly a caring person. To be an encourager does call for sensitivity to communicate genuine interest, understanding, even acceptance, in a loving spirit, to the other person. An encourager can rarely be a condemner.

What a ministry nearly everybody can have as encouragers! The need is universal, but it has to be personalized, on a "one on one" basis. Encouragement can be scattered generally, but it is most effective when one person notices and cares about another person and sustains over as long a time as is needed a loving interest in that person.

I had in mind writing about encouragers to young folk, to old people, to struggling families, to seeking and trying people who have difficult tasks in the church, community, schools and work. But writing space is gone. Please, will you take over and finish this?

If you become an encourager to somebody I think you will have found one of the greatest ministries under God.

Written by Lloyd E. Batson
Published May 1, 2002

Mother's Day is for remembering, honoring and loving

The hurt long ago went away. The love still remains.

I like to think it was curiosity and not meanness that made me do it. At 6 years of age it could have been a mixture of both, I know.

Daddy had bought a new gray felt hat. Getting anything new in those depression times of 1930 was a major event. The hat lay on the hall table in that house next door to Graham Baptist Church in Sumter County, the place we lived until I was nearly nine years old. My, it felt funny, to small fingers, the texture of that new hat!

For some reason mother had left her long scissors on the same table that held the hat. Scissors, a new, strange-feeling hat, and a curious 6-year-old make for an almost predictable outcome. Yes, I found out that funny-feeling hat would cut! Furthermore, so would the scarf, as we called it, on the table under the hat, a hand-sewn cloth with tatting.

My daddy and mother were not happy! Daddy's razor strop, which he kept hanging on the kitchen wall for reasons in addition to sharpening his razor, got a workout. Mother compounded the hurt with her skilled and lengthy use of a peach tree limb.

What do I remember most vividly from that childhood experience? Standing naked on a shelf on the back porch, with mother rubbing some kind of salve on my whelps and whispering in my ear that she loved me!

I know my daddy loved me. He showed it in so many ways across so many years, though I am not sure I ever heard him say it. On this Mother's Day celebration, however, I am remembering that moment when an erring 6- year-old received the discipline of punishment he deserved (though I thought that a razor strop and a peach tree limb was a bit severe!) and the forgiveness of love.

Mother had a way of expecting, and demanding, certain behavior from her children. She could be a stern disciplinarian but I never felt I was the object of anger, or that, in the understanding of later years, she was taking out her frustrations or irritation with other people or things upon me. She held standards, important to her role as mother, which she stood by with fairness. Even her skills with a peach tree limb were instruments of discipline in the truest sense of a learning experience. As a part of the discipline Mother usually sent the erring son to get the tree limb for her to use. The son had to be wise enough to choose one that suit her, but one that would also do the least damage.

Mother was a great lady. She was such a formative influence in my life - as a child and as a man. In one way, the image of that 6-year-old standing on a shelf on the back porch being soothed with salve and a mother's love is one of the most meaningful memories I have.

On this Mother's Day I will recall many times a gentle but firm lady, who expected from her children certain standards, guided them toward achieving them, disciplined them when needed, and loved them through all their good and their bad. How fortunate my mother's children are to have the heritage of a great love!

May God multiply the love of wise and caring mothers! And make it possible that on Mother's Day children will be able, in sincerity, to thank God for their mothers.

Written by Lloyd E. Batson
Published May 8, 2002

Can we play with your worms?

We have been blessed with good neighbors. Good neighbors, even when they move away, leave happy memories.

We still miss two precious boys, five and three, I think they were, when they moved away. They had such inquisitive minds and a high level of politeness, a great combination. Often our doorbell, rung at the garage door, would signal a visit from them and I would open the garage to hear these words from those boys, "Can we play with your worms?" Or they would call to me when I was outside, with the same request.

I keep worms, nightcrawlers, the year round in our refrigerator. I started doing that early in our marriage when my wife was still in love with me enough to allow that! Of course, the worms are in boxes and kept in Ziploc bags. What my two little friends wanted was to get one of the boxes, go out on my driveway, empty out the worms and play with them, often for a long time. When they were finished, they would carefully return the worms and worm dirt to the box, and sound the bell again. It always seemed to me I caught more fish with the worms my young friends played with than any others!

"Can we play with your worms?" is for us a symbol of the joy children put into our lives. I think my own life would be greatly impoverished if I did not get to be around children. I like to look at them, to talk with them, to react to their differing personalities and interests. I see them at church, in stores, riding in cars. To have one of them smile at me, wave at me, call to me, tarry for a moment to visit with me is a precious gift to me.

Children come in all kinds of packaging. Some of them are outgoing, some shy, some mischievous, some lighthearted, some serious-minded. Some smile easily, some have to be cajoled so to do. To use the phraseology I have sometimes heard adults use about children, some are devilish and some are angelic. I like them all!

What label would you put on a couple of youngsters in our neighborhood now that like, sporadically, to ring my doorbell and disappear? They apparently have not figured out how I can step out the back, slip around the side and spot their feet, movements, or shadows behind the automobile, or wherever they are hiding, and make a loud and noisy charge at them. What do you call children who do that? I call them my friends! And what would you call me? Probably a child, too!

People of all ages put so much pleasure into my life, but I especially enjoy children. Oh, I know all encounters with children are not pleasant! But neither are encounters with adults all pleasant.

Children do not stay children, and what those I know become in their ever-changing progress through the growth process is exciting and rewarding to me. Yet in each level of their development, as interesting as each level is, I still can impose upon each of them the image of the joy these folk give me as children.

I can watch, as I stand in the hallway at the church, the "lighted up" eyes and smiles on the faces of children as they pass by me. I can hear, in my mind, "Can we play with your worms?" in its various forms. As I do so, my spirit looks toward heaven and says, "Thank you, Father!"

Written by Lloyd E. Batson
Published May 15, 2002

A place to take flowers

Memorial Day! One of the most popular of each year's national holidays, but not particularly for the reason it was established! Designed as a special time to honor people who died in the wars our nation has fought, it also has been called Decoration Day, from the practices by some of placing flowers on the graves of military service personnel.

While some ceremonies are held honoring those that have died in service of our country, Memorial Day now appears generally to be a "'holiday' holiday," a time to make trips, go on family outings, take short vacations, and a variety of such activities. Are we missing something important?

Because Memorial Day, at its best, brings up the subject of death, I have been thinking of times I have tried to talk with children about death. Once to a group of small folk I asked, "Do you know what a cemetery is?" I got a variety of answers.

The response of one bright youngster still is in, and on, my mind, "It's a place you take flowers," said he.

"A place you take flowers!" It is not just because it is time for Memorial Day that I ask you to think about that. Nearly all of us have had someone close to us to die. All of us have known and appreciated some people who have died. "A place you take flowers" is the burying place, but it is more than that. Whatever it means, it says that you have not forgotten so soon someone or some relationships that made your life better.

It means that though there are some obligatory things in life there are some things you do because you want to. When a loved one or a friend dies, great emotion stirs you to do special things at the moment, but "it's a place where you take flowers" means that long after the obligatory things are done you show appreciation because you still are grateful and you do it because you want to.

It means you knew a love that still blesses, and you are grateful.

It means you can take flowers as a means of touching the past again so that you can leave the flowers to go on with the living of your own life, the better for having known and loved a special person.

It means that flowers are not really for the dead but are ways of expression of love and appreciation from the living. It means that flowers are for the giver, not the dead. The dead, by what they meant to you while they were alive, allow you the privilege and the joy of receiving good from taking flowers.

Since children notice, it means that you teach them of some ideals and values that can be valid and precious in their own difficult world.

It seems to me that seeing a cemetery as a place to take flowers says more about living than about dying. Remembering and being grateful for the past gives meaning to the present.

It seems to me that all of us need to discover afresh the value of "a place you take flowers."

Written by Lloyd E. Batson
Published May 22, 2002

The healing powers of 'setting'

I think he was smarter than many of us are.

In the town where I served for a long time I was often in the local hospital. The hospital, in my early days there, had an entrance to the lower floor just off a small side street. One day as I came down the lower floor hallway, I saw a small boy, about ten I guess, sitting on the bench outside the emergency room, just across from the entrance, staring vacantly toward the door. He was resting his chin on his hands with his arms propped on his knees. I thought he looked so sad and lonely.

Not liking anybody to be sad, and thinking to cheer him up, I bounced up to him and inquired, "Son, what are you doing here in a hospital? You don't look sick." Without moving any part of himself except his mouth, he softly said, "I just came in to set."

"Setting!" What an essential and positive activity that can be! While it may not be good English, it often is good sense. In the frenzied activity of today's world of work, recreation, social activities and multiple involvements in many things, a time of "setting" may be the most valuable thing one can do. The body needs resting. The soul needs quietness. The mind needs relaxing.

Planned "setting," even for a brief spell, would be a rewarding segment of most people's lives. Some say they don't have time for relaxed sitting, but some who practice this "don't have time" wind up with unplanned time in burnout.

I think that though I have not always been a consistent practitioner of "setting" time there have been many times when I became more valuable to myself, to my family, to others when I did stop to "set" just like that boy. Many programs of relaxation are on the market today, and some are very expensive, but an age-old one is free, and available. It is called in that boy's terms, "setting."

"Setting" is at its best, I think, when absolutely nothing is going on except sitting or resting without frenzy of body or mind.

A variation of "setting" is also rewarding. Once I was in my office, with the door slightly ajar. I was sitting, reared back in my chair at the desk, staring into space. Into my office came one of the deacons of the church. Proclaimed he, with too much glee, I thought, "Ah, I caught you goofing off."

"On the contrary," I replied. "I am doing the hardest work I know how to do. I am thinking."

A kind of healing comes from a proper use of "setting." Little boy, I have often used your recipe and it is a good one.

And, decon, periods of sitting still with the mind alive and thinking work pretty well too!

Written by Lloyd E. Batson
Published May 29, 2002

About fathers and storms

It had been a delightful outing on Lake Hartwell with my two sons. The fishing had been good and we had enjoyed riding around in the boat. Then, not long before we needed to go home, a storm quickly blew up, a vicious one with high winds and hard rain. We were caught on the other side of the big water away from our car.

Several times I tried to leave the relative security of a cove to start to cross the big water and had to turn back. Finally, with it getting dark, and my thinking it had calmed a bit, we started out. Wow! What a beating we took! I have at times been in some rough stuff, but this was one of the worst, and I was very apprehensive. My older son sat "glued" to the middle seat and was able to hold to each side of the boat. My younger son, then about six or seven, sat in the prow, doggedly holding on while being severely bounced. Using all the skills I had developed across the years, I managed to maneuver the boat across the open water and to a safe landing. What a relief!

As soon as the boat touched the shore near where we had left the car, my younger son turned and called back to me, "Let's go back and do it again!"

I have thought about that many times. Though he knew it was rough, terribly rough, he apparently had no concept of the real danger we had been in. What really was happening, though, was that he trusted his dad. Somehow he felt secure in the midst of a tough time. Trust in his father made everything manageable, and, strangely, fun!

This Sunday we will be celebrating Father's Day, a pleasant and enjoyable corollary to Mother's Day. Many a son or daughter will find a surge of joy remembering his or her father, perhaps expressing sentimentally his or her love in some way that each receiving father will cherish. In all candor, not every child will have good feelings remembering his or her father, for not every father has done well by his children. How sad that this is so.

What more beautiful and finally meaningful relationship can be established between children and parent than trust, a belief in the dependability and integrity of the father and the mother. Trust, not just in the capacity to handle a boat, but an uncluttered belief in the parent to do what is right. Such a belief is easy for the child to give for it is his nature so to do. But in the end, trust is an earned thing. A child, or a grownup for that matter, cannot keep on trusting somebody who proves undependable and untrustworthy.

Whatever Father's Day offers, it is a time for fathers and children to see where they are in this trust factor and to do the necessary things to make sure that a child, whatever his age, can always, in things little and big, trust his or her father.

In a larger sense, it seems to me that all of us who are children of the Heavenly Father can ride out many of the tough times in our lives simply because we have learned we can trust the Father. Whatever else God is to us, he is one we can believe in to do what is right!

"Let's go back and do it again!"

I would not have dared try, but I am glad my son thought we could.

Written by Lloyd E. Batson
Published June 12, 2002

Awesome!

Awesome! I do not know how many times I heard that word "awesome" from the crowd of excited, energetic, and greatly involved young folk. All I know is I began to feel that I myself was a part of something very special.

Where were the excited young folk? At one of the recent blockbuster movies? No. At a fast-paced concert? No. At a ball game? No. At a party? No. I saw all this fun and fervor at something some folk in our society would dismiss, without understanding its potential for the good of so many. It was something called Vacation Bible School, in a church.

Yes, something at a church in the summertime. Something every day for a week. Something planned primarily for young folk of all ages (but sometimes also for grownups, even very old grownups!)

What were the happy and excited sounds about? The discovery of truths about God which relate meaningfully to young lives in our challenging local and world situations. The feeling that there are spiritual principles that can indeed be understood by young folk, in their own terminology, as being strengths and guides for them in an increasingly complex world.

Awesome! Dealing with spiritual matters in the context of fun! Enjoying a great variety of exciting activities as a shared time with others who, too, were in the discovery of awesome matters made understandable and rewarding!

Vacation Bible School! Sound "old timey?" Some, I would assume, even may think it sounds somehow out of touch with the real world. However, just ask those youngsters I saw about that and they would laugh at such a thought! And probably invite you to join them in the school.

Such experiences, described by the young folk themselves as "awesome," do not just happen. A Vacation Bible School like that I saw first hand is a major investment by a church involving long preparation by many committed adults and older teenagers. The very large number of older people who invested untold amounts of time and energy in itself could be shocking for cynical folk who have no way of recognizing why people would give so much of themselves in such a way.

I'll tell you what I did. Before I went home I went into a dark room of the "basement" of the church and thanked God for busy older people, for young parents already with unbelievable heavy demands on them, for teenagers whose lives are so greatly involved in many things, all who worked so hard. These folk chose to give of themselves so that young folk could discover that the concept of the awesome relates to who they are, what they need, and what they can become, and have fun doing it.

While the younger folk were involved in their exciting discovery and experiences of the awesome in their lives, there was another "school" going on. A large number of older people were in another section of the church studying, seeking, facing the many challenges in their own lives, and discovering for themselves fuller understanding and meaning of the "awesomeness" of God possible in their own needs. There was not the outwardly exuberant, energetic expression of the youngsters but there was the same discovery of the presence of God in their own needs.

All around us in our area there have been, and will be, signs in churchyards, ads in papers, and invitations being circulated about something called Vacation Bible School.

Take note! Something "awesome" may be going on!

Written by Lloyd E. Batson
Published June 19, 2002

Soupy Klondike bars

Have you ever been aware that your just-purchased two packages of wonderful Klondike ice cream bars were doing what Klondike bars do in the hot sun? And you did not worry about them doing so?

A few days ago I was pushing my full shopping cart through the parking lot of a grocery store headed in the general direction, I thought, of where I had left my car (I, a supposedly educated and intelligent man, seem rarely ever to pay attention to where I leave my car in a big parking lot). I met a man, whom I had never seen before, walking slowly toward the store, his head down. I made some lighthearted remark to him and he stopped to respond. Well, the Klondike bars in the shopping cart took a beating as we visited together, two strangers who later walked away as friends.

In the conversation with this man, not long a resident of Easley, it was discovered that we knew mutually many folk in other places, people we have admired and enjoyed. This chance encounter with an intriguing and gifted man will remain a special memory for me. By the way, as we parted he asked me, "Why did you happen to speak to me?"

My reply was something like, "You just looked like somebody I'd like to know." After a lengthy conversation, the final words I heard, as I walked away, were, "Whenever you see a person walking along with his head down, please be sure to speak to him!"

I doubt that this bright man with an engaging personality was having some difficult and disturbing moment. It is true, however, that many people carry heavy burdens that could be made a little easier by a greeting, a smile, or a friendly word. I know, of course, that there are times when a person does not welcome or need the intrusion of insensitive people. I also know that there can be a bit of grace, even healing grace, in a genuinely expressed greeting or smile.

I do not know anybody that can be a blessing to everybody under every situation. I do believe, however, that there is not anybody without some capacity to relate in some way to somebody whose head is down. It takes noticing. It sometimes even takes a bit of courage. It certainly takes genuineness (artificiality strikes out fast!). It does not take specialized skills. It does take alertness and it does take sensitivity about the other's feelings.

I left, with my melting Klondike ice cream bars, with a renewed joy in my own day that resulted from a casual overture to the stranger walking with his head down. In our crazy, busy, and impersonal world, it seems such a tragedy that we miss out on the pleasures of meeting some of the interesting folk that we often pass without any kind of acknowledgement!

Said the man of my delightful encounter, "Whenever you see a person walking along with his head down, please be sure to speak to him." That just may be a need of us all!

And you know what? Soupy Klondike bars taste pretty good!

Written by Lloyd E. Batson
Published June 26, 2002

Celebrating Interdependence Day

Many will fly flags and express some patriotic sentiments on July 4!

It is probably so that July 4 is the most widely recognized and observed, in some form, national holiday. July 4 is commonly referred to as Independence Day.

Regrettably, the percentage of folk in our land who know much about the historical background of the reasons for the holiday seems to be declining.

Apparently, fewer and fewer people can remember ever reading the entire historical document, the Declaration of Independence. Fewer still can quote an appreciable amount of it. Those who can quote from it are usually limited to some version of those eloquent and memorable words of the second textual paragraph, the words being:

"We hold these truths to be self-evident, that all men are created equal, that they are endowed by their Creator with certain unalienable Rights, that among these are Life, Liberty and the Pursuit of Happiness."

The major part of the document, generally regarded as one of the most brilliantly written of human documents, details the reasons why separation needed to be made from the control of Great Britain.

The next to last paragraph is the actual declaration of independence (not here quoted). It is the one sentence paragraph, at the end, that is the reason I believe that July 4 should also be celebrated as Interdependence Day. Here is that sentence:

"And for the support of this Declaration, with a firm reliance on the protection of divine Providence, we mutually pledge to each other our Lives, our Fortunes and our sacred Honor."

Fifty members of the Continental Congress signed the document, including four notable citizens from South Carolina. Writing the document, however, would not guarantee that independence would be gained. The citizenry of the American colonies, represented by the signers, would have to work together in sacrificial commitment to secure the coveted independence. The signers knew the struggles ahead to establish an independent nation. They made their own declaration that they would together do what it took to achieve such independence. In essence, they declared that interdependence among all of them together was a necessary part of the implementation of independence.

The making of a truly independent nation is never a finished product. In 1776, there were many conflicting political positions, a sizeable portion of Loyalists (to Great Britain) still in the land, and many and diverse problems to be worked out, but with committed supporters, interdependent with one another, an independent nation could be established and flourish.

On July 4, 2002, are not we still, as a nation, a diverse people, with many problems, internal and external, yet to be solved? It seems to me that finding some way to engender in national recognition a sense of interdependence, a commitment as diverse people working together to secure the fundamental rights declared in the Declaration of Independence, is still the way to go!

Maybe it is indeed time to have some national holiday known as Interdependence Day!

Written by Lloyd E. Batson
Published July 3, 2002

Two zeroes

For years I have heard essentially the same story, from folk who had been students there, about a professor who once was at Clemson University. He was one I would liked to have known, but probably not to have studied under. His students apparently spoke of him as Professor Zero, or simply "Zero."

The professor had a custom of calling on students, randomly, to stand to recite answers to questions about the lesson for the day. If the students didnít know the answer, the professor would stride to the chalkboard and make a show of drawing there a big zero, proclaiming as he did so, "You get a zero!" It was a humiliating tactic.

Once, it is said, the professor called on a student to recite. Rather than admit he did not know the answer, the student attempted to bluff his way. In the midst of his rambling pretense of knowing the answer, the professor stopped him, strode to the chalkboard and drew two huge zeros on the board, announcing, "You get two zeros, one for not knowing the answer and one for not knowing you didn't know!"

Ignorance, meaning without knowledge, is not necessarily a bad state in which to be. It really can be a positive factor, provided the person knows he or she does not know and will seek enlightenment. In fact, most major advancements in any field come from awareness that something needs to be learned or discovered and search is set in motion.

I thought about attempting to write some "learned" words about recognizing limitations and trying to do something about them. Instead, I got sidetracked by thinking about some people I have known that probably would have gotten, for one reason or another, two zeros from Professor Zero. I will just list, randomly, some of them. Perhaps you could recognize some of them (but, hopefully, not be one of them!).

The person who seems to think he or she has the final answer on everything.

The one that everybody but the person himself knows he does not know what he is talking about.

The individual who, immediately after a person finishes telling a story, announces, "I know one better than than."

The one who obviously does not listen to what is being said because he seems to be waiting until he can make a pronouncement on the subject.

That one who gets hung up on something with which he does not agree and pays no attention to the reason or logic for why the speaker is saying what he says.

That difficult person who thinks he already knows more than the one to whom he supposedly is listening.

The person who apparently is ashamed to admit that there is something he does not know and talks anyway, proving he does not.

The final answer type, the one who, no matter what is being said, comes on with a "I'll top you" stance.

The "center stage" type who seems not be able to let some other person get more attention than he does.

The person who "makes a fool of himself" and is oblivious to the fact.

That difficult person who seems to have a closed mind about nearly everything.

On the list could go!

Professor Zero, we need you still—even if we do not know we need you!

Written by Lloyd E. Batson
Published July 10, 2002

A chaw of tobacco

In the spring of 1947, I was in my final year at Furman University. I had two "side" jobs in addition to being a full-time student. I was teaching a class of veterans (I being one, too) in the afternoon at the then Parker High School, and I was serving as supply pastor at one of the larger churches in Greenville, though I was not yet ordained.

One day I went to the old General Hospital to visit an elderly member of the church I was serving. She was in one of those two huge wards the hospital had at that time, with sixteen beds in each, my possibly errant memory tells me. While I was visiting the lady I had gone to see, another elderly lady, two beds down and two beds over from where I was, kept calling to me and beckoning me to come over to her.

I suppose at that time in my inexperience I may have thought I could help anybody with any problem. I do not know now as much as I used to! So, hurriedly, I finished my visit with the one I had gone to see and went over to the lady still calling and beckoning me with her hand. As I went, I prayed to God asking for help with dealing with whatever apparently difficult problem the woman had. By the way, I learned later that she was 90-years-old and had been brought in that day from what then was known as the County Home.

As I got alongside the bed, the lady kept beckoning me to get closer. I was already as close as I thought I should be. I began to get a little nervous and began desperately praying that God would help me with whatever was of such great importance to the poor soul. Perhaps she wanted to confess some grievous sin or talk about dying or something that would require me at my best.

In the midst of my anxiety about having the right things to say, the lady reached up her hands to my head and started pulling it down near her lips. I really started praying then! As she got my ear close to her lips, she asked loudly, "Is you got a chaw of tobacco on you?"

The inexperienced but eager young preacher learned a lesson that day that in remembering it has helped me many times in the 55 years since. One part of the lesson is that I do not know as much as I perhaps sometimes I think I do. The important lesson, however, is that people's needs, or perceived needs, are not necessarily what I think they are, and I should be patient until I understand things better.

It is important for someone in a position to be of help to others not to pass out instant, ready-made answers or advice to the situation at hand, though it is an easy thing to think one knows what the other's needs are without bothering to find out what they really are. It can be hard to put the brakes on our answers to another's problems and to wait until we learn what the real questions are.

Ready-made answers, though possibly good ones, seldom fit every situation. The person who truly wants to help another will pay attention to the other, will listen carefully, will try to learn what the person really needs, or at least thinks he or she needs.

Back to that lady long ago. I am sure she needed my prayers, which I finally got to pray with her, but now I think I wish I had also had a chaw of tobacco on me!

Written by Lloyd E. Batson
Published July 17, 2002

The role of a 'Pop' Gradinger

The barracks was empty when I went in, except for the "old man" of our outfit, one we in our unit affectionately called "Pop." "Pop" Gradinger was from somewhere up north. I strolled over and sat on the bunk across from where he sat, apparently thinking.

He did a lot of thinking.

Our outfit, in World War II, was getting ready to go to Europe to join the fighting there. For me, I thought "Pop" was too old to go to war. I instinctively liked him. We were friends throughout our combat experiences.

"Pop" abruptly asked me, "Did you ever play any sports?"

"Well, yes," I answered, "I have played baseball, football, tennis and done a little bowling."

"Pop" proceeded to tell me he had been director of a YMHA (Young Men's Hebrew Association). Then he invited me to demonstrate certain actions and movements related to the four sports I had played, saying that, from his experiences in coaching, he would evaluate my skills. I wanted to hear his opinion, and told him so. As he called out what he wanted me to do, without any ball, bat or equipment, I tried, as awkward as it was, to do my best.

When the demonstrations were over, he said nothing for a time, apparently thinking again. Finally, he said, matter of factly, "Well, I think you are pretty good at a lot of things and not very good at any."

Pretty straightforward stuff! But "Pop" Gradinger probably had it right. I did not know whether to laugh or get mad. I think I laughed at his honesty - and the accuracy of his assessment.

There is such a negative sound to the verb "criticize" that one may forget that the first listed meaning in the dictionary is "to consider the merits and demerits and judge accordingly." Another is "to evaluate."

Many things would never be improved upon, or be as good as they are, if there had not been criticism at work, meaning analysis or evaluation. Just about everything, in order to be made better, must be criticized, be examined, be judged.

An athlete will get better if he has a coach or instructor that can properly criticize him or her. Training classes in all fields have to use criticism. A teacher will improve under proper criticism. A minister can get better if he will ask for criticism (but, of course, the kind he often gets without asking for it, the negative, bitter stuff, can break or kill him!).

In the work sector and business world, on nearly all levels, criticism and evaluation regularly go on. It is an absolute necessity for success.

The second meaning of the word "criticize" in the dictionary is "to find fault with, point out the faults of." This, of course, is very commonly done, and so often is destructive. It is often mean and ugly. But I am not writing here about this kind of criticism.

It is not always comfortable to seek criticism, and profit from it. Pride and ego have to be ready possibly to take a beating. Yet, proper criticism, sought, accepted, and acted upon can certainly be helpful to nearly everybody.

A "Pop" Gradinger, by whatever name, can be a most useful person, properly sought and used!

Written by Lloyd E. Batson
Published July 24, 2002

About some common social diseases

It had been many years since I had seen him. I was interested in learning about his family and so I inquired about them.

"Well," he said, "we've got two bad diseases in our family that are about to wear everybody out."

As I expressed some kind of regret about that, he continued, "My father is so afraid things are going to get so bad and he'll starve that he wears everybody out talking about it."

"My sister," he continued, "has turned into such an instant authority on any subject which comes up that nobody likes to be around her."

When I realized he was serious, I was perplexed as to how to continue the conversation. In a way, it is easier to deal with infection, pneumonia and a great variety of illnesses than it is to know what to do with diseases like these. And diseases they are, at least in terms of the damaging effect on the people who have them.

Most of us recognize certain developing symptoms that tell us it is time to take some medicine or to see a doctor. Unfortunately, one seldom recognizes developing symptoms that indicate he or she is catching a disease like the two that the family member told me about. Furthermore, and still unfortunately, one developing these diseases often reacts unfavorably to somebody suggesting he or she might be having a problem.

Social diseases are not just those we used to whisper and snicker about. Social diseases are also those which affect a person's relationship to other people. Irritating habits, obnoxious attitudes, thoughtless practices, consistent disregard of the feelings of others, and such, are really social diseases.

A good person, and a religious one, is not immune to certain social diseases, though there should be no good reason he or she should fall victim to them. It will be by his or her own disregard or imperceptiveness that he or she will be caught by these diseases. A person by the very nature of the love to which he or she has been introduced in faith should be the most likeable person around, the one most easy with whom to identify. But sometimes that person is not, because of losing sight of the outgoing touch of love. When one becomes obsessed with his own troubles, increasingly that one feels sorry for himself and less aware of others. All manner of factors enter into the making of a person who is obnoxious or irritating in pronouncements, opinions, and judgments.

A sad part is that the person seldom realizes the way he or she is. But the need to know it is imperative! A self-curing process can start when one realizes he or she has developed a social disease like these mentioned. There is no medicine that one can take, or a doctor to whom one can go. One has to do it himself!

Regularly we look at our bodies to see if there is a rash, or a peculiar looking mole, or something abnormal. Perhaps we should occasionally do a self-check for signs of social diseases like those mentioned herein. If we are praying persons, it would be a proper prayer to God to ask him to help make us likeable and "sweet" (a very good term!) to others. Perhaps we should be courageous enough to ask somebody else if he or she sees any evidence of any kind of a social disease in us and then to be gracious enough to receive the diagnosis and act upon it.

Lovelier and healthier persons can emerge from the curing of some common social diseases.

Written by Lloyd E. Batson
Published July 31, 2002

The power of images

There is power in images.

In one period of less than twelve months, two images have been embedded into the lives of most Americans. Powerful images that have the possibilities of shaping much of our nation's life for an indeterminable time to come!

The image of the destructive power of terrorism and hate fixed itself on September 11, 2001, in the soul of America, and much of the world as well. In all of history, there probably has never been an image with such dramatic impact as the horror of watching the twin towers in New York City disintegrate.

The second image of potentially great power is the most recent one of nine coal miners emerging from entrapment, and nearing certain death, to face again the unfolding of life with family, friends, and all that our nation has to offer.

Two powerful images, perhaps not with equal evocative emotions but with, I think, equal possible strength in what they could mean!

The affairs of September 11, 2001, and all the acts of heroism and massive effort connected, properly replayed in the fixed memory of us all, may be considered by many as the more powerful of the two. I am suggesting that the power of the recent image of coal miners rising from tragedy to victory could finally be as important as that of September 11, 2001.

Why?

The image of apparently doomed miners emerging from such a desperate predicament was made possible in part by the fortitude, the will, and the corporate strength of nine men who refused to give up. Beyond that, however, the power of the image remaining reflects some others of the strengths and resources that will be the hope of our people and nation in present needs and tough times sure to come.

What does the image of the emerging coal miners reflect? The reaction of a society of people who care enough to get involved quickly in impossible situations, seeking solutions to tragic problems of others! Look at the intellect, the knowledge, the latest technological and scientific developments and the unrestricted use of available materials and resources brought to bear to work for a solution of a grievous problem.

In a sense, the September 11 image of terrorism reflects a defining moment of our nation's life. The image of the emerging miners reflects a way, perhaps the only way, our nation will survive in the yet to be revealed crises that surely lie ahead.

Can anyone do anything but marvel at material resources already at hand in our country, and those surely to be developed? What about the accelerating pace of knowledge and skills capable of addressing almost any imaginable circumstance?

Always there must be recognized, respected, and appreciated the hand of God available in and to all human situations! The human side of challenge and response to tragedy, however, is the role of people and nations. Is not the image of emerging miners a reflection of a reality, the reality being that people, when they want to, when they commit the best of themselves, their knowledge, their skills, and their wills to dealing with great human need, can be a solution in apparently impossible situations?

Yes, we must keep fresh the images of September 11 and all that followed, but let us be acutely aware, too, that the images of emerging coal miners reflect both hope and meaning for dealing with the future and its unpredictables.

There is power in images!

Written by Lloyd E. Batson
Published August 7, 2002

Bereavement's multiple faces

The immensity of their loss brought tears to my own eyes as I stood there with them. The fire had been devastating. The accumulation of the years, things precious to them, gone! Irreplaceable personal things gone with all their belongings. It was a time of poignant grief.

Bereavement is a strange and demanding experience. And there are many kinds, the death of a loved one being just one of them. This family, for example, was experiencing bereavement not unlike that known in the loss of a loved one.

Not many lives are untouched by bereavement. Witness the agony of the parent, having loved and cared for a son or daughter, having nurtured high hopes and ambitions for the one to whom so much was given, and now that one goes astray in an apparent wasting of life. That parent knows great bereavement. See a child of the home try to cope with a parent who violates the love of the home. That is a bewildering bereavement.

The loss of a job, which provided security and family well being, may bring a deep grief. The crumbling before one's eyes of the high image in which a friend has been held brings sorrow. Failure, of a variety of kinds, may introduce real bereavement. A church may know a special kind of grief when one of its members goes astray from Christian principles or performs unbecomingly toward the fellowship.

People who experience bereavement, on any level, have certain identifiable needs. They need to have the sustaining sense of the presence of God as they walk through the valley of the shadow. They need the understanding and the support of others who, not affected directly, can sense their trouble and minister in love, through love, to them. They need to be allowed to let certain processes of bereavement work themselves out without intrusion, and to experience the respect and acceptance of others as these processes are working.

There are many kinds of ministry to others. One of them is the developing of sensitivity to the many kinds of bereavement through which people around us are constantly going, and showing a respect for them in love and kindness. The bereaved can find strength in such understanding, respect and kindness.

Most of us have some instinctive sense of sharing with others when bereavement because of death comes, but what of all the other experiences of bereavement? There is a loving ministry there, too — for all of us.

Written by Lloyd E. Batson
Published August 14, 2002

Beauty in missed notes

A grandson was singing that venerable and beloved hymn, "Amazing Grace," at the funeral service for his grandmother whom he adored. In his gifted voice, with clarity and beautiful expression, he sang, providing for all in attendance the ministry of that wondrous affirmation of faith. He was singing for the glory of God and in honor of one precious to him.

Then, suddenly, near the end of the last line, his voice broke as tears flowed. Notes normally so easy for him to sing were missed as he struggled to conclude. Not a person present was unmoved. When he went to his seat with the family, I went to the speaker's stand to do my part in the memorial service. I looked at the bowed and still teary-eyed grandson and thanked him for his beautiful and moving ministry to us all. Then, to him, I said, "I think the most beautiful notes you sang were the ones you missed."

There are circumstances where the capacity to be stoical, to be fully in control of one's emotion, is desirable and helpful. Yet, I have long believed that the capacity to cry, to be emotionally stirred, is one of God's greatest gifts to his creation. Suppose it did not hurt when a loved one dies, what would that say? And suppose there was no desire to express deeply felt emotions of sorrow, what would that reflect?

Had that grandson completed with perfection his masterful presentation of that great hymn I would have carried away the memory of something powerfully beautiful. That memory, however, likely would soon have lost its impact. It has been several weeks now but I still sense the deeply felt surge of my own emotions, and the tingling thrill of them, as I received the gift of missed notes of that magnificent hymn, blessing me because they were portraying great love for a dear one, a love that needed not perfect expression, only deeply felt emotional release.

Missing notes as I sing is not an uncommon experience for me. As a matter of fact, those around me in church, when we are singing the songs of faith, know it is my normal procedure. Yet, there are times I can't finish my standard "messing up" because I suddenly feel deeply what the song is saying to me, or what I remember about what the song meant to somebody I knew, or how the song reflects the love of God to me. Spontaneous "tearing" in the presence of something that reminds me of love, goodness, and, yes, of grace gives precious blessing to me.

The capacity to love is priceless. To feel deeply is a precious journey of the spirit. A few notes one misses in the expression of deep feeling is likely to be the most beautiful notes of all.

Yes, grandson, your singing was great, but the few notes you missed because of your deep feeling were gifts of blessing to all of us present.

Written by Lloyd E. Batson
Published August 21, 2002

Was Ritzy really a dog?

Was Ritzy really a dog? Was she ever a dog?

I suppose one would have to say, biologically, Ritzy was a dog. She looked like a dog. She had the characteristics that normally are identified as canine. But was Ritzy really a dog? I am not sure.

Ritzy got to be old, very old. She got to be infirm, blind, deaf, stiff-jointed, cranky, incontinent and possessive of many other less than desirable conditions. But so do people! Was Ritzy really a dog?

Ritzy was loved, and she loved in return — and sometimes she loved before love was given. She had capacity for spontaneous joy, responding to multitudes of events and situations. Often her spontaneous happiness was contagious to those "beings" around her. Was Ritzy really a dog?

Did Ritzy require care? Yes, and she got the best of it! Was she expensive to have around? Yes, for maintenance of dogs as well as people is costly — food, medicines, professional treatment and a variety of the unexpected.

Did Ritzy have a personality? Yes, similar in many ways to others of her kind but one that was also distinctly her own. There were along the many years of her life changes in her personality, some delightful, some irritating, but, like beings called people, her personality was her own and that, in part, made Ritzy Ritzy. Was Ritzy just a dog?

Was Ritzy just a part of the family structure or was she really family? Didn't she have a major niche in family activities, family planning and family budget? Didn't along the way Ritzy take a protective role of the children of the home as being her children? In fact, wasn't Ritzy continually an identifiable member of the family, with all the pros and cons coming into play?

Can Ritzy be replaced? No! No family members can be replaced. Family members remain even after they are gone. What they were, what they did, what they gave, what they meant remain in memory and appreciation. Like it is with human family members, there is grief, even crying sorrow, when members like Ritzy leave, but the hurt finally goes away and the joy remains.

Was Ritzy really a dog? Well, I think the answer is "Yes" and "No."

Written by Lloyd E. Batson
Published August 28, 2002

Publisher's note: This was written for Batson's grandchildren right after he learned that their dog, Ritzy, in the family for 16 years, apparently had slipped away to die.

A home homecoming

What a privilege it was for me just recently to be invited to a "Homecoming" as guest speaker in a church I helped organize many years ago! A well-planned service (but with the speaker probably not living up to his billing!), great fellowship and the indispensable "dinner on the grounds" (such hardly ever being outdoors nowadays!). All made for a delightful day.

Homecomings, festive occasions as they are, while differing in many ways, all have some things in common, whether they be at churches, or colleges and universities, varying kinds of institutions, or workplaces or anywhere old friends enjoy one another. Memories are stirred into fresh meaning. Disbelief at how old some folk have gotten is on every hand. New acquaintances are made. Programs are tolerated, and even enjoyed, while the pleasures of "being home" fill the air. At colleges, as it will at my alma mater when I go there this fall, football will be prominent. On the list goes!

Some wonderful opportunities are offered at homecomings of all kinds. Using as an example the "Homecoming" at the church I just attended, the very nature of the gathering called for remembering what the church had meant in times past. Sensing again the values, the strengths, the directions for living gained from the ministry of the church called for reaffirmation of those factors and fresh commitment to them as essential for the days yet to be. Reaffirmation and fresh commitment to the cause of a homecoming is often the spin-off of such a gathering.

There is another kind of homecoming that may not be scheduled as an annual event, or a big and festive occasion. Yet, it just may be the most important of all, the one most needed for attendance and attention. It is the going again, even while living in one, to the home! The home where the family is. Home, where relationships are, or have been, of great value. It is the deliberate, conscious return to the strengths and values of the home! Regrettably, many folk, while still living at home, have let the goodness, the joys, the values, the blessings of the home slip away.

I can be invited to many kinds of homecomings that others have planned. I can enjoy and benefit from them. The fact is, though, that no outsider can plan and invite me to the homecoming I regularly need in my own home. I must do it myself. No one can plan a home homecoming for another. The person, or persons must do it.

Look at what can happen in a home "homecoming." A person, and the persons of the home, even in homes deemed good ones, need to identify afresh the virtues, the qualities, the values that contribute to the welfare of the home. Attention to them can result in affirmation and fresh commitment to them as being strengths in the home and in the lives of the individuals of the home.

Deliberately going to a "homecoming" in one's own home will provide encouragement, strength, and shared love and appreciation for the home as being a major factor and force in the shaping of the lives of all connected to the home. A frequent home "homecoming" is essential to the well-being of the home!

Let us enjoy and benefit from all kinds of homecomings but surely priority must be given to the home "homecoming!"

Written by Lloyd E. Batson
Published September 4, 2002

9-11 and 911

It has been one year since that day of infamy, Sept. 11, 2001, a day that has affected nearly everything we as a nation and what we as individuals are, and do, and will do. 9-11 is now a part of our national vocabulary. It is also in the language of much of the world. May 9-11 ever be our teacher!

9-11 likely will never, in the lifetime of most of us, need the year 2001 to be affixed to it. It is a day unto itself and a universal symbol.

All around us on this Wednesday, Sept. 11, 2002, observances, relating to that somber day a year ago, are being held in public places, in churches, in schools, in workplaces, in family gatherings, in government on every level. 9-11 will go on in our lives! We have seen in 9-11 parts of humankind at their worst. We have also seen in massive and heroic response by countless folk a picture of humankind at their best. 9-11 must become a symbol for a nation and its people finding their way to the best!

Is it a good time now to recall and appreciate the same three numerals, only slightly differently presented, the three numerals relating to the needs of individuals and communities all over our land? These numerals are also instantly identifiable. They are 911. It is the number to call in emergencies to receive help. 911, identified with response to urgent needs! Behind 911 there are resources and personnel ready to respond to accidents, fires, medical emergencies, criminal activities, and a whole array of individual and community crises.

The number is 911, but behind the number are people who choose to be available, often at less than adequate pay, to deal with the hurts, problems, and needs of our local community. These are people we may take for granted that they will be there when we call. Could 9-11, in addition to what that portrays, be suggestive to us to be also thankful for the resources behind 911 and for the men and women who do this generally unheralded work (until we have an emergency that affects us!)?

The number 911 is written on many phones for use when needed. It is taught to children. 911 is an integral part of a community prepared to help its people. It seems to me that today would also be a good time to recognize, to be grateful for, and to express thanks for the many men and women in ministry to the welfare of others at the 911 call.

Out of the horror of the events of 9-11 have come multiple examples of heroism, of courage, of sacrifice. Our thanks must go on!

Perhaps somewhere in and around the intense sense of presence of 9-11, and all that that reflects, we should find time to give thanks for what 911 reflects, and for the men and women involved therein.

Written by Lloyd E. Batson
Published September 11, 2002

A bad hair day

I hear frequently a phrase that I am not sure I understand what it means. It has to do with something called a "bad hair day." My limited understanding makes it appear to me not to have anything to do with hair.

What it seems, to this uninitiated writer, is that it has something to do with a personal feeling that nothing is going right, that everything that comes up is an irritation, or the person just seems not to be able to get his or her act together.

I know that such feelings pop up regularly in many people, but what does that have to do with hair? I guess I will file "bad hair day" with the long list of other things I do not understand.

If I knew a proper definition of "bad hair day," I probably would more easily have sympathy with those who have them. Let me tell you, though, the ones with whom I do have sympathy. It is with those who are the victims of somebody else's "bad hair day." From my general observation there often are victims of somebody's hair going bad. A basic question with me involves whether there is ever any fairness in making others suffer through the frustrations of another's such a day.

While I never use "bad hair day," whatever it means, about myself, it is likely that there are times others think I must be having one. If I am thin-skinned and take everything around me as a personal affront, am I having a "bad hair day?" If I am grumpy, discourteous, or short-tempered to other people, without any apparent reason, is my hair messed up?

If somebody is nice to me and I do not even smile or respond with a "thank you," should I look in the mirror to check how my hair looks?

If I wake up wishing I could skip the day at hand, has this thing called "bad hair day" already descended on me, especially if I spend the day making others around me miserable and wishing indeed I had skipped the day?

Could it be, when I feel that nobody understands me, and I proceed to act out reasons for such non-understanding, that I have signed up for whatever one those messy hair days is?

Is it possible that when I mope around, feeling sorry for myself, what I really am doing is blaming my peculiarities on some shape my hair is in?

I guess what I am dealing with is that, whatever a "bad hair day" is, human personality and frailties make it inevitable that I have one occasionally. What I question, though, is that when I have one, do I have a right to inflict such a day on others around me.

On the other hand, perhaps I need to discover afresh, and hope others will also, what love, friendship and acceptance are all about--including recognizing a person's "bad hair day" and adjusting gracefully to it, or, at least, something pretty close to that!

Written by Lloyd E. Batson
Published September 18, 2002

A shovel degree

A shovel has many uses!

Having voluntarily enlisted in the army in World War II, I was sent to Camp Wallace in Texas for basic training. That camp, built up on the marshlands near the coast, had enough mosquitoes to make the rest of the world's ravenous insects jealous for a similar base of operations.

When I finished the survival course of basic training and mosquitoes, I was given the option of applying for Officer Candidate School or a college program called Army Specialized Training Program. Thinking to serve my country and get further college education (I had completed two years of college), I chose to try for the college program. After taking a battery of tests, though I had never held in my hand a slide rule, a basic tool in math and engineering at that time, nor looked through a transit, I qualified to go to Texas A & M University as an advanced Civil Engineering student! Wow!

Wouldn't my parents be proud of me, and perhaps astounded? Off I went to that prestigious university to sit in those huge amphitheater-type classrooms and somewhere along the way become a civil engineer.

Upon my arrival at Texas A & M, I waited eagerly for the first assignment to this supposedly brilliant student. Know what it was? Texas A & M had a horse cavalry unit. I was sent down to the barns, given a broom and a shovel and told to go to work cleaning out the horse stalls!

Yes, I did sit and study in those prestigious classrooms - until the whole college program collapsed because replacement troops were needed for combat in the war going on in Europe and the Far East! After school hours, though, I became well acquainted with a broom, a shovel, and horse manure!

Many times, while pushing a broom or a shovel at Texas A & M, I laughed out loud at the picture I must have been making, of a "bright" young man doing his thing with a shovel in a horse stall.

In all honesty, I think a "broom and shovel" experience can be some of the best education one can get. I have had the privilege of earning several degrees, but there may not be a degree to be earned more important than a "shovel degree."

It may be that the true measure of a person is determined not in how well one performs in the "plush" and privileged places, but in the inevitable difficult and unsavory experiences. The greatest of all teachers talked about one who aspired to be great having to learn to be "servant," to do the lowly things that need to be done. The great interpreter of the Great Teacher wrote, "... I have learned, in whatsoever state I am, therewith to be content," meaning he had to learn to make the best of whatever was at hand.

In my opinion, the best education available anywhere for those who want to make their life good and to count for others needs to include a "shovel degree" of some sort.

Written by Lloyd E. Batson
Published September 25, 2002

An Old Census Can Live Again

I now know what my father was doing on April 11, 1930! He was taking a census of all the people up and down our road in rural Sumter County, South Carolina.

A friend, doing some historical research, found the census record from 1930 of the people who lived in our community in Sumter County. She sent me photocopies of several pages. My family was listed in the official record — in my father's left-handed, leaning greatly to the left, handwriting. My father was counting me on that date and putting me into history! Me, listed as five years old.

The census record has a lot of information for each entry — about family, age, occupation, specific kind of work within that occupation, whether one could read and write, whether one had gone to school the day before, race, head of house, age when married, et cetera. All of it was handwritten by my father, the enumerator, as he is listed in the record.

In my excitement at getting to see this census, I found myself being a nearly six year old again. I began visiting again, in my memory of that year, the homes up and down the road on which we lived, homes in which I had been many times. I mention here just four of the homes, the ones closest to us.

I went to see Uncle Black and his family again. They lived just below us on the road. He was not my uncle, but everybody called him "Uncle Black." Uncle Black was a farmer, with a rather large family. I am not sure I ever got them all figured out. Uncle Black also chewed tobacco. Once, with my father's permission, he cut off a slice from his plug of tobacco and gave it to me to chew. My father knew exactly what he was doing when he let me have the "chaw." I got violently sick and never in my life took another chew!

We always had a milk cow. One of my jobs was to take the cow to the fields around us to stake her out with a rope. Once I took the cow to Uncle Black's field. I was driving the stake down when, from a nearby fenced pasture, a huge bull broke through the wooden gate and ran toward me, snorting. Terrified, I ran home to tell my folks what the bull had been about to do to me. As a six-year-old, I did not know bulls were interested in cows, not me!

"Miss Leila," a lady on down the road, always had some of the world's best fresh baked cakes and I was always welcome. And how I tested her hospitality! I was at her house when somebody came from our house to tell me I had a new baby brother, the one listed in the census of 1930 as one year old. I was more interested in the cake I was eating than in the news about my new brother.

Just up the road from us was Uncle Brown. Obviously, since he and I were listed in the census as being of different races, he was not my uncle. What a gentle, loving man he was, living in a small unpainted house in a field. How welcome I was in his house. One day, when I was about six, I went to see him. His weeping wife took me to his bed where he lay, with a white sheet covering most of him, dead. She and I stood, holding on to one another for a long time, weeping together. My friend was dead and I could not take it in. How bonding is shared grief!

Just up the road, in the field beyond Uncle Brown, lived Lottie, with her large family. Lottie's occupation was listed in the census as "wash woman." My, I liked to slip into her house when hot "hoe cakes" – large, flat biscuits or cornbread -- were on top of the stove. Lottie always pretended not to look when I sneaked a piece of that wonderful bread. It was John, her younger son, who found some cigarette "butts" and we sneaked off to a deep ditch and tried to be grownup people smoking. We nearly choked to death!

Whether or not one finds in a census people he or she used to know as a child, I think it would be greatly rewarding to go visiting again to the homes of people of childhood days. Why should precious experiences ever cease having meaning?

Most of us have a lot of visiting again to do. Let's do it! It will be great – again.

Written by Lloyd E. Batson
Published October 2, 2002

I want you to need me

It came vividly, and tellingly, to my mind again after many years when I saw a father abruptly brush off his son who wanted to help him do something.

What I relived was a time when I was out in the backyard of the house we lived in next door to the church, doing something that was frustrating me. My son, about five or six years old came out, stood by me, and asked if he could help me. I told him I did not need him and he could go back in the house. He left, with his head down.

Shortly he was back, standing close. With a tear or two slipping down his cheeks, he said, "But I want you to need me."

Bang! The son had nailed his father with a truth I knew but had not acted upon. What I was doing I could really do better by myself but my son was articulating one of the great needs of most people, the need to be needed. I wish I had had sensitivity enough to recognize what my son felt, and to find a way to let him constructively be involved in what was going on.

Rejection is a terrible feeling, for any age, whether it is caused intentionally or thoughtlessly. Children, and grownups, too, are hurt when they feel they have been rebuffed, put down, rejected, ignored, unwanted or dismissed as irrelevant.

There is an attendant despair, that of feeling one is just a "bump on the log," that feeling of, though present, not really being a part of what is going on. There is an inherent need in most people to be included in conversation, the social activity and exchange at a dinner party, for example, or any other gathering or activity. Not to feel included, even while present, makes one feel awkward, ill at ease, and even unwanted.

There are, of course, differing personalities in any group, with the extremes of the extrovert and the introvert, and in between. Wise is the person with enough sensitivity to others around to make sure all are made to feel both wanted, included, and needed.

The Bible, for example, in teaching about the strength of a viable, healthy church, stresses that no part of the body is unimportant, that the "small" part has an invaluable role in the welfare of the whole, as much as any other part.

Back to the parent and the child. Among the many responsibilities, and certainly one of the highest privileges, for parents, is to instill in their children a sense of worth, in the family, yes, and in the children's own personhood. A child, whether he or she ever expresses it or not, has a great need for feeling needed and included in the family structure and well-being. Busy parents can easily bypass opportunities to enhance the sense of self-worth and usefulness in their children.

A healthy sense of self-worth, and a sense of usefulness to others, is not only important for children; it is fundamentally essential for all folk in every stage of life.

Yes, son, I am sorry I did not see where you were coming from. And for whatever it is worth, I want you to know I really did need you, then, and I need you now!

Written by Lloyd E. Batson
Published October 9, 2002

It is creeping fast

It was one of the most appropriate and appreciated prayers we ever had prayed for us.

Shortly after I retired from the active pastorate thirteen years ago, and facing what I hoped would be many other years of ministry of a variety of sorts, my wife and I were guests in a small church in the beautiful hills of northern Pickens County. I had enjoyed being in that church several times across the years. I was to preach in the morning service and was sitting out in the congregation, as I like to do in the churches where I go to preach.

Just before I was to go to the pulpit to speak, one of the men of the church was leading the morning prayer. In the midst of the prayer, he began praying for Dr. and Mrs. Batson, expressing thanks for them, asking God to take care of them, and praying for the Father's blessing on them every day. Then, as he continued, he said to God, "...for you know, God, old age is creeping up on them."

He was right! And it was creeping up fast then, and the pace has now picked up! He knew that "old age creeping up" presents new and differing challenges - and opportunities.

You know what I think? I think God's ears perked up as that man spoke honestly and plainly. Do you think God ever chuckles? I think he must have chuckled then, and enjoyed the prayer as much as we did. I do know also that he has over and over answered for us the needs expressed in that prayer on our behalf.

One of the things I appreciate about that "old age is creeping up" prayer is that it reflects something important and encouraging. It recognizes that there is no one way that is the "right" way to pray. I do not believe God places a premium upon how a prayer is constructed, phrased, or uttered. I believe he hears and receives, equally, prayers of sincerity, honesty and faith.

It is a biological fact that one, for example, in his seventy-ninth year, as I am, must recognize that naturally developing processes impose some physical limitations, changing dimensions of lifestyle, even varying degrees of health needs. This biological fact, however, is not restricted to those of us in "old age."

A brand new baby starts immediately into aging, and aging brings changes. Look at all a child has to learn in moving through all the stages of development. The baby, then the child, next the teenager, then the young adult, then the business or career formations, the family establishment period, middle age, then the senior years, and finally "old age." Every one of these "aging" periods has changing demands and challenges.

So, life itself is a process of "age creeping up," with varying needs all along. Who can say what is the best age in which to be? I, for one, have been through most of the "ages" that appear along in life. Know which one I vote for? Right where I am now!!

Certainly, my current stage introduces the probability of some differing health needs, physical limitations, and even some very difficult problems. Yes, my "age" needs special help and attention from the Father God, but there has not been an "age" in which I did not have special needs, and there will not be one.

The bottom line is that, with the help of God, and people who will pray for me, and give me encouragement and assistance as the need arises, I have the opportunity to enjoy "old age" that already has crept up on me. I intend to do the best I can to make it the best age yet - and find fulfillment in it!

What comes next? Well, I will see, because it is creeping up - fast!

Written by Lloyd E. Batson
Published October 16, 2002

Joining by Resurrection

I was walking on the sidewalk of that wide Main Street in Pickens. A man on the other side of the street, one I recognized as belonging to a church of another denomination from mine, called to me to wait.

After he had made a hurried crossing, narrowly missing being hit by an automobile, he said he had been hoping to see me. He proceeded to tell me about a trip he had made down in Alabama, I think it was, doing research about his family lineage. He had found where his great grandfather had joined a Baptist church there long ago.

"Tell me," he asked, "what does it mean in a Baptist church to join by resurrection?"

He went on to explain that while the handwriting was a little difficult to read, it was written beside his name that his great grandfather had joined "by resurrection."

"Well," I replied, "that's a new one on me! You probably need to go look at it again to see if it said he had joined by restoration. Sometimes, back then, a person lost membership for some reason and later he or she was restored by the church."

I have to admit that I laughed a bit, and told my inquiring friend that, while I never heard of joining a church by resurrection, I did think, though, that it would be a great thing to see happen many times! If resurrection means coming alive from the dead, I told him, it would be great in the church where I was pastor to see a good many join by resurrection. We had names on the church roll, I confessed, that represented people who for all practical purposes, as to interest, attendance and activity in the church, might as well be dead.

Yes, if resurrection means "coming alive from the dead," it is likely that most churches in our area have members who no longer seem to have any meaningful relationship to the church. "Joining by resurrection" would be cause for thanksgiving, for the church and for them.

"Joining by resurrection" is a good idea, not just for people whose identity with a church has become non-existent. Civic clubs, eleemosynary (charitable) organizations, public service committees, community project organizations, for example, often need some of their members to join up again "by resurrection."

"Coming alive again" is also a need for many individuals who, for whatever reason, have let die many of the things, values, activities and feelings that once gave excitement and pleasure to living. A "resurrection" could bring meaning and pleasure again.

Some folk have allowed to go dormant some of the things that used to put joy into their lives--like reading good books, visiting friends, interest in new things to see and do, writing letters of encouragement or expressed interest. Some who once gave pleasure to others with a sweet, loving spirit have allowed dullness, apathy, or crankiness to deaden their lives. To "come alive again" would greatly improve the quality of life.

Yes, "joining by resurrection" might just be a decision many of us need to make!!

Written by Lloyd E. Batson
Published October 23, 2002

Why does one vote?

In the election processes of 1936 I had become interested in the whole concept of citizenry voting, though as a twelve year old I guess I understood very little of it. On voting day of that year I went to the local voting place set up at the depot that served the Atlantic Coastline Railroad in our village, and watched what went on.

At that time in South Carolina there was an abominable thing known as a poll tax. The word "poll" originally simply meant "head." A poll tax was levied on adults and had to be paid before one could vote. A basic problem was that the tax was the same for rich and poor, and, unfortunately, was considered by some as a way to keep some folk from voting. An amendment to the Constitution in 1964 eliminated the poll tax for national elections. In 1966, the Supreme Court declared it unconstitutional in state and local elections.

Another ploy available, in my observations as a youngster sometimes unfairly used, was a requirement that before one could vote he or she had to be able to read and understand the Constitution. That left a tool in the hands of the vote managers for possible discrimination in enforcement, and in the decision as to who could properly read and understand the Constitution.

One indelible memory I have from watching the voting process on the deck of a train depot in a small village in 1936 was seeing an elderly man come up, obviously very uncomfortable about being there and about not knowing what all he had to do to vote. I saw him take from his pocket a wrinkled paper, appearing to be a mimeographed letter or form of some sort. He handed it to the approaching poll manager and said (I recall his exact words!), "I want to vote for this man. He is the onliest one who writ me."

Why do people vote? A corollary question is why people do not vote. That man long ago, unaccustomed to voting and not knowing whether he would be allowed to vote, had interpreted a form letter of some sort as somebody being personally interested in him, and he wanted to support him.

We are a long way from mimeographed contact from a political candidate to these days of unbelievable amounts of money spent on multiple kinds of advertising, including the assault of negative ads and innuendos.

Why do people vote? A part of the reason still ought to be, even in the "bigness" of elections in our time, that the individual citizen comes to believe that somehow a candidate and the candidates are genuinely interested in the personal welfare of the people, that the candidate and candidates really do care about him or her and will honestly attempt to represent the welfare of the citizenry.

People, of course, have vested interests in certain candidates and issues and come to vote. Some come to vote against certain ones. Some truly are interested in the welfare of the local, state, and national welfare and come to vote.

In candor, I get fed up with much of the machinations of politics, but I will not allow such to rob me of my responsibility to vote. To be able to vote, to have a say, however minute it may be, is a privilege I cherish. Voting, on every level, is a responsibility and a privilege!

As egotistical, and perhaps naïve, as it sounds, I think my single vote is important to the welfare of my country! I do not intend to default on my obligation and privilege!

Please, citizens of our area, join me on November 5 in voting, for whatever reason you do so. You do not have to vote for whom and for what I vote, and you may not, but, please, be a responsible citizen and vote.

Written by Lloyd E. Batson
Published October 30, 2002

The sturdy oak

Writer's note: My mother died in October, twenty-three years ago. Remembering this called to mind something I wrote for our church paper a few days after her death. I want to share it here.

I turned my car in the circular drive until I was facing the highway and turned off the lights. With no lights on in the lonely house behind me, I would sit there in the late night and wait until the family got home from the hospital where their precious family member had died. Because I had been in another hospital with my very ill mother, I was not reachable when the sudden death had come.

It was a magnificent night, with a nearly full moon lighting the night from behind me, and bright stars, gloriously sparkling, in front of me. Out in the highway, the headlights of cars going in both directions pierced the darkness. To my right, in the shadowy darkness, I could see the cemetery where I had been many times with grieving families, including my own. As I waited, I alternately prayed for the family, thought of my own mother in great suffering, and simply enjoyed the loveliness of the night.

It seemed to me that those cars were going in several directions as if nobody could decide which was the proper direction, and the cemetery to my right spoke of the confusion, the hurt, and the lack of stability in the lives of people of this earth. As I pondered this thought, I began to note something. Silhouetted against the starlit sky in front of me was a great oak tree, its branches and leaves reaching up into the brilliant sky. I watched, fascinated. Then, so quietly, but so clearly that it was almost eerie, there came to me the assurance that, in spite of all the appearances of confusion, hurt, and lack of stability and direction in the earth, it is possible to know certainty, security, and well-being. That oak tree, itself a symbol of sturdiness, right in the midst of all I was watching, reached up in the night toward the stars!

I need to know that there is something dependable, something strong, something I can count on, because there surely is enough around me that is transitory and confusing. Some people are to me like the oak tree, reminding me of dependability and strength. My mother was one of these people. There are others who encourage me everyday. Most of all, I need, myself, to reach out to the heavens. While my feet are on the earth, I can know heaven's strength. What are some things I can know and depend upon? They are many:

"The Lord is my shepherd."
"He calleth them all by names by the greatness of his might."
"He giveth power to the faint."
"Come unto me, all ye that ... are heavy laden."
"I am the way."
"... [nothing] shall be able to separate us from the love of God."
"Be of good cheer; I have overcome the world."
"Thanks be to God which giveth us the victory."
Thanks, oak tree. I am glad I saw you!

Written by Lloyd E. Batson
Published November 5, 2002

A memorable catch

Because I had not been able to attend the first football game of the season at Furman University, I did not know where my seat was. When I located the area, I found that my seat was in the middle of the longest row in the stadium, and the row was already filled except for my seat.

A lady was sitting in the end seat on the aisle. My first decision? How to present myself as I sidled down the crowded and narrow row of seats. My front side or my backside? I decided on my front side as being more presentable. Just as I neared my seat here came the lady who had been sitting on the aisle! Her problem? My foot had caught in the strap of her purse and I had dragged it unknowingly to my seat!

After I made peace with the lady, I sat down to enjoy the game. Seated in front of me was a young couple with a baby, obviously bringing him for the first time to a game. They had brought what appeared to be everything but the kitchen sink to take care of him, including a huge supply of diapers. No kid could use that many diapers during one game! It was a precious youngster and I spent a lot of time doing the silly things adults do to attract the attention of a baby.

I had not seen before the bazooka type gun the Furman cheerleaders were using to shoot rolled Furman souvenir tee shirts into the crowd. I had learned to shoot real bazookas in World War II, and I excitedly followed every tee shirt fired into the crowd, hoping one would come my way and I could grab it. I wanted to give it to one of my grandchildren.

None came near me, and I finally stopped looking every time I heard a gun fired. After awhile, suddenly, I was aware of something flashing through the air above me. I reached quickly and caught it!

Apparently, the father of the baby in front of me had been changing diapers when the gun fired and he had thrown up his hands to catch the tee shirt. A memorable night! The father caught the tee shirt and I caught the experienced diaper!!

How long does something enjoyable last? As long as you need it to! All along, in our earthly journey, unusual and delightful things happen. These need to be stored up in our minds - and some of them in our hearts. Some of them need to be shared with others. Some need to be kept for private enjoyment.

A pleasant memory, a funny experience, an unusual encounter, an encounter with some "character," a rewarding conversation with some unexpected turn! These are but some of the kinds of things that are good at the moment of happening but can become treasures of pleasure if properly stored in accessible files of the mind and heart, and regularly revisited.

I recommend a way to spend profitably a few hours occasionally. Sit down by yourself in some comfortable setting and begin to probe your past, distant and near, to identify afresh some moment or happening that you enjoyed at the time of occurrence. Relive it again. Laugh out loud, or chuckle within. Let your mind see and feel some things you may not have noticed at the first happening.

Reach again for those good times. They can be good again!

You may reach for a tee shirt and catch a diaper, but you know what? Any burden I might have gets a little lighter every time I catch that diaper again!

Written by Lloyd E. Batson
Published November 13, 2002

Lost in the crowd

On one of its busiest days, I was in one of the big local stores, dodging clusters of people in every aisle I went down. Suddenly, from behind, a small boy brushed me as he ran by me. While he was making no crying sounds, I could see the tears flowing down his cheeks. He disappeared to the right at the end of the aisle.

When I got to the end of the aisle, a hurrying man with a troubled face started toward me from another direction. Sensing what was happening, I touched the man on his shoulder and said, as I pointed where I had seen the boy go, "He went that way!"

Thanking me as he turned, he added, "My son got lost from me in the crowd."

A bit later, I saw the happy father and son walking together, clasping hands and exchanging smiles. I imagine the father had mentioned me, because each of them, with his free hand, waved at me.

That anxious and worried father had said to me a sad thing, but one that I have heard, in a great variety of forms, across the years. "My son got lost from me in the crowd," the father said. Restoration to the father of his son in the store was relatively easy. It has not been so in many of the "lost" situations I have known, some of which I have attempted to assist in restoration.

In the case of the father and son in the crowds of the store, it was more separation than being actually lost, and could be resolved rather quickly. Separation, however, between family members, an all too common occurrence in so many varying forms, may not be so easy to resolve.

Getting "lost in the crowd" from families, values, principles, relationships is, of course, a figure of speech. In practice, though, that sometimes is exactly what happens, for example, when a son or daughter, getting involved in alienating activities and life styles away from the home, breaks parents' and other family members' hearts. Separation then cools or destroys ties that bind a family together.

Separation, or "getting lost in the crowd," is not just a youthful thing. Our world offers so much alienating involvement to men and women as well.

"Getting lost" is not necessarily a physical separation. Families living under the same roof can become separated from one another. Such separation may be a result of some single incident, but more often there is a drifting apart from common interests, shared activities, caring attention to one another, and even love.

Parents, children, families can lose so easily the most valuable relationships of closeness, loving, sharing - and usually so unnecessarily.

I heard that father's anxious voice and I saw the joy of separation being mended. I, standing in one of those crowded aisles, also experienced a quick flash in my mind and spirit - of some happy resolutions to being lost or separated from one another that I have seen. I said a thank you to the Father God.

Restoration may not always be easy, but determined effort, not sidetracked by panic, can sometimes bring solution. It surely is worth a concerted try - by all concerned! The rewards can be great!

"Lost in the crowd." Sad!

Reunited. Wonderful!

Written by Lloyd E. Batson
Published November 20, 2002

Identifying Thanksgiving

This Thanksgiving I have been remembering a hitchhiker I saw between Easley and Pickens. Hitchhikers aplenty I have seen. In my college and military days I often was one. In days safer so to do, I have picked up many hitchhikers, but now do not. Still, something about this one impressed me. Perhaps it was because I had a hunch that that green bag and that brown bag the hitchhiker had with him contained all the man's earthly possessions.

The thought crossed my mind, "Lloyd Batson, if you had to discard everything you own except what you could put in one green bag and one brown bag, what would you select to keep?" In times of war or natural disaster, many people have had to flee with just what they could carry in their hands. Now I ask you to react. If, for whatever reason, you had to select from your belongings just what you could carry in two small bags, and these would be your total worldly possessions, what would those things be?

Frankly, for myself, I do not know. It probably would depend on how long I had to think about it. This thought pattern led me to thinking about the blessings of God and country. Both have been good to me and I know that on Thursday we will celebrate a national day of Thanksgiving. In all probability, I will do as many people will, do more celebrating than giving thanks. And that will not be right!

Many of us take so much for granted, without thankful acknowledgement. Now I ask another question I finally got around to asking myself. Does your happiness and well-being depend upon the quantity of material things? Does the quality of your life depend upon how much you have of things so highly prized by most of society? Do not be too hasty about answering that, for you are likely to be less than honest if you really do not think it through.

Me? I am still agonizing over it. Somewhere in this I must get down to basic stuff. Creature comfort is important to me, as I suspect it is to you. But, finally, my happiness and my well-being must not depend upon creature comforts.

I cannot put faith and trust in a green bag or a brown one, but my life would not be worth much if I did not make sure I always had them with me. Integrity is important to me but I cannot package it. Without a sense of integrity I could not live very well. With it, I could live with fewer creature comforts and have a sense of well-being. Somewhere I would have to have a Bible, and that I can pack. Yet more important to me is that part of the Bible which I have in my heart and mind.

That hitchhiker was the catalyst that led me on a pilgrimage, one that I had been on many times before, and one I will need regularly to make all of my life. While physical blessings should evoke continued thanksgiving, I must remember and appreciate that the real meaning of life is spiritual. Without the spiritual blessings God allows me to enjoy, life with a thousand and one green and brown bags would not be worth much.

It is Thanksgiving time! For what are you truly thankful?

Written by Lloyd E. Batson
Published November 27, 2002

A second grade crisis

What do I remember most vividly about the second grade in Brogdon Elementary School in Sumter County, South Carolina in 1931? I can easily tell you.

The second grade met in the same room as the first grade, with the same teacher. My seat, a single desk, was on the row next to the window. We were having a spelling test, with the teacher calling out the words we were to write. It was late in the school year and I had a perfect grade in spelling for all the year up to then.

After we had finished the test, the teacher told us she would call out the correct spelling and we were to put an "X" by any we had wrong. About halfway down the list, to my dismay, I discovered I had one letter wrong in one word. I was horrified! My perfect record ruined!

As the teacher continued spelling the words, I did not mark an "X" but erased the wrong letter and wrote in the right one. What a struggle set in! I knew it was wrong, but I wanted to keep my perfect record. My heart beat wildly.

That is not the end of the story. Before the teacher came to pick up the papers, I went back to the word, erased the correct letter I had written in, wrote in the wrong letter again, and marked the biggest "X" I ever wrote alongside the word.

I was disappointed, but, strangely, I felt better.

That is still not the end of the story. When the teacher came by to pick up the papers, she looked at mine and she gave me a little hug. She said she had been watching me and knew what I had done. She said she was proud of me for doing what was right.

That is still not the end of the story. At the end of the school, I got the best spelling award, perfect all year - except for one word. When the teacher made the award, she announced that I had missed only one word all year but that she had put a gold star by that word.

Only the teacher and I knew what she meant!

Many factors influence our decisions in moral and ethical situations. Among them are laws, community standards, religious teachings, "rules" of organizations and clubs, assignment responsibilities and "watch dogs" of many kinds. Yet, the final important decisive factor in what we choose to do about honesty, about matters of integrity, about responsible behavior rests with the individual.

As for me, I cannot say that I have always done what is right, but I do know that a second grader made a decision that has never been far from him in the seventy-two years since then.

Thank God, too, for a very wise second grade teacher!

For that matter, let me thank God and the men and women who have been my teachers on many levels.

Thank God for those who teach today! They still make a difference!

Written by Lloyd E. Batson
Published December 11, 2002

I went outside and cried

I went outside and cried!

My father was a minister and often preached in churches other than the ones of which he was pastor. Once, somewhere around 1930, I guess, because it was some time before we moved in 1933 from out in the country in Sumter County to the small lumber mill village of Alcolu, six miles down the road. Daddy was preaching in a revival service. It was at a church somewhere not far from Brogdon Elementary School. I was happy that I could go with him.

I was, I guess, six years old, or possibly seven, and, obviously, I do not recall the entire service. What I do remember, and remember still with a surge of emotion, is a story that my father told in his sermon to those folk. Daddy was in military service toward the end of World War I. He went to Camp Sevier, near Greenville, for basic training. In that church, near Brogdon School, I heard him telling about his custom at night, while in camp, to read his Bible and then to kneel beside his cot to pray. Once, while he was praying, somebody threw a boot at him and hit him. Another boot or two followed.

I did not hear the rest of the story, because I ran out of the church and cried my heart out. I could not believe anybody would be mean to my Daddy and throw things at him!

I was little, but my tears were as big as anybody's. I hurt terribly and could not stop crying. How could they do that to my Daddy? I loved him.

Out in that churchyard I could not understand anybody making fun of and being mean to somebody trying to be true to his faith, and especially to my father. I still do not understand! I still hurt when I see ugliness toward others. I still cry, inside myself mostly, when I hear verbal "boots" being thrown at others, either in some strange sense of fun or with intent to hurt.

It is not a far cry from throwing boots at one kneeling to pray to the ridicule and belittlement, so commonly heard around us today, of other people's religious faith or actions. Not agreeing with them, or choosing not to believe what others believe, is one thing; ridicule or belittlement is another.

I now am supposedly grown up, but I still do not understand meanness, in any form.

Yes, I ran out of the church and cried! And sometimes now I wish I could run away and cry!

Written by Lloyd E. Batson
Published December 18, 2002

In the darkness a candle

Writer's note: Once, in response to a request to write a favorite Christmas recollection, I wrote about what was for me then, and is now, a treasured memory of a Christmas experience. I want to share it in this column.

Twenty years old. Thousands of miles from home. Hunting for a place to spend the night in a place he had no idea as to where it was. Heading for places he did not know. Bitterly cold, and Christmas Eve!

The Germans, in a massive and desperate effort, had done devastating damage to civilians and Allied forces in a break through in Belgium that came to be known as the Battle of the Bulge.

My army unit, having been in combat in northern France, had suddenly been ordered to make a forced march to join the fighting in Belgium, up there somewhere on the map.

On Christmas Eve, I, with a few of my buddies, found shelter on that bitter cold night in a small railroad car, something akin to an ancient caboose. After making sure every crack was covered, we lit the one candle I had been saving for some special need. Some of us in the feeble light tried, with stiffened fingers, to write a note home. All of us talked about home and Christmas.

The single candle, never big, but lasting longer than we believed it would, finally flickered out. In the darkness, we sat for a time, saying nothing, but acutely aware of our loved ones at home thousands of miles away. Folk having no way of knowing where we were. We ourselves did not know! Yet, in some mystical and precious way, each of us seemed to feel our loved ones were with us, right there in that cold darkness.

I guess I knew what I was doing, but I listened more than I spoke as I began in the darkness to quote Luke's beautiful story of the birth of Jesus. Then I prayed out loud. A few of the others joined me, in halting, stumbling, but genuine, prayers. For at least two of those men, I learned later, it was the first prayer either had ever spoken.

We did not know where we were or where we were going. We only knew it was rough "up yonder" where we were headed. The weather had been so bad that the Allied planes from England had not been able to fly to bomb the advancing enemy forces. Black dark and cold! And we sat silently, not able to see one another. Yet, in the darkness and cold a strange and beautiful light of Holy Presence had touched each of us. Now we could go to sleep, remembering in the midst of our anxiety that God had come to the earth in that Christmas child. Not a one of us could explain it, but peace had come to us!

When the light of Christmas morning came, I stumbled from that railroad car. Then what a glorious sight and sound! The sky of full of roaring planes! The weather had changed and planes could fly again. We could resume our forced march to whatever was waiting for us wherever we were going.

Not a one of us knew whether he would ever see another Christmas, but we had had this one! In the bitter cold and total darkness, we had experienced a Light from God, a precious Christmas gift.

Christmas, 1944. Many years ago, but still as real and precious as the Christmas this year will be.

What is the wonder and glory of Christmas? God comes wherever we need him!

Written by Lloyd E. Batson
Published December 25, 2002

Cleaned out!

I had to laugh when he said it. Later, I did not laugh, because, as I thought about it, it was sad, very sad.

In a moment of greeting I had inquired about his Christmas. In measured cadence, he spoke matter of factly, "Christmas cleaned me out."

Here was a man who felt, I think, that he had overspent for Christmas. Most of us can identify with that! And most of us know we ought to have better judgment. But, we want so much to do nice things for those we love! In our better judgment, we know we are, to a large degree, programmed from outside ourselves to spend more than we can afford. Standards of our day, commercial interests, moods of the times are among the high-pressure influences affecting Christmas giving. Add to these the very real "spirit of Christmas" and we can indeed get "cleaned out." Paying for Christmas often takes far too disproportionate a part of our resources for the whole year.

Do you suppose the man meant he was drained emotionally? Psychologists know that there is more depression at Christmas than any other time of the year. There are many reasons why this is so, but that is not what is on my mind.

What I do wish the man had meant was that Christmas was such a beautiful, exhilarating experience he had been purged of much of the year's accumulation of debris of all kinds, and he felt clean and new through and through.

We are in the beginning moments of a new year, 2003. For me each new calendar year gets here more rapidly than any before it! Would not it be great if we could start 2003 "cleaned out," in the beautiful sense of the being rid of all the old burdens, heartaches, worries, confusions that have built up in our lives? As it is easy to accumulate junk of all kinds in the attics, basements, garages and closets of our homes, so we seem to find it easy to collect in our lives the junk of a thousand kinds that ought to be cleaned out.

Misinformation, prejudices, ill will, animosities, fixed notions, ill-founded alien-ations, all are but some of the "people to people" junk that clutter up a person's mental and emotional premises. Habits that rob the pocketbook and hurt the person, the family, the job should be cleaned out. Carelessness in personal devotion, poor involvement in church, inattention to Bible study are some of the spiritual junk accumulation that should be "cleaned out."

Why should not Christmas be a purging, cleansing experience? I think it should, in the good sense! We all need something big and beautiful to come into our lives to take prominence over the things that would otherwise tend to defeat us. But Christmas as a onetime event is not all we need!

We need Christmas every day. Nobody could afford, or even tolerate, I suppose, Christmas every day, Christmas as it is now generally promoted. However, the Christ of Christmas is not a once a year affair! To "behold his glory" is a possibility for every day. Indeed, if it is not so, then the once a year observance is probably ceremonial and farcical.

2003! May God help us start this year properly "cleaned out." May he help us stay "cleaned out."

Written by Lloyd E. Batson
Published January 1, 2003

A gas tank encounter

While I was waiting at the gas pump for my tank to fill, I spoke to a person I did not know who was at the next pump, putting gas in his car. Idle talk it was.

Something I said about traveling triggered an emotional response in him for which I was not prepared. All I could say was, "I am sorry."

What this man told me was that for years he and his wife had looked forward to retiring. They had exciting plans about traveling to many places. Then, just a short time before his scheduled retirement, his wife got sick. Now he had to spend most of his time taking care of her. As he talked (and he seemed to slow his tank filling process to a trickle), it was evident he was embittered about not getting to do what he had planned so long, and about the heavy burden of taking care of a sick wife. His open resentment was not pretty. I can imagine that it was a big disappointment to the both of them when the wife got sick, but her getting sick was not her fault! Now a lifetime of being together in what must have been a good relationship was being ruined by a growing resentment which almost certainly was showing itself at home and affecting what they said and did.

I did not know the wife, but I felt real sorrow for her. I guess, however, I was more disturbed about what had happened to the husband. Caring for an invalid wife certainly cannot be easy, but that difficult task was made more burdensome by the burgeoning resentment the husband was experiencing.

When I left the gas tank, my mind rambled over recollections of resentments I have seen which have affected people's lives.

I have seen, for example, some folk seem to come to resent the restrictions that married life and home responsibilities make upon them. Such resentments frequently result in alienation, or divorce, or wishing for divorce. Parents who build up resentment about the demands their children make on them may make their own lives and those of their children unhappy. Children who nurse resentment about parental expectations of them often create problems for themselves and everybody concerned.

As a minister, I have even seen the toll that resentment can take in the service of the Lord. God notices, too. He reports in Malachi 1:13, about some of the priests and worshippers carrying out their duties in the temple with festering resentment. They were saying, "What a burden!" Yes, resentment about the requirement of one's religion can finally destroy the meaning of one's faith. To feel required, for example, as one might come to feel, by family, friends, the church community standards, even the Lord, to attend church regularly, instead of being able to do some of the apparently pleasurable things others do, can set in motion a festering resentment that takes away spiritual joy. A resentful religious person is not a happy religious person!

Building up of resentment can cut across many areas of responsibility. To recognize and deal with destructive resentment may be difficult, but this destructive monster needs early attention and rejection! When signs of resentment, about anything, getting a toehold on emotions begin to show is the best time to come to grips with it and replace it with something healthy.

Life is too good, and too short, to spend it being eaten away by something so insidious and destructive as resentment!

Written by Lloyd E. Batson
Published January 8, 2003

Two silly green frogs

Two frogs sit on the edge of one of my filing cabinets in my study, staring at me with silly grins on their faces. They watch over me with unswerving loyalty as I study, write, think, and try to come to grips with a variety of demands with which I attempt to deal.

These small, gangly, "beanie bag" type of green frogs with big eyes represent something greatly important to me. I was having a procedure done in the local hospital that required being put to sleep in the operating room. As I, lying on the gurney and jesting with the driver, passed the nurses' station, one of the nurses at the desk came running and put in my hand a green frog they usually give to young children going into surgery, as a way to alleviate anxiety. Then another came and stuck a frog in the other hand. You can guess the comments of the nurses! I went on into the operating room with a frog in each hand and laughing – until something somebody did to me sent me into "bye bye" land.

A simple act of levity? Well, yes and no. Behind the spontaneous "frog act" lay the friendships of the wonderful folk who work all over the hospital, who with their skills and their pleasant personalities give so much help to so many.

In spite of my being in proximity to my "second childhood," I do not think I really needed a beanie bag frog to handle the hospital procedure. What I did need, though, still do, and always will, is love and caring offered to me.

Those silly frogs represent something else – my need for relief from the burdens, the stresses, even from the toll of "humdrum" matters. What a blessing the gift of laughter, of smiles, of light banter is to me, and can be to nearly anybody. Of course, I know that there are heartaches, troubles, and heavy burdens that need a deeper and serious touch from caring and understanding folk.

In my mind, among the wisest of people are those who know how and when to laugh and when to cry with others. Into my own life, time after time, have come the treasured gifts that people, sometimes in surprising places and circumstances, have given me. They are gifts that make easier the affairs of everyday life and the especially needy times of my life. The givers often do not know that they are exactly what I need for the moment.

Two silly green beanie frogs, sitting in the midst of Bibles, commentaries, books and papers of all kinds, and in the crowded quarters of a guest room turned into my study and "office!" Out of place? No. They are constant reminders that in all that I do, all that I search for, all I plan for, all that I work at and sometimes I am confused by, there are people who care about me and share in my life with friendship and love.

I doubt that I will request that those frogs be placed in my hands when final farewell is said to me, but I will leave this earthly life with gratitude for all the gifts of caring, in such great variety, that people have given me along the way.

In the meantime, two silly green frogs add a precious dimension to my life as they stare steadfastly at me everyday.

By the way, do you have "frogs" in your life? You are blessed if you do!

Written by Lloyd E. Batson
Published January 15, 2003

Some restoration needed projects

Out on the highway near where we live a fascinating project is underway. Set among large and majestic trees, an old house is being restored. I do not know who has lived there in earlier days or who is doing the restoring now. All I know is that I have enjoyed watching the project unfold.

In its prime, that house must have been a beautiful and commodious house and home to its occupants. It will be again. Even when I do not need to go that way to get to where I am going, I sometimes choose to drive by to enjoy the progress being made. For years I enjoyed seeing a large herd of goats that roamed in the nearby pasture, but they apparently are gone. I hope they will again decorate the area!

In my thinking I have moved beyond the restoration of that house to some restoration projects of other kinds that could be undertaken by most of us. For example, are there some friendships that once offered pleasure and goodness to us but no longer are a meaningful part of our lives? Can you recall the warmth, the simple day-to-day awareness of good feelings you had with those friends? Did neglect or busyness with other things and people let deteriorate the bond between you and them? Perhaps a friendship restoration project is in order.

Many folk, young and old, have at times had compelling dreams that kept them on focus in reaching educational levels, financial goals, and vocational interests. Dreams can fall into disarray for many reasons. In a world of reality are not dreams still a valuable force? Could it be that a dream restoration project would provide a challenging background to our lives?

Personal enhancement activities can suffer when inattention, carelessness, or even energy demands from other things, set in. Has reading time, for example, been allowed to fade away? Or rewarding hobbies sidetracked? Or classes offered for self-improvement at libraries, clubs, schools or churches being generally ignored?

Family structures, relationships, creative activities, and personal bonding with needy members within the family can deteriorate or fall into disarray by carelessness or neglect. Should it be that some of us should give attention to a family restoration project? As a building that does not get proper maintenance ultimately will suffer so do many important human things deteriorate by inattention or neglect. Perhaps it is time to consider some personal restoration projects.

Not everybody has the resources necessary for restoration for such an exciting place as that house at the bend in the road on the highway near us, but nearly everybody has enough resources available to work on the restoration to goodness and usefulness of many personal things that have been allowed to lose value or meaning.

It does take noticing as to what has happened or is happening, and the deliberate use of the tools and resources already in existence or easily available, if many personal restoration projects get underway and succeed.

And you know what? Personal restoration projects usually wind up benefiting others as well!

Written by Lloyd E. Batson
Published January 22, 2003

" ... It didn't do any good"

One of the continuing pleasures of my life is the relationship I have been privileged to enjoy with the local hospital. I attended the opening of the hospital in 1958. As a pastor in Pickens for 33 years, I regularly had church members who were patients in the hospital. In visiting them, I came to know the administrative personnel, doctors, nurses, and many of the other people who worked there. Both my sons were born there.

During the more than thirteen years since I have lived here, following my retirement from the active pastorate, I have had the privilege as a volunteer to be related to, and involved in, the chaplaincy services at the hospital.

Regularly I recall many of the experiences that I still treasure, experiences with patients that I have visited while assisting in the chaplaincy program. I tell now just one that makes me chuckle every time I visit in the room where one particular patient was.

Because of the numbers of people involved, I do not always remember whether the patient I am visiting has been in the hospital before and I had been to see him or her.

My custom is that, unless I know the patient well, before I leave a room I ask for the privilege of saying a prayer.

One day, as I was about to leave one room, I said to the patient in the bed, "If it is all right, before I leave I would like to say a prayer."

I saw her purse her lips momentarily before she responded to me. Then said she, "Well, I guess it'll be all right but the last time you prayed for me it didn't do any good."

I quickly replied, "Well, let's try one more time."

My batteries get charged with delight every time I remember that moment.

There are some important understandings, however, pertaining to that incident. One is that I should never start feeling that I hold some kind of power to be transferred by "performing" a prayer. I do, however, believe strongly that prayers, when offered in sincerity and faith, are heard by God who does have power, love and grace to give.

Another understanding of importance in sharing prayer and faith with another is that that person may not have the same understanding and knowledge about spiritual matters as I do. I must not invalidate any opportunity I have by getting upset or aggressive at the person's response, whatever it is.

It is important to understand that, as in the implications of the story I have told, the value of holy things cannot be measured by normal human standards. The Holy One, seeing from a viewpoint beyond our own, may be at work, and often is, even when we do not think he is.

I did, later, see that person again. The first words she said to me were, "You did it! I am better!"

No, lady, I did not, but I believe God and his co-workers at the hospital did.

What a rewarding journey I have had these many years at the hospital! And in privileged relationships anywhere!

Written by Lloyd E. Batson
Published January 29, 2003

Blessings from a blue heron

A single bird, a blue heron, has blessed my life.

Periodically, for most of the years we have lived where we do, a single majestic bird shows up on the lake behind our house, stays for a few hours or a day and leaves for where I know not.

The bird is a heron and, I am assuming, a blue heron, one of the largest of the heron family of birds. I also assume it is the same bird each time that has visited us before. Each time it appears, I say a thanks to the Creator Father that no accident has befallen the bird nor that another created being, called a person, has chosen to destroy such a majestic creation.

Herons are graceful birds, with long, sharply pointed bills that appear to extend right into their eyes. They have narrow heads, long slender necks, and bare storklike legs. In flight, herons stretch their long legs straight out behind them and curl their heads between their shoulders.

In searching for food, the heron stalks along the edges of streams and lakes with a stately stride, silent and alone. Sometimes the heron, as I have seen my visiting "friend" do, will stand for a long time with its head drawn between its shoulders. It appears to be asleep, or resting, but it actually is patiently waiting for fish, frogs, or some watery creature. As soon as the heron sees its prey, it makes a lightning-quick dart and catches the victim in its spearlike bill.

I am no ornithologist, and I do not know all I would like to know about blue herons, but I am writing about the pleasure one such heron brings to my wife and me.

In awe at that bird, and in further awe at the gift in it of the Creator to me of such a majestic creature, I will stand at one of our windows sometimes longer than I thought I had time for, just watching. I, at times, try to slip as near to the bird as I can without frightening it away.

The Creator of the blue heron has countless gifts to give us in the creatures of the earth. The Creator's gifts would take on greater meaning in our lives if we would increase our awareness of the great variety of things and beings around us, ours to find pleasure in watching and appreciating.

It is important to me to remember that the wisest of all teachers who ever lived in the earth talked about things around us being a means of reminding us of a great spiritual matter. Speaking of the "lowly" sparrow, Jesus said that not a one of them falls to the ground without the Father's notice. If he cares about a sparrow, should we not, then, understand how much the Father cares about us, he taught.

Thank you, Mr. Blue Heron, or Mrs. or Miss Blue Heron, for having us in your itinerary. You bring joy to us. Please keep coming!

Written by Lloyd E. Batson
Published February 5, 2003

Homemade Valentines

There might not have been a bigger event in the fourth grade in 1934 in the small sawmill village of Alcolu, South Carolina, than the Valentine celebration!

Miss Lib McCarter, the teacher, had decorated the room with a lot of white and red crepe paper (Miss McCarter, actually a splendid teacher, would sometimes yell at an unruly student, "I'll snatch you bald-headed." She never did, but we surely thought she might!). She had covered a large box with white tissue paper and made an opening in the top so we could put our valentines in the box for the "one by one" withdrawal and distribution of the valentines to the class. The drawing was scheduled, agonizingly late for us, for the last activity before we were to go home.

What excitement! It was still in the depression time of the 1930s, and few of us, if any, could afford to buy valentines in the store. Instead, all the students worked for days making homemade valentines on a variety of kinds of paper (I got one made from a part of a brown paper bag, with a heart drawn with a crayon on it). As we came to school that day, we went by the box and proudly put our valentines to one another in the pretty box.

What an exciting ritual, when the magic moment came for the valentine drawing! As Miss McCarter called a name from her roll, a student would come by the box, reach into the opening, extract a card, and call out the name written on the valentine. Then the boy or girl to whom the valentine was addressed would come, usually running, to claim the card. It took a long time for all the cards to be dispersed. The big prize was that the person who received the last card got to take the wonderful box home.

Some of the more popular students got more cards than the others. Sadly, some got only a few. One little girl got only one. Was she sad? No! She may have been the happiest one there, for her self-esteem was so low I think she did not expect to get a single one. How glad I was that I, for some reason, had tried to think who might not get one and had tried to make my prettiest valentine for that girl.

The crowning moment came when the last card was drawn. My name on it! One of the proudest moments of my life was walking home carrying that big box to show my parents.

Homemade valentines! This year, gorgeous and expensive cards will be bought and given. Tantalizing boxes of chocolates and costly gifts of great variety will be presented to folk special to the giver. In no way depreciating these gifts, in some ways I wish all valentines still had to be homemade, reflecting creativity and personal feelings.

It seems to me that this week called "Valentine's" would be an excellent time for individuals, families and friends to find some way, highly personal, to do some "homemade" expressions toward some other folk who need the care and attention of others. It is the kind of "homemade" expressions perhaps represented by "homemade" ice cream, which may not, in some cases, be as good as "bought" ice cream but it certainly has personal planning and involvement.

A Happy Homemade Valentine's Day to you!

Written by Lloyd E. Batson
Published February 12, 2003

Scissors in his hand

I walked on down the hall with a greater excitement than I had when I started into the hall!

It was Sunday morning, and I had gone earlier to church than I usually do, on my way to teach the class of the oldest men in our church, a class that is one of my continuing joys. No other person was in sight, but when I passed the open door of one of the rooms for small children I saw a man, by himself, sitting on a child's very short chair at a low table, engrossed in using a pair of scissors to cut material for use in teaching little boys and girls.

A grown man, sitting uncomfortably on a child's chair, giving undivided attention to readying himself for a great teaching opportunity – with little children!

Across the years I have been involved in many forms of teaching, including seminary teaching, but I am convinced that the man was preparing for a teaching responsibility and opportunity that has no equal. A grown man, a talented person that can do many things, squatting on a tiny chair with a pair of scissors in his hand, deeply committed to the minds and hearts of little children!

I went on down the hall thanking God, and enjoying imagining the interchange of learning between that man and the small children!

Little children are going to learn. Little children come into the world not only equipped to learn, with varying capacities, of course, but they will learn! From many teachers! Teachers may be people but they also are the environment, physical and social. They are the life styles of others, the practices and cultures of the community, the values of parents, the habits of their friends, the ubiquitous television. Teachers are a thousand and one factors and situations around them. "Teachers" everywhere! Little children will learn! What they learn determines how their lives will be lived.

Look at that gifted man with the scissors cutting out paper things. He apparently believes it is important to invest his time, interest, and talent in being a part of the learning process in little lives that will grow to being big lives. He wants to be a part, for good, in those lives.

There are many "windows" open into the lives of people in their learning process. These "windows" may be open the widest when children are very small. Is not it important that as best we can that we make the most of those wide windows? The character and the welfare of their future are at stake.

Public and private schools, clubs and organizations, churches, public and private playground activities – and endlessly the list could go – operate as teachers. How important they are, and how important for them to be the best they can be!

The fact remains that the best of teaching, on all levels, requires people who want to make a difference in the learning process of young lives. My personal highest gratitude goes to the folk who care enough, with intended good, to invest themselves in the learning process of young lives.

I thank God for a man with scissors in his hand!

Written by Lloyd E. Batson
Published February 19, 2003

Before the I do's are said

Writer's note: Though as a minister I have been performing wedding ceremonies for fifty-five years (and, in my case, as my gift to every couple I have married, I have written an original ceremony), I do not consider myself an authority on what a wedding should be like. I do have many "non-authoritative" observations about weddings, only a few of which I share here, in no particular order.

Before you plan the wedding, make sure that you truly want to be married to each other and can commit yourselves to marriage's long-range implications.

There is no such thing in weddings as a "one size fits all." Your wedding is personal to you, and you need to make it your own.

Wedding etiquette books abound, but remember they are guides, not rules. So, do not allow such books to intimidate or frustrate you. Etiquette books are helpful guides, not slavemasters!

Remember in planning your wedding that you are not in competition with any other person's wedding. Yours is yours!

It is what is happening to the bride and groom, their becoming husband and wife, that makes the wedding special, not the grandeur of the wedding. Keep this the focus of planning! Think through what you really want the wedding to be.

The bride, by custom, takes the lead in planning the wedding, but the groom is important, too! Allow him to be involved in the planning.

A wedding is something to be enjoyed, not overwhelmed by! In the planning process, arrange to take "mini" breaks from the stress of getting ready.

As the bride and groom to be, work hard at being comfortable about "talking" seriously with one another about everything pertaining to your coming life together. Think through any known "touchy" situations that exist, or could arise, and plan judicious ways to minimize problems. "Tricky" situations will not go away after the euphoria of the wedding. Determine, as best you can, that no "surprises" with serious problems can come to light after you have been married.

Decide early in the planning whom you want to officiate at the ceremony, and make proper arrangements with him or her. Do not make all your other plans first and then ask someone to perform the ceremony. He or she may not be available for the time you have decided upon. Besides, the officiating person will be able to help you with some of your plans.

Most ministers, if you choose a minister, will be glad, if you have another minister special to you, to share the service with that one.

Spend enough time with the one to perform the ceremony to feel comfortable with him or her.

Share early with the one you have asked to do the ceremony any ideas you want considered for inclusion in the ceremony.

If the one you choose to perform the ceremony requires premarital counseling, agree to it, with sincerity, and accept it as an opportunity to prepare for your life together. As early as you can after the engagement, make reservations for the place you want to be married, and, from the start, inquire about "rules" for the use of the facilities. Plan to abide by them. Respect the premises and make sure they will be cared for after the wedding is over.

A wedding may or may not be overtly religious, but it is always sacred. Make your plans with this in mind.

Continued on page 106

Before the I do's are said...continued from page 105

If the wedding is to have overt religious expressions, like sacred music, Scriptures, and religious references in the ceremony's text, prepare yourselves for identity with them and for their meaning to you and to your marriage.

Have it clearly understood what the role of the photographer is and respect the church's (if it is a church) requests about photography. The one performing the ceremony may have requests, as well, concerning photography.

If the officiant does not indicate he or she will provide you with a copy of the ceremony after the wedding, you may ask if a copy can be provided. Rereading the ceremony on wedding anniversaries is a rewarding custom to consider implementing.

Remember that a marriage license from the state is required for marriages. Be sure to apply for and acquire it in adequate time (I once came to a wedding time and the couple had forgotten to get a license. What confusion and adjustment!).

A final plea! Please plan to receive, and to delight in, the joy of your wedding, and plan to work at maintaining that joy always in your life together!

Written by Lloyd E. Batson
Published February 26, 2003

Publishers Note: This column was written especially for a Bridal Edition in *The Easley Progress.*

The roll call

It was a special and precious roll call for me!

Last week I called a roll unlike any I have ever done. There is only one possibility, with my mother's family, likely a remote one, that I will ever do again a similar one.

My father's parents had 10 children, my father the oldest. The youngest and last living member of the family, my aunt Myrtle, died in Washington, D.C. and was brought back to the Mountain Creek Baptist Church and cemetery, in Greenville County, for burial. I, having had the privilege to participate in the funeral services of others of the family members, conducted the one for Aunt Myrtle. Mountain Creek Baptist Church was my father's home church, as it was for all of the family. The last remaining member of my paternal grandparents' family gone from this earthly life! The family is not gone, though, from memories, and not from influence!

In my opinion, and experience, my father's family was a great family, having been good citizens, raising fine families of their own, and contributing to the welfare of all who knew them, and to society around them. From the time I was little until now I have believed God connected me to a very special family.

Such a family, and most of them now buried in Mountain Creek Church cemetery, gone! I decided to do something as a part of the farewell service I had never done in the hundreds and hundreds of funeral services I have done in the 60-plus years I have been conducting funeral services. My brother in Kentucky, who has done family research, gave me the information I needed and, as a part of the memorial service for Aunt Myrtle, I called a roll of honor.

Starting with my grandparents, and continuing through Aunt Myrtle, I called the name of each member of the family, giving birth and death dates of each. At the end of the roll call, with joy, and thanksgiving, we, together, offered our prayers of gratitude to God for such a family. Then I continued with a tribute to Aunt Myrtle, at the end of which my brother from Georgia led us in a prayer of blessing.

My father's family was not unique. Families are a part of the Creator God's plan for all his creatures called humans (and, remarkably, with some of the non-human species there seems to be strong family traits at work). How blessed and fortunate are those folk for whom family ties are precious and meaningful, for whom family relationships are sources of character, strength, encouragement and pride.

While there are many, and gratefully many, families with strong bonds, families whose individual members have enhanced the goodness of the whole, there seems now to be a growing deterioration of the family unit as being foundational to a healthy society of people.

So many factors are at work eating away at family ties and values. In our current national "homeland security" awareness, a color alert system has been devised to indicate the level of awareness needed to guard against trouble from outside. Would it be possible, or desirable, for individual families to work out some system to put the family on alert that danger to the welfare of the family might lie ahead? Are not strong families, with meaningful ties to one another and to the community around them, necessarily a part of real "homeland" security?

I called the roll of Aunt Myrtle's family, the family that I am so proud of, the family that put so much into so many peoples' lives, and into mine, and, gratefully, I thanked God.

When I finished the roll call and the prayer, I said to the attending congregation, "Now it is your turn to prepare for another roll call of honor!"

Yes, it is our turn!

Written by Lloyd E. Batson
Published February 19, 2003

Hurt touched by love

She was a pleasant woman, about forty, I would guess. I glanced at her occasionally as she sat impassively, staring into space.

I was in a waiting room of a Greenville hospital. While I waited, I was busy writing a wedding ceremony. The flow in inspiration seemed abruptly to stop and I found myself listening to the conversation of a couple across the room. When the man looked at me, I smiled. Then he eagerly inquired, "Hey, don't I know you?"

It turned out we did not know each other, but we did discover some common acquaintances and enjoyed talking about them.

I asked those two folk across the room if they wanted to make a contribution to a wedding ceremony. That led to a discussion of marriages. They seemed never to have heard of a minister who "went to the trouble," as they said, to write an original ceremony for each couple he marries.

All the time I watched the other woman. Now her interest in things around her seemed to be picking up. A light came to her eyes and a faint smile to her face. Later, with the couple across the room having gone, we talked, that woman and I. She told me about her children, how her husband had left her, and about the hardships she had had raising the children. A series of accidents had been devastating, the latest a broken leg for her tenth grader, 6-feet 4-inches tall, 195 pounds, with a "basketball in his hands all the time."

The daughter was fifteen, and most people thought she was "no good" because she stayed in so much trouble. We talked of a mother's love, and how much the mother wished her daughter would change her way of living.

The doctor came in. I saw the need for privacy, so I left. As I departed, I heard just the doctor's first words, "It's tragic, but we're going to have to — ."

When I went back in, the mother was weeping. Her fifteen-year-old daughter had to have a hysterectomy! The weeping mother talked at length about her wayward daughter, but a daughter who dearly loved children. Now there would never be any children of her own.

We talked. I asked her if I could pray. There in the waiting room we prayed. Then we talked about what resources she, the mother had, about the role of faith, about many things.

I have told this long story to raise questions. What are your strengths? What is real to you? What are your resources when times and circumstances are tough?

Nobody, including a believer in God, is immune from trouble, or at least I have never met one. What I have discovered for myself in some difficult times, and through observation of countless others, is that there is strength and grace in faith and in love, so often defying logic, but nonetheless real. Trust in a living God and a deep human love will not necessarily make the trouble go away, but they provide strength and courage with which to handle the situation.

Such a faith, a trust, so often seems to be the one thing that helps a person maintain sanity. It becomes the "holding on" factor. It becomes the strong arm underneath to catch what is left from a crushing blow, and tends to it, until healing comes.

Dear lady, I wish I knew what is going to happen to this child of yours, but I think I know one mother, hurting terribly, who not only is going to survive but who will have strength and love to give to a needy daughter.

Written by Lloyd E. Batson
Published March 5, 2003

'Insurance' my father left me

I have in some things my father left when he died a life insurance policy from the Life Insurance Company of Virginia, which he had taken out on his brand new son, Lloyd Ellis Batson. The premium payments were 17 cents a week, beginning July 21, 1924.

Because he had never mentioned such a policy to me, I wrote Life of Virginia out of curiosity to learn its history and status. Here is the content of the letter I received:

> "Your policy lapsed for non-payment of the premium
> due the week of November 18, 1929. The policy provides for
> a benefit of $47.00 payable at death."

Imagine not being able to pay 17 cents a week! Imagine something being paid on for more than five years and it taking almost seventy-nine years plus a yet undetermined number of other years before it will be worth $47.00.

It must be remembered that it was in 1929 that those terrible years of the great depression began and many, many people had little or no money even for the essentials.

In my imagination I keep seeing my father, whose income in all of his life was never very high, gathering up 17 cents each week to pay an insurance man who came to the house weekly to collect! All of this for a son whom he loved and for whom he had high expectations!

Times change. Availability of material resources fluctuates. But some things never change. One of them is the responsibility of parents to do the very best they can for their children. By its nature, whether parents appreciate it or children recognize it with gratitude, being a proper parent requires many sacrifices. It often is not easy, convenient, or even possible for a parent to do, to be, to provide all those things that can benefit a child. Still, a parent worth his or her salt, will always try conscientiously to do the best possible for the child. There should be no default on this! This, of course, requires more than just money or things!

While my father could not keep paying 17 cents a week for an insurance policy, I thank God for all those wonderful things he did give me. Love! An example of faith! Teachings of the Lord! Encouragement! Many happy times! Many fishing and hunting outings with him! Appreciation for the role of work! Many, many indispensable things that to this day influence my life!

And you know what? I will not even get that $47.00. My children will, in a sense that says something important to me, that what a parent does do for his children is perpetuated in the lives of those that follow.

17 cents a week! Whether or not you could pay that matters little, Dad. Thanks for being a good parent! You left me many great "insurances!"

Written by Lloyd E. Batson
Published March 12, 2003

The star maker

It was still dark when I went out to get the paper. I enjoyed watching the brilliance of the stars, just about as bright, and appearing to be as near, as I have ever seen them. While I was relishing in my leisurely "eye journey" around the heavens, I was a bit startled at what seemed to be about to happen.

The brightest star in the sky was about to be rammed by the blinking light of an aircraft!

I like to watch the lights of an airplane moving in the sky at night, but I had never seen one headed, as it seemed, directly into a star. In fact, the path of the plane, from my viewpoint, was exactly across the face of the star. It did seem, for a moment, there would be a crash!

Never in a thousand years could an earthly airplane touch a heavenly star, I know, but, for a brief moment, I stood transfixed by the strange sight of an apparent plane and star collision.

I walked for a time in the yard, in the darkness before dawn, pondering the immensity of the universe and the smallness of mankind even at our biggest. What is a star? Well, whatever it is, it is meant to be looked at. One thing for sure, you cannot run into a star. You cannot deface it, pollute it, ruin it, or use it up, as the human race is good at doing with many things. A star is meant to be looked at!

And one cannot see a star while looking down!

That magnificent writing, Psalm 8, in the Bible, speaks of considering the stars, the immense and glorious works of the hand of God, and then wondering about the place and value of man. Surely, he could not be much. He can never reach a star. He can never run into a star. Surely, man is not much!

But he is! There is no rhyme or reason that it should be so, but the star maker God loves the insignificant being of the earth called man and made him (and her!) of angel worth!

That beautiful Psalm 8 portrays this earthly creature, man, as one with great dominion over many things. There seems no limit to his power and his capacity to do and to be. That is what the Star Maker thinks of him.

But a star is made to be looked at, not run into. Never in all his glory, in all his achievement, in all his dominion, must earthly man think he is equal to the Star Maker. Selfish activities, power plays, ego trips, mind boggling achievements and insensitive forays into self-admiration may sometimes make man appear, at least to himself, to be bigger than he is. But he can never run into a star! He may take his blinking lights all over the world and orbit them in the skies, but he will not, and cannot, run into a star. He is not a star maker.

What can a star do to a person? It can remind him that though he can never be a star maker the one who is the Star Maker loves him, and has important plans for him. To look at a star can make one intensely grateful for the privilege to be responsible to the one who put mankind in charge of so much that God cares about. A star enlarges the understanding of how wonderful it is to be visited on this earth by the Star Maker.

It would be great if we could always plan to look at a star and not appear to think we can run into one!

Written by Lloyd E. Batson
Published March 19, 2003

No home to go to

Two contrasting images, recently implanted in my mind and heart, continue to get my attention.

A little girl, across the aisle from me in church, was sitting with her family. When time to leave the "big church" to go to "children's church," she got to the end of the pew, turned back, leaned across her father and kissed her brother, a little older than she, and quickly left.

I am sure I heard and benefited from the sermon which came later, but I had already seen a beautiful one that was still speaking to me while the pastor preached.

Family love! There is no time span in one's life journey when family love is not needed, or does not make positive contributions to the welfare of the individuals in the family and to the family as an entity. Of course, the expressions and experiences of love have varying ways of impacting developing ages and situations but the blessings and strengths of family love, where it exists, can be continually good and nurturing, adjusting to situations all along. Family love! Thank you, precious little daughter of a loving family, for your portrayal to me.

The second image. The forlorn look on the man's face told me he was having a tough time. Because I had gone into the hospital chapel to deal with my own needs, I could easily begin a conversation with him.

Though he was dressed in street clothes, I discovered he was a patient in the hospital. In response to my inquiry about how he was getting along, he, with a quivering voice, answered by saying, "How can you feel when the doctor tells you that you can go home and you have no home to go to?"

The story he told me pulled at my heart. For reasons he did not elaborate upon, he told me that all of his family had disowned him and would have nothing to do with him. No home to which to go! It is difficult for me to imagine many things more tragic!

I had no desire to ask him what all had happened, and neither did I have a right to speculate upon who was at fault, he or the family members. I only knew I was witnessing a sad moment in a grown man's life.

We did talk, I trying to do "encouraging listening" as he, apparently sensing I was not sitting in judgment on him, poured out his brokenhearted feelings. At one point, I asked if I could pray with him. "Would you, would you really pray with me?" he questioned. "It has been a long time since anybody prayed with me," he said.

Here was a grown and troubled man, needing family love and he had none! I know there is no magic wand to wave over the brokenness of that family love. I know I had no such wand, but when I asked the Heavenly Father to touch him with his love, the troubled man did reach over and put his arm around me.

A family where a little girl will spontaneously kiss an older brother and a man desperately needing the ministry of family love and having none! Two graphic images! Little girl, you and all of your family, please find a way to keep your family love strong and viable - all of your life. You need one another all your days.

Please do not, as it seems so easy in our world to do, let happen to you what that grown man is suffering from now!

Written by Lloyd E. Batson
Published March 26, 2003

Praying for military service people

War in any place, caused for whatever reason, and fought by whatever people and nation, is a horrible experience!

Countless folk, whether or not they have family members, friends or acquaintances in military service, feel a great need to pray for the men and women who serve.

Many churches have already compiled lists, or are now doing so, of men and women from the congregation's membership and from known people related to individuals and families in the church. Lists also may include known service personnel from the community. Names are added as any requests are made by anybody for inclusion in the prayer listings.

The church of which I am a member has had for years an organized Intercessory Prayer Ministry, with a large number of men and women having accepted a specific time to come each week to the Prayer Room to pray regularly for people and their needs. Additionally, a thick binder has been prepared for praying for service personnel, with a single sheet for each name and giving as much information as possible.

This past Monday morning, early, I was seeking some way to pray for those men and women listed. In the hours I was there, I went through the thick binder four times. The first time I "walked" through the book, reading the information about each, trying to learn as much as I could about the people listed.

The second time I "touched" my way through, putting my hand on each name, attempting thereby to establish some kind of identity, symbolically at least, with the individual.

The third time I "prayed" my way through, beseeching, the best I could, the Father God to take care of each person and his or her family.

On the fourth move through the book, I "hurt" my way through, trying to imagine and to feel the emotions and hurts of each person and each family at the separation from one another and the anxiety about mutual welfare.

Praying can be done in many forms, there being no prescribed way or "best" way. I have noted what I did Monday, and will do again many times, in some fashion, with the belief that it is a matter of great need for people to pray for our military personnel, no matter what one may feel about the war itself. I feel also that putting as much of ourselves into identity with the one and ones we pray for, however we pray, will assist in intercession with the God to whom we pray.

Certainly we can, and should, pray generally for God to care for and protect all those away in service or war, and for hurting people of all nations, but it is important that we personalize as much as possible our prayers for the men and women away from home and country during these difficult and demanding times of war.

Please, God, hear our prayers!

Written by Lloyd E. Batson
Published April 2, 2003

The wonder of an 85¢ ball

Times were hard in the spring and summer of 1936. In the sawmill village of Alcolu, where I grew up, men with families worked in the mill for 10 cents an hour.

The boys in our school formed a baseball team to play anybody who would play us. We made our practice balls and pickup game balls out of string we collected, wound as tightly as we could, and taped with black tape when it was available. We made our own bats. Pretty good ones, too!

If we were going to play teams from nearby communities, as we hoped, we needed a real ball. I, who was the catcher, was named captain, and put in charge of helping us get a real ball. After working at odd jobs, which sometimes paid as much as a nickel, most of the team contributed a little money. I earned and contributed 20 cents. "Pender" Brown gave a dime. "Plug" Scott put in a nickel, I think. Others gave what they could, some only a few pennies.

When we had raised all the money we could, we sat together around a Sears and Roebuck catalog, went through it until we found a baseball that we could afford, and sent off 85 cents, postage included, to buy our hopes for a good summer. Every day a gang of boys surrounded me at school with, "Has it come yet?" Finally, in about two weeks, our genuine, leather-covered baseball came. What a day that was! We passed it around the team, letting each one admire it.

We got to play most of the summer with that ball. We never practiced with it, in order to prolong its life. That ball had a magic life, but, finally, when the cover could not be sewed any more, we taped it, too, with black tape. We had a great summer with our 85-cent ball! Won a good many games. Lost some, too. Somehow, we had a special bond between us, win or lose, because we had worked together to get it and use it. Not a one of us by himself could have bought that ball, but together we did!

That 85-cent ball still shows up often in my mind and heart. What those boys did then is still a key to getting worthwhile things done.

Local governments, civic clubs, neighborhoods, schools, churches, and nearly everything that impacts society are at their best when there are people who accept a common goal and work at it, together, to bring it to pass. Similarly, they are at their worst when people get crossed up with competing agendas and find no way to work together successfully.

Every person who reads this simple observation of mine can likely cite instances in each of the above normal groupings when either the best or the worst has been in evidence.

May the number of 85-cent balls increase all around us!

Written by Lloyd E. Batson
Published April 9, 2003

Bad music but beautiful memories

Nearly every time I plop down on the piano bench to try to play one of the few hymns I learned to play when I was a youngster a precious memory cancels out the bad playing that is still bad.

The memory is of Mrs. Robert Alderman in the 1930s in the small sawmill village of Alcolu, South Carolina, where I lived as a youngster. A niece of Mrs. Alderman had offered to give me piano lessons. One problem was that we did not have a piano. Mrs. Robert Alderman, widow of one of the early owners of the sawmill, lived near us in what we young boys always thought was a mansion. She offered to let me practice on her grand piano if I would take the lessons.

Can you imagine the torment I inflicted upon that genteel lady! Bang, bang, bang I went on the piano in her lovely living room while she sat, listening, in either the den adjoining or out in the opened sunroom next to that.

I am not, and never was, a musician. Her patience and forbearance did not succeed in making me a pianist, but Mrs. Alderman contributed more to my life than she ever knew. Nearly always, even after a session of my banging away monotonously at something called scales (they never made sense to me), she managed to make me think I had done well and had brought music to her. What an encouragement to a little boy!

I lived in a pretty ordinary world, largely among unsophisticated folk, in a small village. Mrs. Alderman let me have a glimpse of the lovely and the genteel. Without ever, in word or action, appearing to be aware of what she was doing, she encouraged me to appreciate beautiful things, to sense that there were good things beyond what many of my associates settled for, and to work hard to be the best I could be.

In my first visit, with my parents, as an eight year old, in her home to have a meal served in her splendidly appointed dining room, I was awed by the beautiful silver, crystal and starched linen tablecloth and napkins. When it was served in a small thin glass, Mrs. Alderman asked me if I liked tomato juice. I told her, to the embarrassment of my parents, that I did not know, that I had never had any. Then, during the meal, I further embarrassed my parents by attacking the corn on the cob with such vigor that I ate not only the corn but nearly all the cob. Mrs. Alderman's reaction? She made me feel I was an honored guest!

Many times I sat in the sunroom with that elegantly attired, white-haired lady and we talked, talked about many things, in her world and in mine, and talked as equals. How she could receive me with such grace when I must have tracked her carpet with my dirty bare feet (we almost never wore shoes back then) I cannot know. I only know that she made me feel I was wanted and that I was somebody!

Every youngster needs a Mrs. Robert Alderman in his or her life! In our modern society, things have changed a lot from those days, but not the need for a person, particularly a child or youth, to be touched by the patience, the love, the interest, the faith, the grace of another person.

May God bless all the folk who are seen by somebody as a Mrs. Robert Alderman!

Written by Lloyd E. Batson
Published April 16, 2003

An after Easter reflection

As I write this, Easter is just a few days away. As it is read, Easter is over by a few days.

Or is it? Must Easter be over until another year?

In my pondering about the quick disappearance of holidays, I have been remembering an early experience with one of my sons, then five. He and I had prayed together, alongside his bed, and afterwards something was said about God hearing everything we say. My five year old son then observed, "Yes, and God sees me, too."

I asked him if God always saw a good boy. He volunteered, honestly, that God sometimes saw a "bad" boy. Then he continued, "God watches everybody."

I was not prepared for the next comment. "There sure must be a lot of Gods."

Naturally, I asked him why he said that. "Well," he replied, "there sure are a lot of people who have to be watched."

Perhaps I will never be sure of what he meant (there are many possibilities) but my thought is he was recognizing something tremendous in scope. There are so many people in the world with so many problems that it is difficult to conceive how one God could "see after" them all!

We live in a world with so many problems of every conceivable variety, social, economic, cultural, racial, religious, nationalistic, many of which invite mistrust, anxiety, even hatred between individuals and people.

In such a world it is indeed hard to take in the greatness of God. We tend to think of God in anthropomorphic terms — people terms, conforming God to our own limited concepts.

Perhaps the greatest idea a person can have, and perhaps the greatest hurdle in one's earthly journey, is the one reflected in the basic reason for celebration of Easter. It is not that there is a God who watches every person to determine the quality of behavior, but that the God who watches every person truly cares about that one! God loves everybody! That seems almost beyond grasp! But Easter says it is true!

Certainly there is a context in ancient celebrations of Easter pertaining to new life coming yearly in many forms. Yet, widely in all of the world it is recognized that in Christian faith Easter pertains to the crucifixion and resurrection of Jesus Christ.

What we have celebrated this Easter will have been that God does see the struggles, the hurts, the needs of people, and that he cares and he loves to the point of giving his Son on a cross and then breaking open the tomb of death to give life and hope! Easter is Resurrection Celebration!

The pall of war, animosity, anxiety of many kinds hangs heavily over the earth, but Easter says that God cares greatly. It says that this God meets the worst in the world and in people with the Cross and the Resurrection.

Need hope rise on Easter and quickly diminish? It is to our great detriment if we allow it so to do!

This God who "watches" what is going on everywhere has offered to us all a better way than sometimes we choose.

Written by Lloyd E. Batson
Published April 23, 2003

Singing the same song

I saw them standing together in church, young daughter and her father. She had her right arm around the waist of her father and with her left hand was helping hold the hymnal, which her father also held and from which they were both singing. She with her youthful voice and he with his mature one were singing the same song.

It was Easter and I was celebrating the Resurrection, but I found myself also celebrating what was being pictured for me across the aisle. A child and a father had found a way to sing the same song!

Within a few minutes I was again in awe. A well-coordinated youth group of boys and girls, without singing themselves and using movement of long "sticks" in their hands and appropriate movement of themselves, were doing for the worshipping congregation an interpretation of the recorded song being played, "Arise, My Love." As unversed as I am in interpretative movement I found myself deeply moved in my spirit by the portrayal before me of the Christ dealing with death and life. In the coordinated movement of the sticks, I could identify with the redemptive love being celebrated.

At one point, I became aware that each of the young folk was, with his or her sticks, portraying a different musical instrument "singing (playing)" the same song as the others. Through misty eyes and a rejoicing heart, I was witnessing a precious moment. Different "instruments" in the hands of young folk were "singing" the same song!

It seemed to me I had watched two related parables being acted out, both portraying how important it is for people, differing in many ways, to find something important to experience together.

Much is made today of difficulties between older and younger people, between parents and children, between varying social interests, between apparent contradictory community demands, and a host of other differing interests. A young daughter's voice is different from her father's and she may like different kinds of music, but how beautiful and important to both that they can find a way, at times, of "singing the same song" in their own ways but bound together with the same song.

An orchestra, with many instruments performing with the varying qualities of the instruments, but playing the same song, can make beautiful music.
Families who are made up of many interests and activities are healthier families when, with all of their differences, they can find a "same song to sing together." A family that seeks out and fosters shared core values and strengths can allow a great variety of interests by family members as long as they can have some "same songs" they can enjoy, and to which they can contribute and receive blessing therefrom.

Any group of people, social, religious, political, community, national, with all their diversity, are the better and the stronger when they regularly can find a "same song" they can sing together!

I will continue to celebrate Easter, and I will continue to celebrate the ties that can bind people together while differing in many ways!

Written by Lloyd E. Batson
Published April 30, 2003

Mothers and children at their best

      Mother's Day is a very special experience every year, prompting recognition of, and expressed love for, one's own mother and motherhood in general. Before I had gone far into thinking of all the joy and love my own mother gave me, I was "side-tracked" into remembering so many beautiful people who have blessed me along my journey.

      I want to share with you an experience which, by extension, may express some of the relationships of mothers and children at their best, relationships which may be enjoyed and celebrated on Mother's Day.

      Long after I passed them on the street the image of the two stayed in my mind, a beautiful teenager and a bent, elderly lady walking together. I followed behind them a bit longer than I needed to for I was simply enjoying the two who were enjoying one another as they walked along.

      I have no idea who they were. I think I do not want to know. I think I want to imagine them as representing the way youth should look at older folk and older folk should look at youth.

      I saw the youth and the elderly one laugh together. Nothing forced or artificial, just happiness coming out. I saw youth and age conversing, sharing something of common interest. Each in turn listened attentively to what the other had to say, with no pained annoyance at having to wait a turn, no semblance of mere toleration of one another.

      I saw, in the fond side-glances, a gleam of delight that youth and age could be sharing something apparently special to both. I saw two disparate ages touch one another, with a soft and loving hand laid so gently upon the other as if touching something priceless and treasured.

      I saw a span of many years dissolve in an eager inquiry from each about what the other wanted to do next, sensitivity to the other's possible interest and need showing them how very much alike they were. I saw young life and advanced years naturally and simply respecting one another. I saw, and tingled with a kind of subdued electricity moving through me, love gently and beautifully portrayed in a walk down the street together of one in the rising years and one in the going down years, with each finding joy in the presence of the other.

      After a bit I picked up my pace, passed them on the left, and for once did not speak. I did not want to. I could not. A thing of beauty was happening to me and to them and I would not dare interrupt either.

      Long after I passed them the image of the two stayed in my mind, a beautiful teenager and a bent, elderly lady, an image no longer saying much about the vast differences in ages but saying much about the mutual joy and goodness of loving and caring, saying much about what people of all ages have to give one another, given a chance.

      Have a wonderful Mother's Day experience!

Written by Lloyd E. Batson
Published May 7, 2003

A carpet speaks

Yes, I listened to the brief, and the beautifully stated, speeches of appreciation for the great host of volunteers being honored for their services, in an amazing variety of responsibilities, in the local hospital. While I did so, with lowered head, I was fascinated by the carpet design in the huge room where the luncheon was being held.

The speakers recounted the remarkable and invaluable role of volunteers who are involved with the ministry of the hospital. The carpet was at the same time also "talking" to me about volunteerism, and about the characteristics that make it at its best and most workable value.

The carpet that "spoke" to me was of simple design, a series of circles and "heart like" shapes. The strength of the carpet's "speech" to me was that all the shapes in the design seemed intertwined! I could not spot a single disconnected shape, or one that stood out above the others.

All over our area there are organizations that depend upon people who, as volunteers, will give of their time, knowledge, and skills in helping accomplish their ministries to people. These organizations cover a wide gamut of activities, all designed to do something specific for the welfare of others. They include, yes, hospitals. There are multiple youth organizations and civic clubs with charitable and community projects. Sports teams and their activities use volunteers.

There are clinics for medical assistance, and organizations for providing food and clothing to individuals and families in need of help. Recreational opportunities for varying ages and money raising projects in all sorts of local and national causes use volunteers. Volunteers deliver hot meals to homebound folk. Churches do most of their work with volunteers. The list goes on.

Volunteers are at their best when they come to feel they are individually important to the whole. They feel that what they have chosen to do is not just a way to fill idle time, or give them something to do, but that they are integral parts of the purposes and work of the organization or activity to which they have committed themselves.

Volunteers, at their best, are team members, putting the welfare of the organization's objectives above any need for "petting" or special attention. They are helpers in objectives, not objectives themselves.

After the speakers had completed their expressed feelings of appreciation for the invaluable contributions of the many volunteers in many varied facets of the hospital, the carpet kept on "speaking" to me. The attractive and serviceable carpet "spoke" of the goodness of working together for the benefit of others. At the same time, volunteers who are connected with worthy objectives and are connected to one another in meeting the objectives are beneficiaries of fellowship, friendship, love, and camaraderie with one another. Volunteers who help others are the better themselves for helping others, and generally are happier people.

There are so many needs, in so many causes, for volunteers in our area. Is it possible that you should consider becoming one? You will help others and help yourself! The carpet "told" me so!

Written by Lloyd E. Batson
Published May 14, 2003

Monday, May 26

Over the course of a few days, before one Memorial Day, I asked numerous people a two-part question about Memorial Day, "When is Memorial Day and why do we have it?" The answers I got were interesting, but not surprising.

"I think it used to be May 30, but I think they changed it," said one. "It's when you're supposed to remember people."

"It's coming up pretty soon, but I forget exactly when. It's when they have the big car races," answered another.

"I think it is at the end of May and I know it's got something to do with honoring veterans," was another reply.

"It comes in a couple of weeks. We get off work that day. We're going to go on a family trip somewhere. I know we're supposed to remember service people who died in war," another responded.

One person said he thinks it is also called Poppy Day, but he did not know the significance of the poppies.

"I get mixed up about holidays now since they tied them to weekends. All I remember is when we were kids we used to put flowers on graves. Seems to me we used to call it Decoration Day," was one reply.

I confess myself to some confusion about days for holidays, but I do know that Memorial Day now comes on the last Monday of May. This year May 26 is the date.

Memorial Day is a national holiday to commemorate people who died in the service of their country.

As a holiday, many people do celebrate Memorial Day, and it is one of the most popular of our holidays. The day, however, though decreed for a certain purpose is, in a way, somewhat akin to Sunday, known by many as the Lord's Day, a day of worship.

Nothing on paper or in a decree can make people do what the day is designated for. People must still decide for themselves whether they will honor the intent of the day or whether they will use it as they themselves choose.

A mandated and required memorial would likely be a hollow one, just as mandated worship would be.

While nobody can make you or me do a memorial to others, we sadly are the losers if we never do. Nobody can make a person worship, pray or even respect a day of worship, but in my mind he or she is the loser if such is not done.

Memorial Day!

A nation does not come into being without the grit and the courage and the heroism and the sacrifice of many folk. It is not sustained and strengthened without the grit and the courage and the heroism and the sacrifice of many folk.

In our time, we are beneficiaries of those, in military duty, in civilian service, in practiced ideals, who have done their best, and given their lives doing it. Memorial Day is one opportunity to express our gratitude.

Gratitude is not just something expressed toward dead people. All around us are people who have blessed our lives.

If Memorial Day is a remembering day, I hope our remembering will also extend to those who, across the years, and who do so today, have touched our lives in meaningful ways.

Not many of us would be much without the help of many people. Let us discover the goodness of remembering — gratefully!

One more word. A nation does not have much promise for the future without the available grit and the courage and the heroism and the sacrifice of its people.

It is our turn!

Written by Lloyd E. Batson
Published May 21, 2003

Disappearing hearing

In my mind one of the greatest tragedies to befall a person is his or her disappearing hearing.

Often I have heard raised the question, "Which of your physical senses would you hate most to lose? Hearing, seeing, feeling, tasting or smelling?" To lose any one is a devastating experience! Probably with me my answer would vacillate between seeing and hearing.

When I write now about disappearing hearing as a great tragedy I am not talking about experiencing the physical loss of hearing.

So many innovative and exciting developments in electronic equipment, surgery, and medicines that just a relatively short time ago would have been unbelievable are now available to treat and help with the physical senses! There is, however, a hearing problem with which none of these can help.

The disappearing hearing that I consider a great developing loss has to do with hearing what one has heard!

Did you ever hear your parents say to you, or have you ever said to your son or daughter, "This is the fourth time I have told you...."? The problem was not hearing what was said but letting the hearing evoke action. The hearing just disappeared into nothingness.

Many of us have so often sung the beloved songs we learned in church, in singing groups, or in family gatherings that we can sing them without paying much attention to the meaning of the words. We can get so familiar with them we can sing the words without hearing afresh their message. This, tragically, to me, is disappearing hearing.

In most families there are wonderful words of wisdom that parents or grandparents shared with their children but only occasionally they are used for guidance. Disappearing hearing!

Great literature that once brought surges of delight, wonder, awe and meditation may still be filed away in memory but seldom used as it once was. Disappearing hearing!

Lectures, discussion group subjects, speeches, sermons and programs of many kinds that for a time brought help to us as they were listened to again in the mind get little
attention anymore. Disappearing hearing!

Memorized verses from the great book called the Bible can often be quoted without paying attention to their meaning. Disappearing hearing!

It is easy to sit in church and hear every word but go away without remembering anything. Disappearing hearing!

Schoolteachers regularly face situations, and often despair about them, involving students' disappearing hearing.

The litany could go on, but I am here calling attention to a problem that one who has been victimized by it can himself or herself do something about.

The Greatest Teacher that ever lived regularly said, "He that hath ears to hear let him hear."

I think he was addressing the problem of "disappearing hearing!"

Written by Lloyd E. Batson
Published May 28, 2003

A favorite place to visit

One of my favorite places to visit is the "trash dump" (I think it probably has a more refined name!) that the City of Easley provides for the convenience of its citizens in disposing of household "trash" and certain recyclable materials. Because it is funded for the residents of Easley only, non-residents cannot use it. There are county facilities elsewhere.

Access to the facility is easy, the grounds are generally kept clean, the "open" hours are convenient, and the availability between the weekly pickup services at my residence is often a great help.

The primary reason that the disposal facility is one of my favorite places to visit, however, is not because of the above stated reasons, but because the people who work there have become my friends. They are helpful, courteous, interesting, and friendly folk, and like people everywhere, are differing personalities. I enjoy "howdying" with them.

A very human factor is at work at the city facility, as it is everywhere. Businesses and service organizations may have the best of facilities, merchandise, and prices, but the most common lasting impression that affects future dealing with them is of how the "customers" feel they were treated by the people who served them.

Churches, too, though divine in origin, have a very human element to them. They may have the best of many things, buildings, programs, sermons, and music, but if people visit and feel the members have not been interested in them, or not been friendly to them, their interest in the church diminishes. Sometimes it goes away completely.

Most people could, at a given moment, make a list of places they have visited during the last week and grade them according to the pleasantry and efficiency of the people who served them. The reason that they can do so quickly is that they, in fact, already have graded them, consciously or subconsciously.

Employers and employees, yes, and even churches, alike could benefit from an occasional self-examination as to whether the "best foot is put forward" when dealing with the public. "Customer satisfaction" is important in the long and the short run. Some businesses do in fact have professional evaluators, to pose anonymously as "customers" for the very purpose of assessing the status of friendliness as well as efficiency.

I know well that some jobs "try the soul," but grumpiness, discourtesy and unpleasantness are generally inexcusable and everybody is the loser — the business or institution, the employee or representative, and the "public."

Being nice is not nearly as difficult as some folk seem to feel or act!
Of course, I know well that nice, friendly, and efficient workers often have to deal with grumpy, discourteous, and unpleasant "customers."

Being friendly and pleasant works best when it is two-directional. Yet, while I cannot control what others do, I certainly have a say-so about my behavior, whether I am the worker or the customer.

Yes, one of my favorite places to visit is the city operated "trash dump!"

Written by Lloyd E. Batson
Published June 4, 2003

A cap's angle

Recalling it brings pleasure to me.

I watched him, sitting on the wall. Still hot from running and playing, he now settled down alongside his father already there. Beads of perspiration moved dirt along with them as they rolled down his face.

With the jerking, sliding motion one makes with the whole body when feet will not touch the ground, he moved closer to his father. At the same time, turning to see that he did it exactly right, he adjusted the angle of his cap to match the angle of the cap his father wore. Now, cap sitting on his head just like his father's, his shoulder stooped exactly like his father's, he gazed intently at the same world his father watched.

Is not it beautiful to see the love and adoration of a child for his or her father? We really do not need a special day such as Father's Day, on the third Sunday of each June, to make us appreciate the special person a father is. Just ask that little boy!

A child's relationship with his or her father, through the growing years at home, runs to extremes — from "father can do no wrong" to "father can do no right." Whatever the feeling may be at a given moment, there never has been a child who has not been affected by his or her father if the child has spent any time at all with him. Negatively or positively, one's character, outlook on life, moral behavior, and religious concept are influenced profoundly by the man called father. Let not a father among us forget that! Some of us may still have time to make sure fathering is done at its best.

What is the most expressive word we have for God? Is it not "Father?" Not a one of us can be God the Father, but surely God has a high opinion of human fatherhood if he wants us to know him as father. Would your child who knows you as father think well or poorly of God as a father if the child thinks in terms of the only father he or she knows, the earthly father?

The angle of the cap is not right unless it is exactly like father's! Think, will you, of all that says! May God the Father help us earthly fathers be the right kind.

Would it be possible this year on Father's Day, June 15, to look beyond the gifts, cards, and considerate acts of attention and appreciate afresh the inherent goodness possible in a father, son and/or daughter relationship?

If so, this Father's Day might be the very best of all!

Written by Lloyd E. Batson
Published June 11, 2003

I got 'bababatized'

I was near the exit of the local hospital a few days ago, getting ready to go to conduct a funeral, when I saw a bright and pretty youngster skipping through the lobby toward where I was. She was singing softly to herself and moving her arms in beat with her song. Behind her at a short distance were two people, possibly her mother and grandfather, though I did not recognize them.

As the youngster passed me, I said, "My, you look happy today!"

Turning back from the door, she came quickly to me and excitedly declared, "I got bababatized!"

The conversation that followed was precious to this old man who got "bababatized" seventy-one years ago but remembers the experience with clarity and joy. I cannot sing like my new friend, and certainly cannot skip and move in cadence as she can, but I went away meditating upon what things, if any, make me as happy as that youngster was.

Are not there along every person's life journey basic experiences and discovered core values that should remain a constant factor in shaping one's feelings and well-being? It seems to me that a basic faith, for example, should continue to hold value, in all extremes of living, through all ages, including advanced years. It seems to me that such basic faith should impart the goodness of living now and give meaning to the future, including dying.

It also seems to me that happiness, and happinesses, should spill over in relationship to others (not necessarily as that youngster's did!). What could be easier to share than happiness? I know, of course, that some folk apparently find bitterness and unhappiness easier to share!

I went away from that newly "bababatized" and happy youngster attempting to identify some of the key events and moments that have influenced my life, and, pondering them, realize that they still do.

There are such things as "benchmarks" in people's lives, events or experiences that can establish points of reference for reflected joy and happiness. Such benchmarks vary in kind and magnitude but can result in life having continued meaning and happiness.

Some benchmarks, for example, could relate to one's discovery of faith, or the strengths of a good marriage, or achievements such as graduation, or commitment to a fulfilling vocation. The discovery of certain precious friends can be a benchmark, or some kind of service to the less fortunate, or fulfilling decisions for community service. The possibilities are limitless as to what may be one's own "benchmarks" for happiness!

I am too old to skip, and my singing is terrible, but should not I be able to demonstrate in my demeanor what some basic things in my life have meant to me?

"I got bababatized," she declared, brimming with happiness. Well, young lady, some great things have happened to me, too!

A question now. What are your benchmarks for a good life?

Written by Lloyd E. Batson
Published June 18, 2003

No, but I can smell

It was years ago, but every detail is fresh and sharp, still brightening whatever situation brings the recollection to mind.

I had been called to come to the hospital, that a member of our church had had some kind of "spell" or attack and was unresponsive to doctors or family. When I got to the hospital, I found the wife of the elderly man sitting in the hall in a chair by the closed door of the room where her husband was. She was upset and worried. Three doctors were in the room, working with her husband who had been in a coma of some sort for nearly an hour and had neither opened his eyes nor spoken nor reacted to anything the doctors could do.

After a few minutes with the wife, I told her I was going in to see my friend that I had enjoyed for a long time, particularly for his unusual and wry sense of humor. When I entered the room, the three doctors, all of whom I knew, moved away from the bed and motioned me to the bedside.

There he was, wan and pallid, eyes closed, and totally "out of it." What I hoped for was that there somehow could be some awareness that I, his pastor, was there. So, I leaned over him and said one of those senseless things that often come out when one does not know what to say.

What I heard myself saying, as I called his name, was, "Can you see well enough to know who I am?"

To the shock of the doctors and to me, without eyes opening, or change in appearance, there came this surprisingly strong and clear voice saying, "No, but I can smell!"

As quickly as I could, I went outside to the anxious wife and told her to stop worrying, that her husband was going to be all right, and he was!

Several years later, a week or so before he died and I conducted his funeral, that man was recalling and laughing about what he had told me in the hospital room. He knew at the time what he was saying! I delighted in telling this story at his funeral!

I sometimes use this story with families and friends to remind them that they had better be careful what they say around sick people that they think cannot hear what is being said. They may be more aware than they seem to be.

In my mind, a true sense of humor is a priceless possession. It can be a strength in one's own difficult times. It can be refreshing and blessing to others. I use the word "true" because I am not talking about silliness, frivolity, or "performance" (these things can be obnoxious and unappreciated by others). A true sense of humor is rooted in one's personality, one's capacity to know when to take things seriously and when to see the lighter side of what is going on. A true sense of humor is connected with whatever sense of joy is in one's life. A true sense of humor gives not only a pleasant orientation to living but provides encouragement to happiness in others.

Thank you, friend, for your sense of humor, still a blessing to me after the many years you have been gone.

By the way, is not it so that every person seems to have a distinctive "smell" to him or her?

Written by Lloyd E. Batson
Published June 25, 2003

Are you going to the Fourth?

In my boyhood days in Sumter and Clarendon Counties during the 1930s, at this particular time of the year, a very common question was voiced while greeting friends and acquaintances. The question was, "Are you going to the Fourth?" or a bit later, "Did you go to the Fourth?"

The question simply was asking if the other was going to the picnic, the ballgame or whatever it was that the community, the church, the sawmill, or somebody was having on the Fourth of July.

I have not heard that question in years. It would do me good if I were to hear it again, in the same way of those 65 or 70 years ago, but with an additional understanding. Oh, I hear variously, "What are your plans for the Fourth?" Or, "Where are you going this year for the Fourth?" Or, "What are your holiday plans?" Or, "What will you do on your day off?" What I do not hear is "Are you going to the Fourth?" of "Did you go to the Fourth?"

I think we ought deliberately to go to the Fourth! The Fourth of July is a national holiday, celebrating the major event of our nation's history. Most people are aware of the holiday. Many seem to care only that it is a holiday, a day off or the focal point of a vacation, making little or no effort to go in search of something meaningful and good about our nation to celebrate. Holidays are increasingly like that, including Christmas, being mainly times away from work or times of planned trips or activities.

Commemorative holidays for so many seem to have become just holidays with little or no commemoration.

I will make a conscious effort this year to go to the Fourth! I confess that I will have a hard time doing so, with so many other things to which I am committed. Let me share what I plan to do, to go to the Fourth. I will read again the full text of the Declaration of Independence. I will read accountings of the early days of our country. I will spend time praying for our great country (a country having so many needs). I will try to feel for myself what it would take to be like those people who signed that historic document, the Declaration of Independence, knowing that their very lives were jeopardized in so doing.

Yes, I will try to go to the Fourth! I will attempt to discover the Fourth as a commemorative holiday.

How easily we appear to take important things for granted! American citizens cannot afford the luxury of ceasing to learn from the nation's past.

In meaningful fashion we must keep going to the Fourth to discover afresh the hopes and dreams and principles of people who believed in something so strongly that they could conclude our nation's major document, the Declaration of Independence, by avowing, "and for the support of this declaration, with a firm reliance on the protection of Divine Providence, we mutually pledge to each other our lives, our Fortunes and our sacred Honor."

Are you going to the Fourth?

Written by Lloyd E. Batson
Published July 2, 2003

A special gift

Within the hour, as I write this, I have received a precious gift, still in the cardboard box, sealed at the corners with tape to keep the contents from escaping. I am excited! It is not an anniversary gift, our wedding to have in two days a 53 year history. It is not a birthday gift, in recognition of my entrance, eight days ago, into the eighth decade of my life.

No, this box contains a very special gift, which I hope I can use in the next day or so. Though excited as I am to open the box, to "ooh and ah" at the contents, and to handle them fondly, I will wait until the proper moment because the gift calls for special circumstances for it to fulfill its purposes.

What was delivered to me, by my college professor nephew, is a box of catalpa worms, freshly gathered from a catalpa tree, from which comes their name! Ah, catalpa worms!

Catalpa worms, by the way, are seasonal. Out of nowhere, at the time assigned to them by nature's clock, they appear in one kind of tree only, the catalpa tree. With ravenous appetites the worms can denude a tree.

Catalpa trees are not as common in our area as they once were. So, to get a box of fresh catalpa worms delivered to me is special for several reasons.

To start with, gifts tailored to one's interest are always well received. Catalpa worms might just be the world's greatest fishing worms! They do not appeal to the aesthetic tastes of some people, or even to some fishermen. To put it mildly, they might be called ugly, similar in some degree to unwelcome caterpillars. They become distasteful to some if they are turned inside out to put on the fishing hook as they are often done. Fish, however, at times will bite catalpa worms when nothing else seems appealing to them.

So, now you know why I am so pleased with this special gift! I hope to see, shortly, if there is still magic in catalpa worms!

This gift has another valued dimension to it. Because of their scarcity, my catalpa worm fishing is largely a remembered early segment of my life in lower South Carolina. Regularly, as a youngster, I fished with my father using catalpa worms. Fishing times with him are among my most treasured memories. So, that gift box of catalpa worms will bring alive some joys of the past to become present blessings.

Among a person's most influential possessions are his or her memories. Memories are many-dimensional, covering a wide range of emotions. Bad, or unhappy, memories sometimes have to be treated with special attention to minimize their detrimental effect! Happy memories can show up frequently as blessings! Happy memories can at times be healthy prescriptions of healing for which medicine can neither be prescribed nor brought. They can be enjoyable and therapeutic entertainment.

Fortunate is the person whose life has built up a storehouse of pleasant memories! I wish every person could have catalpa worms in his or her background! But, if catalpa worms are not there, I hope something equally as rewarding is! And I hope that memories of whatever it is shows up often enough to add pleasure and goodness.

As for me, my gift of catalpa worms has brightened my day with memories, and I hope the worms will turn into fish!

Written by Lloyd E. Batson
Published July 9, 2003

For the present, a story from the past

Stories about early days in Pickens County delight me. I was fortunate to be pastor for 33 years of a delightful man, who lived into his nineties. His telling of stories from his early days were, in his own slow and soft way of speaking, as funny as any I ever heard anywhere. In whatever gathering he was present, if he started to tell something about his early life in rural Pickens County he immediately became of the center of interest. A truly great storyteller is a rarity and a delight!

Once I heard him tell how he and his teen-age friends got their smoking and chewing tobacco, which they could not normally afford. In his laconic, "laid back" way he said that during the summer, when all the country churches had their "protracted meeting," as summer revival services then were often called, he and the boys would learn when each church in the area was having such services. They knew that it was the practice of the visiting revival preacher to preach against tobacco once during each revival "meeting," often on Thursday night. The boys always managed to learn which night that an "against tobacco" sermon would be delivered in each church. So, on the "tobacco" night, wherever the church was in the area, the boys would hide in the nearby woods. It would be hot in the church, with no air conditioning, and all the windows would be open. The boys would wait out the often long, loud, and emotionally charged sermon against tobacco. Then came the altar call, the call to repentance.

Many of the men in attendance (no woman then ever admitted she used tobacco) would "repent" and come to the altar. As a display of repentance, they then would go to a window and throw out their tobacco.

The boys, hiding in the woods, would then slip up close to the church and gather up all the tobacco. That was the way they got their own supply of tobacco! And had fun doing it!

The surreptitious gathering of the tobacco, though, was not nearly as much fun as what happened the next morning.

Before daylight, the boys would again be at the church, hidden in the woods. This time the fun was to watch the men come at daylight to look for the tobacco they had thrown out the night before!

Though I have seen firsthand some of the implications of this story working out in people's lives, I think I will leave whatever understandings of human nature that can be drawn from this story from the past to the ones who read this, if indeed there are any readers.

Written by Lloyd E. Batson
Published July 16, 2003

Dealing with partiality

For many years while I was pastor in Pickens I had one "job" I do not know how I got. It was just expected, and assumed, I would do it. And I did.

My "job" was to have some area minister at every football game in the Pickens High School stadium to give an invocation over the speaker system before the game. It seemed right, and totally accepted, during those years, to have such prayers there.

Once it dawned on me that we had never had a black minister to do the invocation. I went to the newly arrived minister at one of the churches, and one I had not met, to ask him to do the invocation for the next Friday's game. He readily agreed to do it. I explained to him, as I did to every minister, that there were some things of which he should be aware. He should not try to catch up on his praying at the game, and that he should not show partiality in his praying because there would be another team playing besides the Pickens Blue Flame. He said he understood and would take care of it. At the game, I took the minister by the announcer's booth, introduced him there, and left to take my seat in the stadium. At the proper time a magnificent voice, full and deep, came over the speaker with a wonderful prayer! I was feeling so good I had thought to ask him. Then I heard at the end of the prayer, "May the flame of courage rise over us tonight!"

I kidded my new friend about his prayer ending. He said, "I didn't say Blue Flame!"

Later, it occurred to me we never had had a Catholic priest to do the prayer. I went to my friend, Barney Lohman, the priest at the Catholic Church which served Pickens and Easley. I asked him to pray at the next game, which would be between the Pickens Blue Flame and the Easley Green Wave. I told him what I had told the other minister and he, too, said, "I'll take care of it."

On the game night, after taking Barney by the booth, I sat in the stadium. The priest's prayer was short, as I knew it would be, and a beautiful one. I was thinking how pleased I was I had asked Barney. At the end of his prayer, I heard come over the speaker, "...and may the flame of courage wave over us tonight."

I told Barney that, yes, he did take care of my request! I also told both of those ministers that I think God has a sense of humor and he honored these prayers. Some newcomers to our area may not know that at one time the rivalry between the Pickens and Easley communities was so great, and the fans on both sides got so rowdy, and some into fights, that the two schools had to stop playing one another for years. Such a situation seems ridiculous now, given the wholesome relationships that generally exist in our area between all our communities. Differences of opinion do exist between municipalities, organizations, political entities, and groups, but our citizenry seem to have found ways not just to get along with each other but also to benefit from working with one another for the common welfare.

May it ever be so!

Written by Lloyd E. Batson
Published July 23, 2003

About coons and a coffee cup

Few young ministers ever have the privilege I had while attending seminary of serving the same congregation, a wonderful one, for seven and a half years. The church was fifty miles from Louisville, Kentucky, in Commiskey, Indiana.

Many times during those years, I would go up on Saturday afternoon to go coon hunting that night with some of the men of the church. Fun!

Occasionally, after we were married in 1950, Joy, my wife from New Mexico, who had never been exposed to coon hunting fun, would go with me. She enjoyed tramping in the woods in the night, listening to the dogs hunt, and hoping, like the rest of us, to hear the dogs tree a coon, with all the excitement that that generated. She especially liked to shine the powerful light high into the tree to try to spot the eyes of the coon!

Some of my friends in the seminary envied me and begged me to arrange a coon hunt in which they could take part. Once I did so, and, on the drive up, I told the men, one a big, redheaded man from Alabama named Charlie, that the home to which we were going to begin the hunt was one of my favorite places to visit, and I often had eaten there. The family, farmers, lived a long way from anybody else, at the end of a road. What a delightful and happy family, with a fifteen-year-old daughter and two younger sons! I told the men that after we came in from the hunt we would sit around the stove and be served hot coffee and refreshments.

In the pleasantry of the ride up from Louisville, I told them also that the family had only one cup with a handle still on it, and that I would watch which one of the visiting hunters the lady of the house would take a liking to, and, after the hunt, serve him with the cup with the handle.

Well, after we had had a great time on the hunt, and had treed four coons, we came in from the cold, sat around the stove and enjoyed visiting. The lady of the house made coffee and served the welcomed hot and stout brew. I watched as she gave the one cup with the handle to the redheaded Charlie from Alabama.

In the camaraderie, and in fun, I told the hostess, knowing she would enjoy it, what I had told the men on the ride up and that she apparently liked Charlie above the rest because he had gotten the cup. We all laughed heartily, especially the lady, and the pleasantry continued. But, I had forgotten about the fifteen-year-old daughter who was still up and listening!

Several weeks later, I was having Sunday dinner with that coon hunting family. During the meal, I noticed that there were new cups and plates all around the table. I said something about all that pretty new china. The lady laughed and said, "That Saturday night you fellows from Louisville were here and you teased me about the one cup with a handle, and that I had given it to that redheaded guy, my daughter was so embarrassed that she took her money out of her savings jar and went to town with us the next Saturday and spent it all on the new stuff!"

I nearly died! With no intent to embarrass anybody, and enjoying a happy moment, I had carelessly overlooked the sensitivity of a precious teenager and had embarrassed her greatly. By the way, I am glad to say she remained my dear friend, in spite of my careless insensitivity.

I tell this lengthy story to make one simple appeal. Please join me in trying to recognize that insensitivity to the careless things we say, and comments we make, can easily embarrass, even hurt, others.

My appeal? Please stay alert to how "loose talk" can offend or hurt others, and, particularly, to be respectful of the needs and feelings of young folk!

Written by Lloyd E. Batson
Published July 30, 2003

'Aren't you some kind of preacher?'

I was leaving the hospital in the gathering night, headed to my car in the upper parking lot. Near the steps, I saw the man before he spoke to me. I guess he thought he had seen me before. "Aren't you some kind of preacher?" he asked.

How do you answer that? I replied, "Yes, I am some kind of preacher. What kind do you need?"

This man, one I had never, to my knowledge, seen, forthrightly declared, "I need one who will talk to me, but mostly will listen to me while I talk."

In the semidarkness, I replied, "Well, start talking and find out if I am the kind of preacher who will listen."

Well, talk he did, and listen I did! Pretty soon the darkness had dropped the "semi." My what pent-up feelings in that man poured out! If I had the same burdens that that man appeared to have, I would probably be looking for "some kind of preacher" myself! I am not sure that the "preacher" I am could handle his problems if they were mine.

But listen I did, never taking my eyes off him or giving him the appearance of token attention. Only occasionally did I make any vocal response. I was listening, yes, but I was also concerned that when he finished he would expect me to tell him how to deal with his problems!

When he finally finished, and a brief silence ensued, he blurted out, in surprise it seemed, "Hey, somehow I feel better! Somebody finally actually listened to me!" Well, we did talk a while longer. I never did have to confess my inadequacy for good advice to him. I did, in the darkness, pray with him before we parted. Once in awhile I still pray for "that man" whose name I never heard. God knows who "that man" is. What "that man" needed from that "some kind of preacher" is what many people need — just somebody who actually will listen to them.

Listening is not always convenient, easy, or pleasant. Yet, listening, sincerely, is often what a troubled person needs from another, and not just from "some kind of preacher" either. Everybody can be a "listener," even if it is hard to squelch the urge to pass out instant advice. One can, by trying, discipline himself or herself to "listen out" a troubled person.

When "that man" turned to leave, he gave me one of the warmest handshakes I ever received, and to me, who had hardly said a word about his problems, said, "Thanks, you helped me more than you will ever know." He in the darkness apparently walked away in light.

"Listen to me!" can be a cry for help! Help that can often be given purely in the listening! Did it ever occur to you what real help you might be to somebody by being a "listener?"

Written by Lloyd E. Batson
Published August 6, 2003

The Broken Plate

It was cause for a lot of pleasure when, in the difficult days of the early 1930's, during the Great Depression, the Graham Baptist Church, my home church, purchased two new offering plates. Everybody was excited.

They were beautiful, particularly in contrast to the two old battered ones the church had had for many years. Highly polished mahogany (or stained to look like mahogany!) plates with wide rims surrounding the bowls! My, they looked good on the communion table.

One Sunday, soon after the church bought them, for some reason, I, either eight or nine years old, was asked to take up the offering. Proudly I took the two bowls from the table and started down the aisle, excited and feeling important. About two-thirds down the aisle, to my horror, a horror I can still feel seventy or so years later, one of the plates slipped out of my hand.

I can see it now. When the plate hit the floor the rim and the bowl separated. The bowl part wobbled a few times and settled still. The rim went rolling off somewhere, teetering sideways.

I stood, transfixed, in the middle of the aisle, terrified, as tears burst from my eyes. I had broken one of the precious new plates! I was painfully aware of some demeaning whispering in a nearby pew about why they let a little boy handle the new offering plates. I could not move!

Then, from the middle of a nearby pew, I saw Mrs. Lois Brogdon get up, slide in front of others on the pew and come to me, still frozen in the middle of the aisle. She put her arm around me, and whispered in my ear, saying, "That's all right. I will take the offering plate home, glue it back together, and next Sunday nobody can ever tell it was broken."

Then that dear lady whispered in my ear something I will never forget. She said, "I love you." She then picked up the parts of the broken plate and went back to her seat. I do not remember whether I completed taking up the offering. What I do know is that that Sunday, standing mortified in the middle of a church aisle, I experienced the redeeming power of love. In the midst of shame and grief, I was loved!

Mrs. Lois Brogdon's expressed love in a dark moment of my life had healed my own brokenness.

Mrs. Brogdon was right. The next Sunday there was the offering plate on the communion table as good as new!

And so was I!

We hear preached the wondrous power of God's redeeming love, but a young boy, now old, can tell to this day that human love given to hurting folk has healing power, too!

Written by Lloyd E. Batson
Published August 13, 2003

Watch those buttons you push!

Just recently, I was on the elevator at Greenville Memorial Hospital, remarkably being the only passenger on that usually crowded conveyance. The elevator stopped at one floor and a woman got on. What she did instantly reminded me of a similar thing that happened many years ago in the old Greenville General Hospital. I recorded that "happening" at the time and tell it here.

When a lady got on the elevator on one of the middle floors at Greenville General Hospital, I noticed she appeared to be haggard and distraught. She punched the button for the floor she wanted and stepped back to lean against the elevator wall.

"Lady," I said, "that is the floor you are already on."

"O Lord," she exclaimed, "deliver me from that floor. That floor has been nothing but trouble for three days and nights. I don't know what I'm doing."

Poor lady, but her predicament is more understandable than some folk I have known who have had some bad experiences but keep on punching the same buttons they always have.

Here are the folk who are wearied by monotony day after day but will not do any creative things to change it. There are the husband and wife who know their life together has gotten in bad shape but still keep on doing the same things that irritate and alienate. What about the person who knows well all the problems created by alcohol but keeps on punching the buttons that keep him or her in a mess? The one with an alienating temper but keeps on blasting anyway?

And look at the young folk, whose basic sensitivity tells them that drugs, in whatever form, have nothing but trouble for them but hang on to them anyway. Look what "bad company" leads to, and one may know it and still do nothing about changing friends and associates. Witness the difficulty some have of standing up for what they know is right in behavior and practice because of the "everybody's doing it" syndrome.

Observe the parents who see trouble brewing in family conditions and still hang on to the circumstances contributing to it. Notice the families who see what is happening to them because of their indifference to church life and to spiritual needs, yet go on with whatever it is that has caused the slackness.

The lady said, "Lord, deliver me from that floor!" More of us could deliver ourselves to a better level of living if we really wanted to badly enough. And though she did not mean it that way, she also said, "Lord, deliver." A committed faith will indeed help us move to a better level of living if we will let it.

Watch those buttons you punch! They may be getting you nowhere!

Written by Lloyd E. Batson
Published August 20, 2003

'I caught you goofing off'

I was sitting at my desk, reared back in my comfortable chair, and with my feet propped up on top of the clutter on the desk. Without knocking, or any note of his presence, into my office came one of the deacons of the church, a friend (most of the members of our church were also my friends, believe it or not!).

"Ah," declared the deacon, "I caught you goofing off!"

My quick reply was, "On the contrary you caught me doing the hardest work I know how to do. I am thinking."

Next Monday, Sept. 1, will be observed as a national holiday called Labor Day. As a holiday, it is one of the most popular of all our holidays. For many folk a holiday seems not important so much for what it represents, but simply because it is, that it exists, and that it can be enjoyed, for a variety of reasons.

In summary, Labor Day arose out of organized labor's desire to have "working people" honored. In 1882, Peter J. McGuire, founder of the United Brotherhood of Carpenters, suggested that a national holiday be declared to honor "working people. In September of 1882, the first Labor Day parade was staged in New York City. In 1887, Oregon became the first state to make Labor Day a legal holiday. In 1894, President Grover Cleveland signed a bill making Labor Day a national legal holiday.

As with many words, there has been some shifting of the meaning of "labor." In earlier times it seemed largely to be identified with "manual labor," the "blood, sweat and tears" kind of work. Though indispensable to the welfare of every society, the so-called "working class" of people often had no honored recognition. Admit it or not, consciously or unconsciously, we in a nation espousing "equality" with no "classes" of people have tended to identify and grade our population in "classes" of people.

The word "labor," in our times, probably would better be expressed with the word "work," though "Work Day" would sound strange as a holiday. Among the recognized definitions of "labor" are "the expenditure of physical or mental effort" and "human activity that provides the goods or services in an economy." So, in a proper sense, "Labor Day" is celebration of, and appreciation for, all who are productively involved in personal and societal welfare.

While "Labor Day" as a holiday is generally identified with rest, vacations, and the end of summer, it is an important recognition that productivity, however it comes in its multitudes of forms, is both necessary and honorable.

As it is with other holidays, perhaps we should not only enjoy, and benefit from, this Labor Day but intentionally look afresh not at its existence but at its meaning. And, deacon, I was right. While I have done a lot of manual work in my life, I was at that moment not goofing off but doing what can be, for me at least, the hardest of hard work — thinking.

Know any greater "work" needed in our present confused and demanding world than "thinking?"

Written by Lloyd E. Batson
Published August 27, 2003

"Take me home"

What do you do when you are pinned in alongside a 275 pound cab driver taking fifty minutes to negotiate six miles through the congestion of heavy traffic in the huge city to which you have gone to attend a convention? You talk to him, and enjoy it, though the four other riders, including two who apparently spoke no English, are stoically silent.

At one point, I asked the burly driver what, in the fourteen years he had told me he had been with the cab company, was the most unusual character he had ever had as a passenger.

After a moment of reflection, the man said, "Well, you have your standard types. There is the Crazy Mary, the Do the Job Jud, Tex, the one you take from bar to bar, and the Take Me Home John. I guess it is the Take Me Home John that bothers me the most. He's drunk, or drugged, and tells me to take him home. When I ask him where home is he doesn't know and winds up telling me to take him somewhere, anywhere."

I was intrigued by all those characterizations (these may be standard cab driver characterizations for all I know!), but Take Me Home John is the one that has lingered in my mind the most. Cab riding in Pickens County is not a regular experience for most people, though apparently the Easley area is well served by a taxi company. However, I do see frequently this character, Take Me Home John, in one form or another, in our area.

In Pickens County? Yes. There appears to be an increasing number of people who seem not to know where home is, or at least what home is, and will settle for just about any substitute. Home, at its best, is both a place and an experience, offering strength, encouragement, renewal, love and peace! At least, that is what home is supposed to be. Some people seem not to know where home is, in these terms, and accept a variety of substitutes.

I have known some folk who seem to dread going home because, regrettably, home is not a pleasant place or experience. To me, it is sad when people allow home life to deteriorate to the point that members of the family would just as soon, and sometimes rather, be elsewhere. It is sad to me when a person has to find, or think he or she does, somewhere else what he or she cannot find at home.

What happens to a person that will allow one to lose awareness of where home is, or what it is? I certainly cannot adequately answer that question, the question arising from what appears to be a diminished centrality of the home in our society, with other activities, pursuits, values, interests taking its place.

It is a creeping sort of thing, this substitution of "somewhere, anywhere" for the home.

For many folk, it is important to have some kind of system or program to keep up with budgets, schedules, demands, and multitudes of other of today's pressures. Would not it also seem important to have some system or procedures to look at what is happening to one's family and to work at tending to any deterioration of the home's place in the life of the family?

Perhaps it is time for a lot of us in our still wonderful place called Pickens County to work harder at making home what it is supposed to be, or making sure "there is no place like home."

And always to know where "home" is!

Written by Lloyd E. Batson
Published September 3, 2003

Hope and a box of doughnuts

I bought a box of doughnuts from him, not because I needed or wanted them. It was a hot, sticky Saturday afternoon and I guess I felt sorry for him. Perspiration glistened on his dark face and his ball cap teetered on his bobbing head as he answered my queries about why he was selling doughnuts on such a miserably hot day. The several boxes of doughnuts he was carrying in his not so clean hands appeared to be as damp and disheveled as he was.

My sympathy quickly turned to pleasure and admiration as he answered my questions about why he was selling doughnuts. He was selling doughnuts, he told me, so his ball team could go to North Carolina, as the coach had said they could. Why was his team going to North Carolina? "To go to the series," he said. He could not explain to me all I would like to have known. It was something big, however, and his team had a chance to go to it, and perhaps play in it, I think I understood.

What was taking place in North Carolina I did not know. Perhaps some kind of tournament for youth. It really did not matter to me because I enjoyed sensing the hope that this young boy had about something he was willing to work for to achieve.

Something to believe in! Something meaningful to hope for! How important for every person, young or old! This young fellow with the doughnuts apparently did not have a full grasp on what all was involved in his first trip out of the state, but he knew it would be great, and that he had a chance to experience it.

In our conversation, I discovered that the coach of the team was very important to the youngster. Whatever the coach said and did carried great weight with him. "Coach says we are going to North Carolina" made it certain with him. I even asked this excited young boy who made the doughnuts. "Coach did," he said (wouldn't Krispy Kreme be surprised at that?).

The remembered encounter with the excited youngster came alive again during the recent days of the Big League World Championship Series competition here in Easley. That event brought not only broad media attention to our area, but a sense of joy and pride to our citizenry. Additionally, and perhaps more importantly, the Series brought alive in many folk an awareness of the rewards of getting constructively involved in the lives of young people.

Are not we as a community, and people in organizations, churches, clubs and groups, potentially something like that coach to that doughnut-selling boy who dreamed of the trip of his life? How important it is, it seems to me, to teach, to motivate, to instill confidence in others! How potentially life impacting it can be to play a role in creating vision for living and for finding happiness in every day. For giving to young people something in which they can believe, and for which to work.

To be a part of influencing the setting of goals which create hope, and engender enthusiasm in working for these goals, is a challenge and opportunity, all around us, in many and varying ways.

I do not know who the coach was for the perspiring youngster with the doughnuts, but I admire and appreciate him to this day.

Does it make a difference what "coach" says? I think it should!

By the way, I ate those doughnuts from the battered box I bought. I think they were the best doughnuts I ever ate!

Written by Lloyd E. Batson
Published September 10, 2003

The Asafetida bag

Phew! I could not believe my nose! In a crowded store a few days ago, a person brushed me as he passed by in a hurry. I did not mind the brushing. What I was shocked by was the smell he left behind.

I stood in disbelief. Did I actually smell what I thought I smelled? It had been sixty-five or so years since I smelled that edition of unsavory odors. Did I smell an asafetida bag on that hurrying person?

An avalanche of unpleasant memories erupted in my mind and "smeller," what as youngsters we used to call the smelling senses.

In the small village in Clarendon County where I lived during the 1930s, there were many traditional procedures, practices and substances that some folk believed could ward off diseases and "evil spirits." An asafetida bag was one of them. Asafetida is the correct spelling, though few people I lived around could spell it correctly or give the dictionary pronunciation. Usually I heard some version of "fetidy" or "fetty bag."

"Asafetida," by dictionary explanation, is "the fetid gum resin of various oriental plants ... formerly used as an antispasmodic and in folk medicine is a general prophylactic against disease." "Fetid" means "having a heavy offensive smell."

I am uncertain of the source of supply of asafetida in our village, but what I know was that some people made a small cloth pouch, put asafetida in it, and tied it around their necks with a string, and wore it all or most of the time. Within a few days, perspiration and body dirt added another offending smell to the fetid stuff in the bag. Every asafetida bag wearer in a schoolroom, or anywhere, was quickly identified, but there never was any escaping the odoriferous assault until recess or dismissal came!

I cannot attest to whether an asafetida bag ever warded off an evil spirit or disease, but I can attest that such warded me off when I could possibly avoid it.

Folklore is a rich treasure to be used and enjoyed. Modern medicine has discovered many useful and effective materials in studying folk medicines and practices of times gone by. Something that appears to today's world to be superstition often had roots in practices that at the time had some useful role.

In my mind and memory, I have difficulty believing that a smelly asafetida bag was one of them!

Though superstition and peculiar understanding about many things still exist in surprising number, I am grateful for the disappearance of "asafetida bags" (or, at least, I thought they had disappeared!)!

I walked out into the parking lot, stood by my car, bowed my head and gave thanks for the marvelous medical help we have in our time! I gave thanks for the nearing breakthroughs in dealing with some of the devastating diseases of our times, and I asked blessings upon our skilled medical personnel in our area and upon all our medical treatment facilities.

I do not need memories of long gone (I think!) asafetida bags to make me grateful for the status of medical treatment today, but one suspicious whiff did end in one parking lot thanksgiving!

Written by Lloyd E. Batson
Published September 17, 2003

Magic in the night

What can compare with the pure contentment of a father sitting on a log with his son before a glowing and warming campfire, with no other people within miles of a backpacking camp along a river flowing through a mountain forest?

In a nostalgic conversation with one of my sons, on a recent visit home, about special memories from the past, we both identified one special event as one of the most treasured we have.

My then twelve year old and I had been thwarted time and time again in our plans for such a night, but then it finally came to pass, though some frustrating last minute calls had made us late getting away to our chosen destination.

There is magic in such a night. Food you would hardly tolerate on the table at home becomes delectable. The hard ground becomes a pleasant mattress. Outside a tiny tent, the noise of some unknown animal plundering in your gear becomes an intriguing part of the noises of the mountain forest blackness. The exposed feet of the knotted ball you know to be your son turned headfirst into the foot of the sleeping bag next to you becomes a special lump in your throat. Feet that will not get warm serve only to give more waking moments to enjoy the gurglings of the river's waters nearby.

Magic in a mountain forest! Yes, but greater than that! A father who cannot sing and a son who can, sitting on the log, spontaneously singing at full strength for more than an hour all the songs and hymns we know and some we make up! And without trying to identify it, having the joy and goodness of the Heavenly Father come down from the bright, nearly full moon so magnificently riding the tops of the tall pines! Worship bursting forth without plan! Peace permeating the soul without search! Faith blessing without asking! God real without describing!

Magic in the mountain forest, then, and now as it is recalled! And that is the point of my writing this recollection.

All through our lives we are storing up treasures, not alone to be revealed in heaven, but for special times and needs here on earth. Songs, both sacred and secular, Scriptures, poems, stories in great literature, memorized in whole or in part, become treasures to be brought forth for pleasure and for ministry to us.

These treasures are for sitting on a log before a fire on the special nights of our lives and they are for the times the shadows of trouble and need want to squelch the joys of living. These treasures become vehicles of strength to us for the good times and for the bad. They interpret our deepest needs. They express our joys. They declare our faith.

That night, long ago, finding stored up treasures to be blessings in the mountain forest, itself now is a stored up treasure still having magic.

Store up treasures! They can be precious blessings somewhere along the way!

Written by Lloyd E. Batson
Published September 24, 2003

Blessings in a funeral

Are there blessings to be experienced in funerals? I say yes.

While I know a few people who in all of their lives have never attended one, a funeral is a universal experience among the people of the earth. A funeral service, varying in kinds of expressions, is a way of saying an earthly farewell to one who has died. It is often called a memorial service.

As a minister, I have conducted hundreds and hundreds of funeral services, including those of my father and mother, my wife's parents, and of grandparents, uncles, aunts, close friends, church members, community friends and acquaintances — and now a brother. I have also attended countless other such services.

Amid the sadness at the death last week of the first one of my parents' six sons, with all the emotional impacts of that, did I find any blessings in the experience connected with my brother's death and his funeral? Yes! And I have seen such happen countless times with others. I have often observed to folk that some of the best things in life happen in connection with death. I am not saying all is good but that some good and precious things can happen, and often do.

In abbreviated form, I list some of the things precious to me that happened a few days ago when my brother died and was buried, and which I have seen happen many times with others.

There came a renewed awareness of the goodness of family ties across the years. Family ties can be among the greatest continuing strengths and resources in life.
A rush of memories of the contributions the one we were honoring made to my life across the years flooded my mind and heart with fresh blessing.

Blessing came in recognizing the futility of denying grief, of "being brave," and all those clichés so often heard in connection with funerals. There is blessing in "letting tears roll."

It was good to sense the need to stay better connected to various family members, and plan to do something about it, even though distances and the busyness of life seem to make such difficult.

What a joy it was to be a receiving part of the expressions of loving and caring people who said and did so many things to touch a grieving family, including what must have been the most food ever assembled in one house.

How precious to hear and feel the expressed appreciation of so many people whose lives have been made better by the one we were honoring and burying. Sometimes, in our own busy lives, we are not aware enough of the many whose lives are touching and blessing others.

There was an emerging understanding that grief can, and should, move from its devastation to a stimulus to make one's own life and journey better, and helpful to others.

It was good, in recognizing the severe loss of one family member, to feel a renewed appreciation for the others that remain.

There was goodness is realizing afresh that there does not have to be "right" words to say or "magic" phrases to utter. Infinitely more important is the sharing of presence, a touch, a smile, or a conveyed love, even without words, of showing one cares.

I stop my listing of blessings in a funeral with one of immense importance. It is the awareness of one's own mortality and the urgent need to be properly prepared for the death that will inevitably come to every person, and for what comes thereafter.

Yes, blessings can, and often do, come from funerals!

Written by Lloyd E. Batson
Published October 1, 2003

I ain't a gonna do it

A friend of mine once told me that when he was the young pastor in a church out from Brevard, North Carolina, an old man, a member of his church, was in the hospital. The man, somewhere near ninety, was critically ill and seemed to be in the process of dying.

The man's family was crowded into the hospital room, standing around the walls, waiting for his last breath. All of a sudden, the elderly man opened his eyes, sat up in the bed, and demanded to know why God had not gone on and let him die.

The family was shocked. None of them knew what to say. Finally, one of his grandchildren said, "Well, PaPa, the reason God didn't let you die is because he's got something else for you to do."

The elderly man, with surprising vigor, declared, "Well, I'll tell you right now I ain't a'gonna do it!"

I would have enjoyed being in that room!

While I have never heard a deathbed declaration like that, I have witnessed, in varying forms, stances taken, sometimes adamant and sometimes subtle, reflecting essentially the same feeling of that old man.

All around us there regularly are situations of many kinds that need help from willing folk. Some quickly do what they can. Others, whether or not they say it in the words of that old man, take the stance of "I ain't a'gonna do it!"

Neighbors get in trouble. Folk get sick. Elderly ones lose mobility. Shut-ins are lonely. Food gets scarce. Crises appear. Charitable organizations for assisting others need volunteers and funding. Churches need workers in their many programs. The list of needs is long, very long.

Wonderfully, some folk sense opportunity for doing what needs to be done, and gladly get at it. Others, even if they become aware of the needs, turn away, apparently feeling that if the needs get met somebody else will do it. "I don't have time." "That's not my problem." "They got into that mess; let them get themselves out." These are some of the attitudes of "I ain't a'gonna do it" folk.

I know that no one can respond to every need that appears, but to take an attitude of "I ain't a'gonna to do it" to an opportunity to be of help to others robs one of some of life's greatest rewards.

Being a participant in some meaningful way of making the lives of others better is surely, in the language of the old man's family members, responding to "God's got something else for you to do."

"I ain't a'gonna do it" is a great thief!

Written by Lloyd E. Batson
Published October 8, 2003

I was it

I have just attended Homecoming at one of the colleges from which I graduated.

Homecomings at colleges and universities are festive occasions, with all manner of events and programs planned for the enjoyment of graduates who come back to celebrate the past, in the context of exciting current achievements, and to enjoy classmates and friends who were in school together.

Specific class year reunions usually are scheduled at intervals of five or ten years, and these are highlighted in the school's celebration. My class was the oldest one being recognized.

So, with interest and excitement, I looked forward to attending my "Homecoming" at North Greenville College, and to the joy of seeing my friends and classmates of my graduating class. On the scheduled Saturday, two weeks ago, I, with my wife, not a North Greenville graduate (she has two degrees from the University of New Mexico), went to Tigerville, South Carolina, for the festivities. I was anxious to see again those special folk of my years there.

When I got to the appointed room for my class reunion, I made a startling discovery. I was it! A one-person reunion!

This was the 60-year reunion of my graduating class of 1943. I did not get to do the usual thing of being amazed at how old my classmates had become. I was the only old one that got there! Sixty years had taken their toll. Shocking! How could so many have gotten too old to attend, and so many to have died!

Realistically, given the normal processes of so many years, I did not expect many to be able to attend, but I was not expecting to be the entire reunion of our class! So, since "I was it," was there a reunion of my class? Yes, there was!

Memories do not have to have flesh and blood present. So, in my mind and spirit, I enjoyed afresh all those I could remember. I celebrated what friends can always celebrate, the contributions that particular people have given to one another. I recalled the fun times, the serious and difficult times, the responses we made to the challenges confronting us, and the refreshing variety of personalities that made life for all of us on the campus exciting and fulfilling.

My "reunion" strengthened again my appreciation for what North Greenville College (then a two-year college called a junior college) did for me. Times were tough, the depression years not being over. The college offered me an opportunity for an education, one that my family and I likely could not otherwise have afforded. The school, even with its limited resources at that time, was exactly what I needed, an environment of learning and challenge, and an opportunity to work to help pay my way.

I was it, as far as the Class of 1943 at Homecoming went, but I was, in my heart and mind, in reunion with some of the most important people and times of my life.
In the fast-paced environment of the day in which we live, I think it important to be able to go back, regularly, in memory and appreciation, to a reunion with people, events, challenges, even defeats, which have helped set the strengths and incentives for the living of our lives.

The past still has much to give us today — if we will take the time and meditative reflection to visit it.

"I was it," but I had a great 60th college class reunion!

Written by Lloyd E. Batson
Published October 15, 2003

My last big brother fight

Writer's Note: For the many beautiful and helpful expressions to me relevant to the death of my brother, Paul, and to the column, "Blessings in a Funeral," which I wrote after his funeral, I am grateful. My grandchildren have always wanted me to tell them bedtime stories. I wrote down one of their most requested stories, one I chose to read at the graveside part of my brother's funeral. I use it today for my column. LEB

My brother, Paul, older than I by eighteen months, and I often as children got into scrapes and sometimes big fights. He was always bigger than I was, but I was wiry, quick and tough. So, I usually got the upper hand in disputes that called for fighting. Sometimes the fights were not very gentlemanly!

The last big fight I recall vividly! Paul and I got into it upstairs in our house in Alcolu. I do not remember the reason. Boys, and brothers especially, do not have to have a legitimate reason to get into fights!

Our house had an upstairs with two rooms with access by a staircase in two sections, the upper part turning at a ninety-degree angle with a flat place, or landing it was called, at the turn. Our fight began in one of the rooms upstairs, went to the hallway at the top of the stairs, then into a tumbling, wrestling match down the stair steps, blows flying in many directions.

We were oblivious to anything but our fighting with one another. When we had tumbled to the landing at the turn of the steps, suddenly, to our horror, we saw Daddy waiting, having heard and seen most of our struggling. We both expected a reprimand, and to get the severe punishment Daddy was good at giving.

Indeed, we got the ultimate discipline! Quietly, but with a firmness that we knew by experience we had better accept without dispute, he handed out the worst of all punishments. He made us kiss one another and apologize!

Paul and I never had a fight again. We sometimes had verbally loud disagreements, but not any more fisticuffs or wrestling! One reason for that, on my part, besides the dread of having to kiss him, was realizing that he was getting so much bigger than I and it would be prudent to negotiate settlements.

I think that last fight helped me realize something that has stood me in good stead all my life, that there are much better ways to settle disagreements than fighting, in whatever forms such takes.

Another outcome of that last big fight was that I began to realize my older brother was actually a pretty nice guy and I could enjoy him as a brother! That has been the case for many years now.

Written by Lloyd E. Batson
Published October 22, 2003

A stolen wallet

A stolen wallet! A major problem anywhere, but magnified when one is out of the country!

One of my sons, a college professor, is in France with some of his students on a semester of foreign study there. For the first time in his years of traveling in foreign countries, a few days ago, while in Paris, a skilled thief took his wallet from his person without his being aware of it until later. While he did not recover his wallet, he was amazed at, and grateful for, the kindness and help he was given quickly in getting duplicates of important cards and papers.

His predicament reminded me of the one time in my life when my own wallet was stolen. In 1943, I had been sent to Camp Wallace in Texas for basic training. I was housed in a barracks with men from all over the country, none of whom I had previously known. My strange new world was a hodgepodge of frenzied and physically demanding activity.

For the security of my very limited money, I slept with my wallet inside my pillowcase. To my horror, one morning when the predawn rude awakening was forced on our barracks, I discovered that my wallet was gone from its "safe" hiding place. My wallet had been stolen in the night from under my head!

Far away from home, and payday still three weeks away (payday did not amount to much but it was all the income I had), I had been robbed of all I had. Frantic searching, with others of my barracks assisting, produced nothing!

Two mornings later, at reveille, during the formal ceremony outside, my name was called to come forward. Afraid I had done something warranting rebuke, I approached the sergeant in charge. With a simple apology for what some unknown person had done, he presented me with more money than had been stolen from me! The men in my barracks had quietly taken up money to replace mine!

I had thought I had been developing into a "tough" soldier, but in unmilitary fashion tears flowed!

A lot is wrong in our world! But a lot is right! It is easy to be obsessed by the apparently growing problems of selfishness, "evil," crime, inhumanity toward one another, et cetera, to the point of overlooking the vast amount of good going on all around us.

Yes, people are "stealing wallets," in the myriad of forms that takes, but there are countless people who are spontaneously helping others, doing acts, little and big, of kindness, and going out of their way to assist with problems and needs.

In spite of the many evidences that there is a vast supply of bad things and people in the world, there are regularly recurring displays of human goodness all around.

It was sixty years ago that men in my barracks, many of whom I not yet gotten to know well, gave me a blessing far beyond the replaced money (I was told that every man in the barracks had contributed!). They made me aware of goodness at work in the midst of evil.

I suppose I could have found a way to survive without the money stolen, but I still am blessed with the awareness instilled then that all is not wrong in this world!

Written by Lloyd E. Batson
Published October 29, 2003

One hundred years ago and from now

Among the recent additions each week to *The Easley Progress* that have fascinated me have been quotations from the editions of the newspaper of fifty years ago and one hundred years ago. My active imagination has let me enjoy many people and events that I was not around to know and experience.

I have "met" some interesting, delightful, and influential people of that time and tried to identify with them and what they did "back then." These reported activities and events of long ago (but not actually so long ago for many of us older people!) have intrigued me.

The way my mind works has also introduced another exercise that I have enjoyed, one of imagining how those folk back then might have reacted had there been some way to have two columns detailing what would be going on fifty and a hundred years from then! I want to quote here one recent item in *The Easley Progress* one hundred years ago: Prof. Langley's air ship has been given another trial and made a complete failure. All efforts so far to navigate the air have been a failure. God made the fowls to fly in the air, fish to swim in the water and men to walk upon the earth, and all efforts to change God's law in this respect, we think, are doomed to failure.

There was no way, of course, for the editor, or whoever wrote that item, to see one hundred years into the future. I wonder, though, what he or she would have thought, not only about the present state of airplanes, but about a man landing on the moon and the mind boggling space exploration, the Internet, the breakthrough in medicine, and a thousand and one other "impossibilities" now commonplace?

Of course, I believe that a human cannot be God, and should not try to be. Yet, Psalms 8 in the Bible, if you would like to read one of the most beautiful and astounding things ever written, declares God's high opinion of his favored creation, human beings. Genesis 1 portrays the given assignment to the creation to have dominion over, and to subdue, the earth and earthly things. I cannot see that God made a law anywhere that people could not fly. Rather, I see God expecting his creation to do everything possible to do the "undoable" and to learn the "unlearnable." All of this, of course, in the role of the created and not the Creator!

As exciting and astounding as are the rapidly increasing "breakthroughs" that constantly unfold in our time in human knowledge and accomplishments, I think that these achievements have only touched the surface of what is yet to be. I cannot see this as breaking or changing God's "laws."

What they may be I do not know, but out there, not far away, are developments beyond our present imagination. I do not see God as limiting what his creation can do and become — except in one absolute area. Though he or she may at times seem to think and act otherwise, a human cannot be God! The creation, though fabulously endowed, cannot be the Creator, and must not assume the role of playing God!

The Creator will honor and bless the creation as long as the created understands Psalm 8.

Written by Lloyd E. Batson
Published November 5, 2003

Five minutes before you hear the dogs

I do not do much of it anymore, but I always enjoy listening to those who do. Within the last few days, I have heard exciting tales of some hunts up in the mountains and elsewhere. Hunting and fishing stories always have a touch of the mythical in them, I know, but they always fascinate me.

I grew up downstate in deer hunting country. At that time all deer hunting was done with an assortment of hound dogs to find and run the deer. Before I was old enough to carry a gun myself, I sometimes was allowed to go along with my father to enjoy the festivities and the sounds. Through most of my hunting days I enjoyed the festivities of a hunt more than the hunt itself.

The first time I was permitted, at about twelve years of age, to carry a gun of my own (a borrowed twenty gauge automatic shotgun) I was taken by one of the older men on the hunt to a stand in the woods, a ditch bank, on the edge of a swamp. I was told by the elderly hunter that the big bucks often ran near that place.

Before the old veteran at hunting left me alone in that vast woods, he very carefully gave me instructions, all kinds of instructions. Among the things he told me was, "Now get ready five minutes before you hear the dogs running. The big bucks often slip out before you hear the dogs."

"Yes, sir, and thank you. I'll be sure to get ready," I eagerly told him.

What I did not realize at the time was how wise he was. Later in the morning, and a long morning it was for a young boy alone in a big woods, as I sat on the ditch bank, I got to thinking about what that old man had said to me. How was I to know when it was five minutes before I would hear the dogs?

What the veteran hunter was telling me, I would learn, was to stay alert all the time!

How simple life would be if we could always depend upon "hearing the dogs" before we had to get ready to do something!

There are many applications of the wisdom of that veteran deer hunter, wisdom that has to do with much more than deer hunting. The person who waits for somebody else to identify opportunities for him or her will miss many chances to excel, or to do something important.

Local governments and institutions cannot afford to wait until a need is suddenly at hand to deal with it. Alertness before "the dogs are heard running" makes proper response easier.

One can, by not staying alert, miss an opportunity to give counsel or guidance to a son, daughter or friend just starting to experiment with drugs. The "sound of dogs" usually means that the deadliness of drugs has already taken its toll.

Some students wait until exams are at hand to study, or a paper is due in the next day or so, assuming that when they "hear the dogs" there will be plenty of time to get ready. It seldom works that way.

Marriages have been destroyed because the husband or the wife, or both, did not stay alert or keep communications open, problems mended, relationships cultivated. Waiting until you "hear the dogs" is to wait too late.

Poor management of one's financial resources will invite disaster when a sudden crisis comes. Waiting until one "hears the dogs" means trouble.

The examples of the validity of that old hunter's advice abound. Think about them, and stay alert.

Just for the record, the veteran hunter was right. A heavily antlered buck slipped up behind me before I heard the dogs. Because I had to pick up my gun from the ground, whirl and shoot from down in the ditch, I missed the first deer I ever shot at, and one that was the biggest I have ever seen in the woods.

My buckshot, however, did topple a small pine tree, and do it neatly!

Written by Lloyd E. Batson
Published November 12, 2003

The pleasures of an aching back

Is there ever a situation where an aching back spells pleasure? Yes, there is! There was the huge garden, a few days ago, glistening in the late afternoon sun. The differing shades of green in a variety of growing things were enticing the sensory anticipation of a transfer of them from the array before me to the table.

Then came the unqualified, and welcomed, "There it is. Go to it," and the "farmer" going away to leave me with my conscience. Will I be greedy and load up? Or deny my inclination and try to be "nice" and not get more than I perhaps should?

Beautiful, the huge patch of turnip greens, gloriously shaped and shining! Waiting! Waiting for one who all of his life has known and enjoyed the satisfying ministry of properly cooked and seasoned turnip greens to his ravenous appetite for such a delicacy. With pockets stuffed with blue grocery store plastic bags, I started into the unblemished sea of glistening greens. I tried to be careful about mashing them down. I was also aware that any cover-up about how many greens I picked was impossible. The path and extent of picking would be clearly evident!

There is no way to pick turnip greens except by stooping, and, by its nature, picking turnip greens is a slow process. So, a back in its eightieth year for some reason began complaining sooner than it used so to do.

I will not record how many greens I picked but it was enough that I came home with a back still complaining in not so friendly terms.

Any sense of guilt about accepting at face value the invitation of the "farmer" to get all I wanted, and could use, vanished when I walked into our house with my full bags and my wife exclaimed, "Oh, wonderful! We'll have plenty for some great meals!" What a surprise and delight it was for me in 1950, when I went to New Mexico to get my wife and brought her back east of the Mississippi River, to discover I had gotten more than I knew in that dear lady. Though she had not been introduced to the joys of "southern cooking," I discovered that she liked turnip greens as much as I did.

The careful washing and fine-tuning of the greens, some to eat for supper, some for the next day, and some for the freezer to eat later, took time. Then came the cooking of all the greens. The anticipation of what surely must be one of the Creator's choice inventions — turnip greens — made those chores pleasant.

Some things give testimony to the pleasures of an aching back. The goodness of friends who sincerely say, "There it is. Go to it." The pure enjoyment of a meal of turnip greens at their best. The engendered memories of the happinesses of other times and places when people have given of their friendship and "turnip greens," here meaning a great variety of gifts to be enjoyed.

Yes, there can be pleasures in an aching back!

Written by Lloyd E. Batson
Published November 19, 2003

Honestly, Thanksgiving

The lady appeared to be embarrassed, greatly.

She had been staring into space, her face so sad and with a slight trace of tears showing on her cheeks. During the brief moment that she was unaware I was around, my mind worked frantically, wondering what I would say. When I did speak, and she recognized me, I almost wished I had turned unobtrusively into another direction.

So quickly as to be almost violent, she wiped at her face, and, with some rush of forced strength, transformed the sadness of her face into another kind of sadness, the unnatural and agonizing appearance of an imposed smile that rested upon a countenance not ready or prepared to be happy.

With embarrassment showing in a smile not yet being done with sadness, and in her uneasy voice, she appeared to be ashamed that I had caught her in the throes of melancholy. Somewhat giddily, she apologized for looking like she did and said something about a person not being supposed to give way to her feelings as she had been doing.

Before I left, things, I think, had changed a bit, but still lingering in my mind is the initial reaction of that dear lady.

Most of us like to be seen at our best. But is being at our best some forced appearance that is not real? Are not there times when we are our best when we are at our worst, if that "worst" means we are being honest and trying to deal with something real that needs tending to?

Nobody ever needs to apologize to me, for example, if that one is hurt, or deeply disturbed, or cares greatly, or burdened with a heavy load of some kind, or struggling with a moral or religious problem, or carrying a great grief. Being human is very normal, you know!

By the way, I encourage people under certain circumstances to cry. I often tell folks that it is all right to cry, just do not "boo hoo" all the time!

Being honest sometimes requires weeping. Being honest also often requires thanksgiving. There are few people who have no cause at all to express gratitude. Even at our worst, there usually is something for which honesty would require that we be grateful.

Something beautiful happens to those who, being honest, recognize in the midst of their troubles something good and give thanks for it. The simple act of thanksgiving tends to give a better handle on the trouble that wants to monopolize our feelings and actions.

For me, as an individual, though I sometimes have heavy burdens I know also that honesty requires me to be thankful for and about many things. When I express thanksgiving I usually am able to handle the other things better, honestly.

It is Thanksgiving season. We, most of us anyway, do not really have to manufacture performed thanksgiving. We just need to recognize, honestly, the real reasons we have to be thankful.

Have a Happy Thanksgiving! This might be the best Thanksgiving season ever — if we are honest!

Written by Lloyd E. Batson
Published November 26, 2003

When hard times come a'knocking at the door

The recent call from a sixth grade teacher in one of the local schools involved her not knowing my age, but needing to find out. Her diplomatic approach was admirable, but I caught on quickly and broke in with, "I qualify. I am old enough. I was there, from the beginning to the end."

What the teacher needed was someone old enough to have been in the Great Depression, beginning with the collapse of the stock market in late 1929 and lasting for a long, difficult time in the life of this nation and the lives of its people. Her classes had been studying about the Great Depression and this astute teacher wanted someone who had experienced it to visit her classes and to talk personally about it.

What followed was one of the most enjoyable experiences I have ever had. I spent the class hour with three separate classes during the day. I have been in many classrooms but I have never had a more attentive, interested and responsive audience, with not a frivolous or insignificant question or comment asked or offered. The respected teacher sat apart from the class with no need for control. I came away with great appreciation for the teacher and the quality of the delightful young students.

In recorded history, economic depression has cyclically come and gone. The one the students had studied was called the Great Depression because it was recognized as the greatest of all — at least in our nation. It is difficult for present-day students to comprehend the burdens and struggles of such a time as the Great Depression because, gratefully, they have never experienced such. I hope they never do.

I did attempt to describe how the depression affected us as a family, and all those around us, in the struggle to provide basic needs in those difficult times. Among the things I tried to do, however, was to portray that there is inherently great stamina and ingenuity in most people that can survive nearly anything. Hard times do not necessarily spell defeat.

I could tell those students such things as that the standard pay for farm laborers was fifty and sixty cents a day, and that for workers in the sawmill, if they could get work, the common wage was ten cents an hour. With that income families had to be housed, fed, and clothed. As a teenager I landed a great job, at twelve and a half cents an hour. After some time at that scale, there came one of the most memorable moments of my life — a call to the manager's office to be told, "Lloyd, because of your hard and good work we are raising your pay to fifteen cents an hour!" Glorious news! Among other things, it helped with my savings for college.

The story I wanted those students to hear, however, was not primarily about the hard times, but about the strengths and goodnesses that can be brought to bear in difficult situations. In my case, I was privileged to have loving, hardworking parents that let us children know about the power of love and faith, about the goodness of sharing together, and that joy and happiness, while affected by hard times, did not depend totally upon the quantity and quality of "things."

Yes, I could describe what we did not have, but it is what we had that allowed me never to feel sorry for what we did not have. We had what I now know was family love, acceptance of hard work as a norm, the capacity to have fun and pleasure without having to buy it, respect for and appreciation of people around us sharing the same struggles, and a working and rewarding faith in a living God.

What I would like those students, having studied about the Great Depression, to learn is that the quality and meaning of life, though affected by economic situations, is still largely up to them!

Written by Lloyd E. Batson
Published December 3, 2003

The Empty Mailbox

I can still see her.

An elderly lady, dressed in green, white hair blowing a bit in the breeze, striding briskly the last few steps down her driveway, and moving quickly across the highway as I slowed a bit to let her pass. From the middle of the road, in the midst of one of her jaunty steps, she turned to wave a cheerful "thank you" to me.

Intrigued by this bright, lively, straight-backed elderly lady, moving with enthusiasm across the road to the mailbox on the other side, I kept a slow pace and viewed her from the rearview mirror. I saw her open the mailbox, reach a hand into its depths, withdraw an empty hand, stand for a fraction of a second, turn and start across the road again.

This time the green clad figure, white hair still blowing slightly in the wind, erect no more, stooped and moving slowly! She seemed more to stumble across the road than to walk. My rearview mirror magnified a picture of disappointment and dejection.

I have no idea who the lady was, on a road I do not often travel, but that green clad lady, on the way to and from the mailbox, came home with me, in my mind.

My imagination tells me she was expecting to hear from somebody important to her, and, with great anticipation, even excitement, the joy of that anticipation showed itself in spirit, body and feet. Then, an empty mailbox. Nothing! Crushed and disappointed, empty-handed and empty-spirited, the walk back across the road reflected the impact of a day without what she needed, or wanted, to make her life bright and good.

Had I known who she was and what her address was, I think I would have bought the most beautiful card I could find, or have written the best letter I could write, and sent it to her.

It seems to me that if folk, in general, understood what a timely note or letter can mean to a person, and sometimes to a particular person for a particular reason, more such notes, letters, or cards would be written. It is such a simple thing to do.

Most of us in our society live such busy lives nowadays, but could there not be developed an alertness to the many people for whom life is restricted or lonely?

Could we start noticing, or start planning to notice, those folk who longingly seek a word of love, or assurance, or encouragement and hope, and see that they get it occasionally from us?

It seems to me that there are times when most of us could deliver, in some form, the kind of word or deed that helps meet the expectations and hopes of searching folk, so that the walk across one's roads is not a stumble, but the joyful step of one who has received good news from somebody who loves and cares.

Lady, with blowing white hair, and dressed in green, I do not know who you are, but you touched my life!

Written by Lloyd E. Batson
Published December 10, 2003

About worms and Christmas

On one of the last pleasantly warm days, I had an itch to "wet a worm," out in the pond back of our house. I rummaged through the back of the refrigerator to see if there was still a box of worms there (I usually keep some fishing worms the year around, properly packaged and enclosed in a Ziploc bag in the refrigerator. Wonder of wonders, my wife tolerates them! She likes the fried fish they sometimes produce!)

While I was in the search, I was recalling an exchange I had had once with the lady at the "bait place" where I was buying worms. I asked her if she ever had Louisiana Pinks. She said she never heard of them. It has been a long time since I have found Louisiana Pinks.

In the event you do not know, Louisiana Pinks are long and tough worms. They stay on a hook better than other worms. They can be broken into smaller, usable pieces if you wish, thus being more economical. They do not deteriorate away from refrigeration as quickly as night crawlers or some other worms do.

I know you needed to know all of that!

After being told that only night crawlers and red worms were available, I was getting a box of night crawlers from the bait refrigerator. The lady came back to tell me I should open the box to check the contents. Said she, "Sometimes people come back here, take the worms out of one box, add them to another, put the dirt back in the emptied container, and come pay for the one they had added the worms to."

"You're kidding, aren't you?" I asked.

"No, it happens often," she answered.

"Sometimes you must wonder who the real worms are," I sadly responded.

It is not fair to worms in general to compare them to the way some folk act! Aside from being great fishing bait, worms have such an important function in ecology! Worms, however, can sometimes cause trouble, and embarrassment. (How many older folk can remember, as I can, having had worms as a child?)

"You worm, you!" is an accusation of contempt, referring, I am assuming, to being "low-down." It is in this sense that sadly we may wonder who the real worms are. As we near the beautiful and exciting time of Christmas, I certainly am aware of much evil in our world, but I will hear again the message of the angels that there is wondrous help available. Announced they, at that first Christmas, "Unto you a Savior is born!" Bad is in the world, yes, but help is available! Good news! That is the essential word of Christmas!

Early in my life, somewhere I read about a sophisticated lady in England that refused to sing Isaac Watts' hymn, "Alas, and Did My Savior Bleed," in which is the line "Would he devote that sacred head for such a worm as I?" Quite testily she declared she was not a worm! By the way, our hymnals now say, "...for sinners such as I."

A truth is that, while some of us act more despicably than others, we all are sinners needing grace, love, understanding, and acceptance. In so many ways we ought to clean up our "worm" actions, but with so much we need help.

At the heart of the Christmas story there is the announcement of where there is the greatest of all help. As the angels declared to the shepherds, "Unto you is born this day ... a Savior which is Christ the Lord!"

What a wondrous time Christmas is! Let us be sure to hear the angels declaring what we need most of all!

Written by Lloyd E. Batson
Published December 17, 2003

What did Santa Claus bring you?

Note from L.E.B.:

With his permission, I am using for my column this Christmas what my older son, Ellis, wrote in the annual book of Advent devotionals prepared by the members of his church, Saint John United Methodist Church, in Prospect, Kentucky.

"I tell you the truth, anyone who will not receive the kingdom of God like a little child will never enter it." Luke 18:17, NIV

"What did Santa Claus bring you?" This was the question that started it all.

My parents had gone all out for the Christmas I was two years old. They figured I was old enough to notice and appreciate what they were particularly proud of purchasing, the educational and fun toys their precious baby boy was getting. Generous at all times, they were especially so this Christmas. But when we went to the church Christmas morning worship service, and I was asked this question, my answer was, "an apple, an orange, a banana, and three pecans."

I had ignored all the toys, noisemakers, and puzzles, all the glitter and bright wrapping, and reported only on what was actually inside my stocking. I seemed perfectly happy with this simple gift.

My answer made my Dad laugh so much that every Christmas since that day every Batson has gotten an apple, an orange, a banana, and three pecans for Christmas. The list of recipients has expanded to include spouses, in-laws, grandchildren, visiting friends, and even pets. Some new to the tradition have rolled their eyes and even thought we were a bit fruity and nutty ourselves.

The real importance of our tradition comes from another family Christmas moment. We have a picture of my little brother in p.j.'s and bathrobe, around age three, sitting in his little red rocker, surrounded by a pile of presents eager to be opened. He is determined to rock and eat his banana until it is gone before he joins the usual Christmas mayhem. I remember trying to get him excited about the presents, but he was perfectly content with his life at that moment.

In Sunday school, we are discussing childlike faith. That childlike faith encompasses so much, including curiosity and fearlessness, but I am thinking now of that attitude of perfect contentment with the goodness of life and the Giver of Life. No worries, no fears, no distractions, no "busyness" that robs us of simple pleasures. Schleiermacher calls it the "feeling of absolute dependence on God." How I wish I could capture that simplicity and contentment all the time, or proclaim with Paul that in any situation I am content. Maybe this Christmas the apple, orange, banana, and three pecans will bring me back to that.

Father, restore in me contentment with your goodness. Amen.

Written by Lloyd E. Batson
Published December 24, 2003

The making of a happy New Year

A household is often a microcosm, a smaller version of the larger world. Relationships and activities within the household are often repeated elsewhere. For example, in a facetious exchange, I said something to my wife about something she had done. Then I observed, "Remember when I did the same thing and you pitched a fit?"

"I don't remember my fits — just yours," was her quick reply.

We are at the end of one year, and the beginning of another. Traditionally, one is supposed to think about what he or she has done the past year and how improvements can be made in the new one with the making of resolutions. Generally, New Year's resolutions are an exercise in futility since they seem so easily and quickly forgotten. I want to suggest here, however, one area of attention that might make the new year one of the best you have ever had.

Time has a way of obscuring a proper perspective. If you have some problem with somebody, or something, if you are carrying an irritating burden, if you feel you have been wronged about something, if you feel strongly about what somebody has done and it has affected your attitude, or if there is some continuing awkwardness in your relationship with somebody, perhaps you have remembered only what others have done and not your part in it. You may have ignored what you have done similarly.

Instead of perpetuating a grievance into the near year, instead of carrying the burden of animosity a bit longer, instead of maintaining awkward relationships through 2004, perhaps you could make things better by honestly reviewing the situation. It might just be that in some way you helped make the situation what it is. Your own attitude and behavior might have played a part in the problem. If this be so, and it probably is, for very few things are totally one-sided, you can do something about it – if you really care. Another trouble with New Year's resolutions is that we may let the identifying of needy areas suffice for the solution. Few of us are ready for the sometimes painful application of the resolutions.

We have no way of knowing many things that will happen in 2004. There will be some things not under our control. But there will be some things that are up to us! Here is a call to take a close, hard look at some of the causes for unhappiness and confusion in our lives. There almost certainly will be some areas that we can alleviate by proper acknowledgement and action on our part.

In a very real sense, a Happy New Year depends upon us!

Happy New Year!

Written by Lloyd E. Batson
Published December 31, 2003

Spoon love

Is it possible for spoons to evoke lasting memories of Christmas? Yes! If they enter the picture as spoons did at our house this year.

For most of our married life, my wife, Joy, and I, in our travels, in this country and abroad, have collected demitasse-sized souvenir spoons with distinctive representations on them of the places and culture of the country and the area we were visiting. Friends often brought them to us, as a gift, spoons from where they had been. As a result, we have a collection of many, many beautiful spoons.

At our retirement over fourteen years ago, we had to remove the spoons, mounted in order, from the walls where we lived. In part because of limited space in our smaller new home, and aided by the plague of "putting off," we never got them on display again. In storage, most of the spoons became nearly black with tarnish.

Our children and grandchildren decided that while visiting with us for Christmas one of the things they would do was to have a spoon polishing night so we could begin to enjoy the hundreds of spoons again. So, one night, gathered at our dining table, all the family took places with individual assignments. Some were to apply and rub the silver polish on a spoon, pass it to another for more polishing, and others to wash and dry. It took several hours to complete the task.

My job? Just to watch and enjoy the whole episode. Laughter and jesting accompanied the constant "oohing and aahing" that various ones, older and younger alike, uttered as the dark tarnish gave way to reveal gleaming beauty. Many questions were asked about the images and words on the spoons. Questions such as "How did you get this one? What does this inscription mean? What is this building? What country does this represent? What did you do on your visit there?" introduced interest not only in getting the spoons polished but also in the story of the spoons.

We, of course, will remember the joy of the entire Christmas visit of our family, but the laughter, the sharing, the pleasures of the spoon polishing night will continue to be very special to us.

Whatever else Christmas means for anybody, family gatherings, enjoying one another, sharing happily, even in an arduous task, and storing up precious memories can go on blessing through times to come when the family is not there.

As my wife and I, alone together for most the year, pass by, and perhaps handle, the now displayed souvenir spoons (arranging and finding ways to attach the holders in the limited space was another lengthy and challenging task taken on by one of our sons), we will enjoy reliving our experiences associated with each one. Past pleasures will be resurrected, about places, events, and people we have enjoyed in past years. In our minds and feelings, we will relive many wonderful experiences.

What, however, will most regularly come back, fresh again, to us? The joy of a very special night, when our family had a "togetherness" in doing something for us! We will recall how precious it is for a family to enjoy one another, to laugh together, to work together, and to love together!

We will appreciate and enjoy, yes, the other wonderful gifts they gave us (and wear a lot of them!). However, as we look fondly at those glistening spoons on the walls, we will be most thankful for the gift of their ongoing love for us, represented in the reflected memories of those glistening spoons!

Blessed is every family that has something akin to "spoon love."

Written by Lloyd E. Batson
Published January 7, 2004

Handmade and Hand-operated

We take so much for granted! Like, for example, a fully functioning "automatic everything" clothes dryer! When something in it malfunctions, we almost take it as a personal insult and an attack on the household!

What a welcome gift was our first clothes dryer, in the winter of 1958. Our first son was newly born. There was no such thing as disposable paper diapers, only the cloth kind that had to be washed over and over … like the obedient husband I was, and am, I was out in the backyard, in a blowing, bitterly cold wind, hanging diapers on a clothesline. Some of the men of the church apparently saw me, felt sorry for me, got together, bought and delivered a brand-new clothes dryer. What a glorious gift! My wife likes to say if it had been she out in the cold hanging diapers we would not have been given the dryer!

Our present dryer, with automatic settings to do many levels of drying, and to cut off at the proper time, has apparently blown a sensor, or something. Now the drying levels of the clothes have to be checked, and tested by hand, until the clothes are properly dried. What an "inconvenience!"

Have you thought recently about all the things in a single day you routinely use which are automated in some form? Perhaps, in an idle moment (and you are supposed to have some of those moments since there are so many automatically programmed things in houses now!) it would be an interesting exercise to look around and to make a list of the automatically functioning things you depend upon. The results will be astounding.

So many things, which affect our lives daily, are automated in some form! I am convinced, however, that there are some important things that cannot be automated and, if they could be, should not be.

For example, where is there a machine that one can punch or program to obtain a set of values in one's life? One's values, upon which he or she builds a life, and from which strength and goodness develop, come from struggle of soul and mind, and are handmade and hand-operated.

Can you purchase or construct the latest models of a faith that automatically gives help in a difficult situation? Faith is handmade and hand-operated, at least as it comes to grip with daily demands.

Is love packaged for purchase (so much in our day seems to be based on the appearance that it is) so that the deepest needs of people can be met by automated "pleasure" machines or programs? Is not love always handmade and hand-operated, resulting from inner resources that do not come in packages?

Has anyone invented a process that will guarantee proper and effective moral behavior in a time of testing? Is not the decision to do the right thing handmade and hand-operated, based on established character and implanted ideals and convictions? Where is there an adequately designed and easily available religion, adequate for this modern world and for eternity, one automatically productive? Only in a personally involved relationship with God is there a salvation daily working in the life of a believer — received hands-on, if you please.

It is a wonderful time to be alive, but there are some things that do not and cannot be made to work automatically!

Written by Lloyd E. Batson
Published January 14, 2004

Blessings that go on

A shock wave swept through our community and area when the word came that a popular young person, widely admired, loved and honored, had been killed in military action in Iraq. War by its nature does not discriminate among those it destroys, but it did not seem to make sense, nor to be right, that so young, respected and outstanding a person, a captain, a commander of a helicopter unit would not come home again, alive, to her beloved family and community.

Our community, in amazing dimensions, expressed its grief, its support of her family, its appreciation for a life well lived, and its recognition of the ultimate gift of her life in doing what she believed she could and should do.

I never had the privilege to know her personally, but Captain Kimberly Hampton apparently was a remarkable individual, one gifted with intelligence, beauty, talent and personality, so genuinely expressed. Through all of her abbreviated life, and without any apparent plan or program to make such happen, she received recognition and respect in whatever activity or relationship she was involved. Expression has come from countless folk that throughout her life she found ways to give blessings to all around her.

A blessing that has come to me, concerning this one I did not personally know, is expressed in a question and its answer. Is such beneficial involvement in the lives of others now to be in the past tense? Not at all, is the answer!

An untimely death, in all its sadness, will not erase what that special lady put into the lives of many, many others. Blessings that come in the gifts of love, encouragement, inspiration, and challenge to others have the capacity to impact the relationships the receivers of those gifts have with other people around them.

This beautiful, talented, vibrant young lady will not again in person have opportunity to do what she apparently did all of her life. Is her life of blessing over? Not at all! All who have been blessed by her will keep on benefiting from those residual blessings. Furthermore, they will be multiplied over and over as those whom she blessed will, in turn, have opportunity to honor her memory by sharing with others the impact of her life on them.

To be sure, the experience of such ongoing blessings will not have Kimberly's personal touch, but the abundantly shared blessings of her life are not over, nor will they be! They will still come to bless others through the ones she so helpfully touched in her life.

In the economy of the Creator God, received blessings can be multiplied as they are passed on to others in the lives of the receivers.

People more gifted than I have spoken and written of this remarkable young person, but a beautiful chapter is yet to unfold in years to come, the chapter being of the results of her shared blessings still going on.

Not many among us will have the remarkable and distinctive capacities Captain Kimberly Hampton had, but every one of us has his or her own blessings to give to others. Those who have received treasured blessings from others have the privilege to pass on those blessings, mixed meaningfully with their own distinctive blessings.

Yes, there are blessings that can go on without end!

May our blessed community become a blessing sharing community!

Written by Lloyd E. Batson
Published January 21, 2004

Fingers on the eyes

Children often do surprising things that delight and instruct me (and they sometimes do surprising things that have the opposite effect!).

Such was the case once when, during a commitment service at Vacation Bible School, I asked all the boys and girls to bow their heads and close their eyes. Predictably, many bowed their heads, but, just like adults, could not, or did not, keep from peeking around to see what was happening. I then reminded the youngsters that I had asked for closed eyes but some of them had their eyes open. I asked them to start all over to see if they could keep their eyes closed.

This time all cooperated, but three different ones quickly put fingers on their eyes to insure that they stayed closed!

Great! I liked that. It does take discipline to keep eyes closed during a time like we were having. I know that. I admire the extra effort the three children made, knowing they could not trust their eyes to stay closed on their own. A childish thing? No, a very mature act!

There are many times in our lives when we should take whatever steps are necessary to make ourselves do right. There are times we need to exercise self-discipline. For example, churchgoers sometimes find it hard to worship because of wandering eyes and wandering minds. Every worshipper, I included, could strengthen the personal regimen it takes to insure giving full attention to the process of praise, prayer, and proclamation.

Many of us are not aware of the little things we do that rob us of some blessings of worship. Looking around, being fascinated with somebody's dress, suit, hairstyle, seat companion or other interesting things, may keep one from full awareness of the flow of worship. Whispering, about some sudden thought or remembrance, is a common interruption of worship. Perpetuating absorption with a burdensome problem one brings with him or her to church may keep that one from an audience with the very One who finally would give some kind of strength for the burden.

The sermon may be perceived as being "dry," "uninteresting" or "irrelevant," and one allows the mind to slip into neutral, thus precluding any good that might show up. Reacting critically to a missed note in the choir or one of the instruments may invalidate the ministry needed from that music.

Playing the old game of surveying the congregation to see what "hypocrites" have come (what hypocrisy this is in itself!) may shut one off from any ministry available. For that matter, are we not all hypocrites if "hypocrite" means being less than we ought to be?

I like what those children did! Knowing that old habits and natural impulses are hard to manage, they took steps to see that they could control them.

I have written here primarily about some things that can interfere with getting the most out of worship, but are not these same factors problems with giving full attention in public forums, school classes, business conference agendas, training classes, meetings of any sort?

Do you suppose that all of us should be as honest, courageous and innovative as those children to help with some habits and frailties? We would probably be the better for it!

Written by Lloyd E. Batson
Published January 28, 2004

A White Rose

I guess it did look a little odd, a man out on the streets of Pickens on a Tuesday morning wearing a "Sunday" suit and with a white rose on his lapel. You can imagine the variety of comments I got! I still chuckle at this memory, though it was years ago.

A member of the church, having picked the rose from her yard, brought it by the office early on a Tuesday, dew still on it. A beautiful thing! I decided to wear it instead of putting it in a bud vase on my desk.

Several times, to the query of why the rose, I replied, "Well, I am ready to do a wedding or a funeral. Which do you need me to do?"

One "out of towner," having heard I had already given notice of my intended retirement after thirty-three years as pastor of the Pickens First Baptist Church (would you believe, I gave a year's notice?), asked, "Are they already pinning roses on you?"

To that I replied, "Yes, and you see what color they chose."

Many folk did speak admiringly of my rose. And so the day went, until the middle of the afternoon when the wilted rose came apart.

When I went home for lunch my wife was busy in the kitchen. Still wearing my rose, I walked around her several times, getting in her way, and generally complicating the last minute preparation for the lunch (one does not gain much from getting in the way like that!).

As I sat down for lunch, still dressed as I had been all morning, I said something about the pretty rose I was wearing. The lady who lives at my house (who, by the way, had fixed one of my favorite meals) said, "Oh, I did not notice you had one."

A rose. That is what is on my mind.

Some people miss out on much beauty and goodness in the earth by not noticing a "rose." How often we allow the busyness of life, the frustrations and annoyances that come along and the myriads of distractions that clamor for attention to shut out awareness of the beautiful and the good things around us.

With the same eyes with which we see a pot about to boil over, we can see a rose. I have not learned enough along the way, I know, but I have learned that usually, no matter what is happening, there is a "rose" somewhere if one would but notice.

Know any annoying people? I think I have learned that even the worst of people have some good things about them. It surely does help when I can see a "rose."

I think many folk enjoyed the rose I wore that day, but the one who enjoyed it the most was I. It really did not matter to me whether other people noticed. My day was better because I could see the rose and smell it.

How important for a person to have something beautiful in his or her life. The personal ministry of something lovely is priceless to the sense of wellbeing and to the integrity of a person. In the midst of a world, often ugly and demeaning, a sense of being touched with something beautiful adds joy and goodness to a day.

If there is a "rose," something beautiful, in a person's life, it is great if other people notice, but whether they do or do not the "rose" does him or her good!

What a dreary world this would be if there were no beauty in it! But there is! So, why not discover something beautiful and precious every day?

"Roses" are renewable, and good every day!

Written by Lloyd E. Batson
Published February 4, 2004

True Love

"Love is in the air!" Is that what is happening as we come again on February 14 to a popular tradition, the celebration of Valentine's Day?

How old does one have to be to feel love strongly? Obviously, love knows no age barriers.

The first compelling, consuming sense of "love" I experienced had disastrous results for me. I was nine years old, in the fourth grade, in Alcolu Elementary School in Clarendon County. We had newly moved, in 1933, to Alcolu, and I had been smitten by love for a pretty, lithe, blond girl in the third grade. My, my, I did like to look at her and find every reason I could to be around her.

There was a major problem, though. A third-grade boy, son of a staff member in the office of the lumber company, was also smitten by her. One day, right after school, behind one of the school buildings, that "other" boy and I had a face-to-face shouting match over our common love. I, a bit larger than the "other" and being a "tough" youngster, thought I had the upper hand until our verbal assault led to a ferocious fight. Wow! Was I surprised, and literally hurt! What I did not know was that the father of that "other" boy had given him boxing lessons! He quickly, with "professional" jabs, bloodied my nose and cut my lip in several places. I was hurt, yes, but my embarrassment at losing to a rival, and a smaller one at that, was more hurtful!

How was I to explain to my parents my "cut up" face when I got home? Fortunately, my father was not at home, and my mother had some guests. To the expressed shock of my mother, as I went through the front room, I "explained," while quickly moving on, that we were playing "pop the whip" and I was at the end of the line and got slung against a tree. If you are not old enough to know how physical that "pop the whip" game could be, I will explain it to you if you wish! By the time my mother's guests had gone I had washed carefully, patched myself up, and mother, knowing how rough sometimes the games were her sons played, never asked for any details.

It was just ten years later, at an army base in Texas, that I met my lasting "Valentine." I have now been married to her for fifty-three years.

Celebrating "love" on Valentine's Day not only is a national tradition, but it can be a personally rewarding experience. How fortunate are the persons who have found "true love" and can rejoice in it!

I may not do anything spectacularly "romantic" this year, like hunt for the prettiest and most expensive card, box of chocolates, flowers, restaurant meal, trip, or anything tangible, but I do hope that I can find some genuine and personal way to let my "Valentine" know I truly love and appreciate her.

Anybody ready to join me in doing the same for your "Valentine?"

Let me suggest one potentially rewarding "Valentine" experience. It is the reading of, and fresh commitment to, the most definitive description of "true love" ever written.

"Love is patient, love is kind. It does not envy, it does not boast, it is not proud. It is not rude, it is not self-seeking, it is not easily angered, it keeps no record of wrongs. Love does not delight in evil but rejoices with the truth. It always protects, always trusts, always hopes, always perseveres. Love never fails." 1 Corinthians 13:4-8a.

Written by Lloyd E. Batson
Published February 11, 2004

A White Handkerchief

A white handkerchief still blesses me.

The church was packed. Folk, crowded tightly together, had come from many places to honor the widely appreciated and loved man now dead, taken in midlife after an unbelievably long and difficult struggle with a devastating illness.

The family, including his wife surrounded by twelve children, sat close together in the center section. One of the children, about 12 years of age, sitting on the end of the pew, began to weep profusely. A tall, lanky man rose from his seat across the aisle, walked over and gently and lovingly handed the grieving daughter a fresh white handkerchief and returned to his seat.

I, from my seat on the rostrum as one who was helping conduct the memorial service, suddenly needing a handkerchief of my own, bowed my head and thanked God for what I had seen.

Thank God for people who know when we hurt, for people who care when our world comes apart. Thank God for the gentle understanding of people who, without a word, know when to touch our lives with gentleness and understanding.

It then occurred to me what was happening. The crowd of folk, come to honor the dead, was grieving, too. And it was precious! It seemed to me that the entire congregation, hurting themselves, was handing to the stricken family a handkerchief of love, one they needed themselves. They could share it as a gift of their own sorrow to the sorrow of the family that had so much loved the husband, the father, the son, the brother, now gone.

A white handkerchief handed to a weeping child. My worry, about whether I was going to say the right thing when, in the service, my time came to speak, was now gone. I knew I did not have to say something that could miraculously ease the heartache. It was already done. The entire congregation, represented by that white handkerchief, had reached out in grief and love to touch the family, and they, the family, knew it.

The family, people of faith, all of them, knew already the presence of the Great Shepherd of the sheep had already sensed the strength in the supporting arms of the Father. In uncluttered simplicity of faith, they already were receiving the ministry of the Comforter. Still, human, so very human as they were in their grief, they seemed to need something else. And the need was met. Friends, neighbors, co-workers, business associates, church people, all were hurting with them. How complete now was ministry in time of great need.

It seems so simple, does it not, the passing of a handkerchief to a weeping youngster, and a gentle touch of a loving hand? But, let me tell you, both as one who has watched it unfold and as one who has needed it himself, there is great beauty and strength in the midst of the most difficult of times from the ministry of shared grief on the part of sensitive folk who care and who touch.

Sometimes you may worry about how you are going to help people who grieve. Do not worry about it. Just make sure you care and you notice. Then, reach out with your white handkerchief, in its variety of forms, and touch the hurting folk with a part of you. God came to that family, and he came, in part, as he often does, through people who care and who love.

And it was good.

Written by Lloyd E. Batson
Published February 18, 2004

About collards and people

Just recently, my lady and I were enjoying a great meal of diverse tastes at our house – collards, rutabagas and turnips, the second meal of leftovers from a cooking several days before. Added to those "old timey" delicacies was a fresh baking of her delicious cornbread muffins. A wonderful lunch!

In the midst of our pleasant feasting, the question was raised as to what family of vegetables each of those we were eating belonged. Our set of ancient encyclopedias (a set we got for our boys to use in their early school years) is close to our dining table. While continuing to eat, we looked up each of the vegetables.

Would you believe that collards, rutabagas and turnips all belong to the same grouping, the mustard family?

While I continued to eat and enjoy the members of the mustard family, with the differing expressions of tastes thereof, I got to rambling around in my memory, recalling some of the diverse experiences of another family that I have enjoyed and benefited from — the human family.

Right here in Pickens County we have a growing diversity of people, coming from many backgrounds and countries. There are people with a great variety of cultural backgrounds, talents, achievements, motivating goals and desires to identify with attitudes and personalities of others. They have come to live among the "old timers" already here. They and we, often differing in many ways, are from the same family – the human family. They have come, and they add greatly to the resources of our community.

Some people, as do my wife and I, like collards. Some do not. Some relish rutabagas. Some have poor opinions of such and reject any opportunity to eat them, or even taste them. Whether or not one likes collards, rutabagas and turnips, they are food and can, and do, contribute to the food supply. Some people eat snails and like them. I do not. Am I qualified then to deny that snails have a place in the food chain!

How diverse the members of the human family are! I think it is exciting to be a part of a community with great diversity among its members. It is not possible, or even desirable, for everybody to be like everybody else. Our "human" problem is to recognize the value of people around us and to find ways to relate constructively to them and, in turn, to receive the contributions they can make to the welfare of the whole.

It is an obvious fact that our community called Pickens County is increasing in the diversity of the people making it up. The "table fare" is not the same for everybody. Our community can be the better as we learn that we are in the same "family" and as we do our best to learn how to relate to, and give to, one another.

We can be the better as we learn how to receive from one another what each constructively has to give the other.

The "human family!" I am glad I am a member.

Written by Lloyd E. Batson
Published February 25, 2004

A choreography of kindness

We hear so much about road rage and bad driving manners all around us that I want to tell you what I saw, and enjoyed, a few days ago, right here in our town!

I saw an amazing performance of what seemed to me to be choreographed kindness. Beginning south of the Wal-mart and continuing, as I moved north with the traffic, almost to Main Street, I think I saw more cars trying to move into the heavy traffic of S.C. Highway 135 (Pendleton Street) from so many side places than I had ever seen.

What I saw over and over, as I moved along, was car after car, though having the right of way, pausing briefly to let other cars, blocked in at various points, out into the flow. Nobody blew a horn, yelled, or appeared upset. Remarkably, it seemed, traffic moved along pretty well, and I think I never saw so many smiles, head nods and waves offered to others. While I was stopped at the traffic light near the railroad tracks, I said out loud, "Wow! I have just seen something beautiful!"

What it seemed to me was that some master design beyond the ingenuity of highway engineers was at work, something called human kindness. Not only did bothersome traffic problems work out well, but also everybody seemed to be enjoying the unplanned but effective attention to others.

Was I watching an unrepeatable choreography of human kindness, or was I watching unfold a solution to many of our problems, problems on nearly every level of relationships with one another?

Nearly everybody recognizes the folly and stupidity of the growing problems of "road rage" when it comes to other people. But what about us? Did I see, at least for one time, that just the simple practices of thoughtfulness toward others could alleviate not only traffic problems but probably would help with most of our unpleasant experiences with others.

There is no governmental or legal action that can require kindness and thoughtfulness on the part of the populace. Kindness comes from one's character and sense of values. Civility is a great word, and a valuable characteristic, but I think the word called kindness, available to everybody if one will act on it, would result in a safer and more pleasant driving experience.

"I have my rights" is a cry we hear a lot. Yes, each person rightly has many "rights" but does it sound like "double talk" to say that there are times when we could forego the right to our rights? Such could be called kindness or thoughtfulness to others, even in traffic situations.

Our community has so much that is admirable and helpful to the welfare of all. Rather than it being a once in awhile thing, like what I saw and experienced the other day, is it too much to hope for, and to come to pass, that our entire community, in traffic matters, and in other ways, could become a choreography of kindness?

For that matter, why could not our area adopt a motto for itself, and act upon it, the motto being "Easley, a Choreography of Kindness?"

If it is to happen, I guess I had better start practicing my part of it!

Written by Lloyd E. Batson
Published March 3, 2004

Memories, how they linger!

Memories! They abound, good and bad.

I have sometimes been asked, "What is the earliest memory you have?" While I have a flood of early memories, it is difficult to say which is the earliest. However, I can easily identify the three earliest datable ones I have.

One involves having been in a big, hot, crowded room where Uncle John Loftis was nearing death. I was there, against a wall, awed by all the things taking place, and I heard Uncle John say his last words. Years ago, I found, with delight, Uncle John's tombstone in the cemetery at Mountain Creek Baptist Church giving his death date. I was four years old when I witnessed his remarkable home going.

Another of the treasured datable memories is of being with my father, riding in an old Chevrolet, nearing Sumter, seeing him take out his pocket watch and hearing him say, "Right now we are getting a new president, Herbert Hoover." I was still four and I am sure I did not then understand much about presidential elections (and still do not!).

I can also recall being down the road from Graham Baptist Church, playing on the ditch bank, when a neighbor came looking for me to tell me I had a new baby brother and his name was Francis Marion. By his birth date, I know I was almost four.

I am not sure how important it is to have datable early memories, but I do know that people all their lives benefit from pleasant memories of their early years. They also sometimes suffer from bad ones. When people having psychological and emotional problems seek professional help, attending psychiatrists and psychologists often try to unearth some unpleasant experiences in earlier years that may be an underlying contribution to the present disorder.

It is not just to avoid later problems that people need happy experiences to remember. Pleasant memories come again and again to be joy, inspiration, and encouragement to folk as long as they live and have mental capacity to recall.

Parents do many things for and with their children. Whether they at a given time are aware of it, they are providing a large reservoir of experiences, reactions, and impressions that remain as constructive or destructive forces in their children's lives all their days. So does a neighbor, a friend, a community, a club, a school, and a church. In my thinking, it would be great for all these just named, and folk, individually, to stay aware that they all are in the memory making business for children.

Let me use one, a church, as an example. A church has a divine mission to perform, but it also is in the memory making business for young folk. A church does this, in part by making such an environment of love, friendship and joy in faith that children all their lives will remember pleasantly having been a part of it.

I think that a church that makes worship a beautiful and rewarding time, its teaching and training times interesting and pertinent, its witness a compelling and natural activity, and its "away from the church" ministry to others a meaningful outgrowth of what is done inside the church will create treasured memories for children. They likely will be remembered pleasantly all their lives wherever they go, and will be the better for it!

In my use of the church as an illustration of memory making for children, I believe the church that loves one another, respects one another, enjoys one another, and speaks well of one another will create for children memories that will affirm over and over that there is strength and goodness to be found in a church family. They had seen and experienced that in their early years!

We are all in the early memory making business!

Good ones are the best ones to make!

Written by Lloyd E. Batson
Published March 10, 2004

On listening to what you say

To the longtime elderly lady, one with impeccable tastes, dress and bearing, I said, "My, you look spry today!"

That gentle lady, not so gentle anymore, exclaimed more than asked, "Why is it you only use that term 'spry' when you are talking to old ladies?"

Well, why do we? Have you ever noticed that people in general tend to have "set" patterns they use for differing ages?

Such often is apparent in talking with older people. Is not it easy, for example, to associate advancing age with hardness of hearing and, automatically, to shift to louder voice levels? Many older folk retain keen hearing and some who do not may be wearing good hearing aids. No person likes to be patronized.

It can get quite comical at times in a home where elderly people with hearing problems live, but choose not to get hearing aids, or may turn the aids off to save batteries, or just plain do not want to bother with them, or are just not willing to admit to a problem with hearing.

Of course, a little deafness can come in handy when one hears the same thing all the time from another!

At the opposite end of the age spectrum are the very young who, if their vocabulary was advanced enough, would feel at times like protesting, "Why do you talk to us like that and say the same things we have heard over and over?"

Some people seem to have adopted a very limited vocabulary to express greetings. Why do we answer the phone always the same way or say quickly to persons we meet some standard remark? Many folk know today what certain people will say first if they see them tomorrow, and, if they are honest, what they themselves will likely say first to them.

It can be difficult to respond nicely to the same old thing one hears often. I always had trouble responding properly when I was away somewhere and people I knew, or even strangers who knew I was from Pickens, would greet me with, "Well, how are the pickings in Pickens?" There nearly always was an accompanying chuckle as if that greeting was an original creation. I had heard it only about a thousand times!

A vocabulary can be a rich resource of communication. Why should anyone, with all the words and expressions that exist, or can be created, be limited to the "same old thing?" A vocabulary is, of course, at its best when it communicates ideas and feelings, but one's vocabulary is usually larger than that part of it which is regularly used. It might be a shocking procedure, but why could not folk intentionally listen to themselves occasionally as to what "rut" they may be in with their choice of words and ways to greet, respond to or converse with others or express opinions? Recognizing an established "rut" might stimulate a variety of pleasurable ways to communicate!

As a minister, I have sometimes challenged a class or congregation to do something rewarding the next time they pray to God. The challenge? Consciously and deliberately to try the next time they pray to use words they do not recall ever using in a prayer, new words or phrases to express their feelings to God. It is not that God needs to hear new words, but that the one praying, in his or her search of new vehicles (which words are) to express their feeling and faith, can come to grips freshly with what their feelings really are. It helps keep one from going into a set pattern, which one can perform without much thinking and feeling.

Intentionally searching for new ways of expression may enrich the experience of praying and sharpens the identity of feelings about God and one's self. And even the loving God might enjoy hearing something different from us!

I guess what I am trying to express is that everybody can easily add pleasure and meaning to what he or she says to others with a little extra thought and an attempt to be creative.

The speaker and the listener will enjoy the process!

Written by Lloyd E. Batson
Published March 17, 2004

Why do woodpeckers peck?

For several days at my house we have been listening to the pecking of a distant woodpecker, enjoying afresh the interesting distinctiveness of one of God's wonderful creatures.

Going back to my childhood, to the word games we sometimes played with one another, I asked my wife at one point, "Why do woodpeckers peck?" She was not particularly excited about such a query!

Well, but why do they peck like they do?

As long as I can remember, I have been fascinated with words. Among the special words of interest to me since I began to notice "big words" are the ones that end with "logy," that interest coming long before I studied Greek. The "logy" comes from the Greek word logos, which means "word." By the way, God's greatest revelation of himself, his Son, is in the Bible called "logos," the Word.

So, when it comes to woodpeckers, if I wanted to know more than I now do, I could have consulted a specialist in ornithology, ornithology meaning the study of birds.

Why do woodpeckers peck? For at least three basic reasons. They peck in search of insects in trees, using the strong, chisel-like bill provided for them by their creator. They can go up, down, and around a tree pecking while using toes designed for the task, two toes pointed forward and two pointed backward. Woodpeckers, while clinging to a tree with their toes, support their activity with stiff tail feathers. With their long tongues, coated with sticky saliva and having a barbed tip, they can extract the insects they find.

Using their "pecking equipment" to create rapid drumming sounds on dead limbs or a hard surface, woodpeckers make their mating call.

Woodpeckers also peck to make holes in trees to make a nest to lay their eggs on the fine chips they leave from the pecking.

The early pecking of our unseen woodpecker has served as a reminder about many other delightful and regular "surprises" of spring, to be enjoyed if they are noticed. I have vowed to look with big eyes this year at all the great gifts of nature already in abundance right here in our area, gifts to be noticed and enjoyed.

Bradford pear trees, absolutely gorgeous, and in proliferation in yards and along streets.

Yellow jonquils coming up from forgotten places. Squirrels playing hide and seek in the trees and bushes. Green arms of new grass edging into the brown of the old. Camellias sitting among waxy green leaves. Amorous activities of ducks on the ponds. People, as well as birds and animals, enjoying digging in the earth. Piles of clippings along the roads waiting to be picked up, clippings from overgrown shrubbery. The momentarily embarrassed clipped shrubbery offering promise of new and shining growth. Buds in varying shades of red, beginning to show on trees, with their promise of green foliage.

Flowering yellow bushes brightening the present bleakness around them. The movement of fish along the edges of ponds, possibly scouting out bedding areas. Rose bushes with tender new growth, promising glorious beauty of full-grown blooms. New green leaves beginning to interrupt the bleakness of naked trees in the woods.

The litany goes on!

Why do woodpeckers peck? In part, I think, to get us to notice the wondrous things to be seen and experienced as spring comes on!

Stop, look and listen for a moment! You might hear a woodpecker pecking!

Written by Lloyd E. Batson
Published March 24, 2004

April's Ides of March

The Ides of March now comes on the 15th of April!

For many years in our nation, March 15 was the deadline for filing taxes. In the old Roman calendar, March was one of the four months that the middle (ides) of the month came on the 15th. On March 15, 44 BC, Julius Caesar, recognized as one of the greatest persons in history, was assassinated. Hence, the Ides of March came to be associated with tragedy!

Tax time! For many folk tax time has the overtones of tragedy!

In a local eating-place where my wife and I often go, the waitress will place our order as soon as she sees us enter the door (what we order is always the same). Included for me is a bottle of RC Cola (My wife has yet to discover the pure delight of a RC Cola!).

I vividly recall the first RC Cola I ever drank. I was twelve years old, in the middle 1930s, delivering all over the small lumber mill village where I lived the afternoon paper called The Columbia Record. On that miserably hot afternoon I came at the "outskirts" of Alcolu to Mr. L. M. Jones's small store. On the outside was a new sign advertising a great new drink called RC Cola, RC for Royal Crown. In big letters, the cost advertised was five cents. I had one nickel in my pocket. I went first to the icebox where drinks were kept in a covered tub of a sort with chunks of ice to cool them. I took out an RC Cola, opened it, quickly drank about a third of that heavenly cold delight, went over to Mr. Jones and gave him my nickel.

That kindly old man, in his slow drawl, asked me for another penny, saying the drink was six cents. I had the audacity to protest, saying that the sign outside said the price was five cents and that was all I had, and besides I had already drunk a lot of it. He attempted to explain to me, at length, something about an excise tax of a penny on that drink. "But the sign says five cents," I continued to protest. I knew nothing about such a tax.

Finally, Mr. Jones kindly told me he would let me have it for my nickel. Somehow the rest of the RC Cola was not as good as the first part.

My problem then was not much different from what tax time is now. That young paperboy had no meaningful concept of the necessity of taxes and no capacity to appreciate them.

When I took a penny to Mr. Jones the next day, he protested but I insisted on his taking it. My difference in attitude? Through his kindly effort to explain to me about the necessary role taxation plays in a society like ours, I had an understanding, however limited, of why a five-cent RC Cola cost six cents. I even felt somehow that my penny was important.

I do my share of grumbling, like most people, about the increasing and confusing tax load on our populace, but, surprisingly, the shadow of Mr. Jones still hangs around to help me.

He helped me understand, a little bit anyway, why taxes are necessary to the welfare of us all. I often feel frustrated, I confess, at what appears to be so much waste as to how my tax money is spent, but when I try to understand the "why" of taxation, and my role in it, I feel a little better.

The Ides of March as tax time, now in April, still is a tough time! Where are the "Mr. Joneses" who can help us?

Written by Lloyd E. Batson
Published March 31, 2004

Easter, Resurrection Sunday!

Few events have drawn more attention and reaction of many kinds than the production and the showing of the movie, "The Passion of the Christ." In indescribably graphic form, the suffering of Jesus during the last hours of his life is portrayed.

This year, during the Easter activities, perhaps more than ever in history when the Biblical story relating to Jesus' death is read, taught, and presented in music, drama and sermon there will be accompanying strong mental images and emotional feelings stimulated from reaction to the movie.

When I am asked what was the scene in "The Passion of the Christ" that most impressed me, I can quickly answer. It came right at the end, lasting about a minute. With limited transition from the awfulness of the cross portrayal, there is seen the stone blocking the entrance to a tomb rolling away, leaving a view to the inside. The white grave clothes, having been used to wrap the body of the entombed, are in place. Then, slowly, the grave clothes begin to settle until they are flat! That is the striking image I will continue to carry.

Evil and death did not win. The beaten and crucified Christ was alive.
Dark Friday has its picture of the horrible death of the Christ. Resurrection Sunday has its picture of the glorious victory over death.

Whatever other practices, and they are numerous, many of them enjoyable and exciting, that have come to be associated with what is commonly known as Easter, the basic celebration is about Resurrection, the resurrection of Christ from the dead. It is about the victory that the Christ who died offers to all who will believe and receive his act of love.

The first long verse from the Bible that I memorized as a youngster is the same verse that many people first learned. It is a verse that summarizes the story of the Bible. It is what many will celebrate this Friday and Sunday. It is the verse often simply called John 3:16. It reads, "For God so loved the world, that he gave his only begotten Son, that whosoever believes in him should not perish, but have everlasting life."

One of the original disciples, with whom many can easily identify, one who apparently had great difficulty with what was happening at the time of the crucifixion, later wrote exultantly in one of his letters, 1 Peter 1:3, "Praise be to the God and Father of our Lord Jesus Christ. In his great mercy he has given us new birth into a living hope through the resurrection of Jesus Christ from the dead ..."

I think this coming Sunday, instead of being called Easter Sunday, should be called Resurrection Sunday.

Happy Resurrection Celebration!

Written by Lloyd E. Batson
Published April 7, 2004

Miracles go on

There is a young man that I have never seen but one to whom I feel very close because my family in Kentucky, where he lives, regularly gives me updates.

Zack, a 16-year-old high school sophomore, one greatly focused on school, family, church activities, his beloved golf and basketball, training for his first Mini Marathon with his dad, preparing for his spring and summer lawn care business, and looking forward to getting his driver's license, now understands that, given the medical history of the rare thing that has happened to him, he may never walk again!

This vibrant, loved, and appreciated young man has suffered a rare spinal cord stroke. After further exhaustive treatment and therapy, he possibly faces a life in a wheelchair.

A tragedy, yes! It is difficult to imagine how devastating this is to him, his family and friends. In the midst of this heartbreaking experience something beautiful is going on! There has been a wonderful outpouring of love and help.

Zack and his family have been surrounded with prayer and physical assistance. Labor has been given for the huge project of creating a handicapped-accessible environment at home. Caring people have set up a fund to help with the enormous and ongoing costs of medicine, medical supplies, and physical equipment.

Zack, remarkably alert to what lies ahead and retaining and sharing a great faith, no matter what is yet to come in his life, is already part of a miracle in progress. It is the beautiful and precious "miracle" of caring people who quickly and unselfishly respond to the hurt and need in the lives of others, often when the needy people are not personally known to them.

I know about the miracles of the Bible, and I have seen many apparent "miraculous" healings in my lifetime of involvement with people, but I am also grateful for another kind of miracle, one reflected in what is happening to Zack and his family, a miracle I see often right around us in our area. It is the "miracle" of folk, often in surprising numbers, who quickly and unselfishly respond to hurt and need in the lives of others. It is the "miracle" of people who, having no obligation so to do, give of themselves and their resources to assist others in critical times.

As a person who strongly believes in the miracle-working power of God, and regularly thanks him for such love and grace, I also am continually grateful for the "miracle" powers of a citizenry who respond to the needs of others.

Yes, "miracles" do go on all around us!

Thanks be to God for his continuing miracles! And thanks be to the people who, whether or not they identify them as such, do "miracles" in helping others!

Written by Lloyd E. Batson
Published April 14, 2004

A stone step to a stoop

It is very heavy but not huge, only about twenty-four inches long, fourteen inches wide and about five inches deep. For many years in the 1800s and early 1900s, it served as a step to the stoop at the back of the farmhouse in Dallas County, Missouri.

Now that flat stone is a resident of Easley!

Geologists can give exciting information about stone and rock formations in their variety of kinds. However, the story of the stone at the back of our house is, for me, about people and events, not stones and rocks.

My wife's father, Dr. C. R. Barrick, was born in the farmhouse in 1894. Eight of his brothers and sisters were also born there. His father had been born there. The stone shows the wear of many feet stepping on it and the scraping of many boots and shoes to remove mud and dirt before entering the house.

The Barricks who lived in that house were hardworking people, farmers and honorable citizens of their rural community. Life was not easy for them! So, in 1899, land having been opened for settlement in Oklahoma, the Barrick parents loaded their nine children and their possessions in a covered wagon and joined others in other wagons headed for Oklahoma to find and claim new land and a new home. Included was their pastor named Dub Fortner.

My father-in-law, whom I admired and respected greatly, was five years old when he made that long and difficult journey. It took them thirty days to do so. Tales of that trip and of early days in Oklahoma, told from his uncanny memory (about everything that ever happened to him!), often regaled my sons and me. Dr. Barrick enjoyed describing the early days in Oklahoma as being where "the wind pumped the water and the cows chopped the wood."

Many years later after that covered wagon journey to a new land and home (a sod house was his first home in Oklahoma), Dr. Barrick went back to the old home place in Missouri and brought back the stone step from the place he, and his family before him, was born.

Occasionally I go out back of our house and run my hand across the stone, trying to identify with those stalwart and good people of long ago whose footsteps wore a path across the stone.

As long as we have that stone step there will be physical connection to parts of the family I never knew. Are such stones, or whatever are similar possessions, important? Yes! Nobody comes out of nowhere. Whether it is ever dealt with or not, there is a deep need in most people to identify with, and to understand, "roots." Both consciously and unconsciously, we are influenced by our heritage. The better we understand people and their lives and times in the past the better we can understand, appreciate, and develop our own role and journey in life.

It is my feeling that it would be greatly rewarding for people to search for and to identify certain reminders of those that have gone before them, and to keep, if possible, some physical possession, some treasured and representative symbol of those from whom they have come.

Few people are likely to have a worn stone step to the back stoop of a house from the 1800's, but most people could, if they wish, find something that would cause them to feel connected with those of the past. Such a connection could regularly add pride of heritage and an encouragement for themselves to leave something of value by which those in time yet to be will be influenced.

Stone steps to a stoop come in many versions. Do you have one?

Written by Lloyd E. Batson
Published April 21, 2004

Watching a wonder

We are enjoying expecting again at our house!

We are so anxious for the birth process to be completed that time seems to be dragging as we watch the developing process. The mother-to-be has vociferously kept me at a distance, but I have found several viewing places from which she seems unaware of me.

Out behind our house, there is a small lake. On the dam, in an open place in full view, a Canada goose has set up a maternity ward. Day and night she sits on her eggs, occasionally shifting positions. Only infrequently does she get up, swim a few minutes in the lake and eat a little grass. Back to her birthing place she then goes.

I have no knowledge of the incubation period for Canada geese but I think she surely must have used up most of it. I can hardly wait. I confess I am not overly fond of Canada geese in general. What magnificent birds they are, but they do not clean up after themselves in the yard! However, the offspring of this particular goose will be welcome at our house. I have enjoyed watching the process too much to dismiss them from my life. There are two favorite viewing places, one from the window by our dining table and the other out in the yard behind the most colorful display of azaleas we have ever had, red, white, pink, and lavender.

From the viewpoint of loveliness I can watch another thing of beauty, new life in the process and ultimately the bursting into birth. What a vision of glory the Creator has provided for us to enjoy, if but we notice.

One morning I saw something that I called my wife to come to watch with me. From somewhere on the other side of the dam from the sitting Canada goose, there came a mallard duck followed by a string of newly hatched ducklings. The mother duck led her flock proudly right along side the sitting goose and into the water in front of her. The ducklings likely were taking their maiden voyage. The mallard then kept her children swimming back and forth in front of the soon-to-be mother Canada goose. In my mind she was showing off her children as if she were saying, "My children are grander and prettier than yours are going to be!"

I applaud the commitment and stamina of that Canada goose. She is giving total attention to the demanding but always miraculous process of birth. I have no way of knowing whether a goose has emotion and feeling, akin to humans. I do know, however, I have appreciated afresh the constant role of rebirth in nature and things of nature.

Often as I have gazed from the window or through some opening in the gorgeous azaleas, sometimes seeing only the long black neck of the goose sticking up, evidence that she was still faithful to the doing of what she needs to do, I have done what I needed to do. I breathed a prayer of thanks to the Creator Father and a prayer that somehow his chief creation, humans, would discover a fresh commitment and fidelity to carrying out all the fundamental responsibilities we have been given.

I do not know when you are going to get here, but welcome, new family, to our neighborhood!

Written by Lloyd E. Batson
Published April 28, 2004

Why are we here?

The 89-year-old man walked with dignity and grace to the podium of McAlister Auditorium at Furman University two weeks ago to address the students, professors, Furman staff and trustees, invited dignitaries and many guests to begin his address for the Founders Week Convocation.

Before he uttered a word, the audience seemed in awe of what he would say. The speaker, a 1935 graduate of Furman University, expressed his appreciation for the privilege of being there, told something of his early life in Greenville where he was born, and spoke fondly of the gifted professors he had had at Furman, a school that has profoundly influenced him. He then announced his subject and proceeded, with the audience glued to every word, to deal with the posed question, "Why Are We Here?"

Who was this man? A minister? A philosopher? An ethicist? He was Dr. Charles Townes, internationally acclaimed physicist, winner in 1964 of the Nobel Prize for Physics. He was the renowned inventor of the process that led to the development of the laser that has impacted in some way the welfare, activity and well-being of nearly everybody on the face of the earth. It is impossible to enumerate the contributions of this brilliant man. Who he is and what he is stands out among the "greats" in the many fields of science.

I was among the awed beneficiaries of his presence and words, having the privilege of hearing him speak twice and attending the luncheon in his honor. I have no capacity to understand the vast knowledge of this humble and fascinating man but there are some things about Dr. Charles Townes that I can receive, benefit from, and be challenged by.

Dr. Townes is a man of faith, a student of Scripture, and practitioner of prayer. I do not need, nor would I dare try so to do, to explain how he understands these areas of his life. I am sure that his brilliant mind explores these areas in ways I could never do.

As I listened to this great man, as measured by many of the highest norms of greatness in the intellectual and scientific world, raise the question, and deal eloquently with it, "Why Are We Here?", I found myself moving from Dr. Charles Townes to a look at myself. Frankly, I am still dealing with his query, "Why Are We Here?"

I have a feeling that, just as Dr. Townes is still involved in dealing with the challenge of the mysteries of this universe and the unlimited discoveries still to be made, my own journey in dealing with "Why Are We Here?" can lead me to some rewarding and challenging understandings of who I am and what I am.

I would not dare claim that Dr. Townes' brilliance and achievements have resulted from his faith, study of Scriptures and prayer, but they have obviously been basic to who and what he is. I know also that these can be basic strengths for me.

Dr. Townes, when the statue of you that is to be erected in downtown Greenville is there, I will pass by it and thank you again for the challenging "Why Are We Here?"

Will some others of our area pass by with me?

Written by Lloyd E. Batson
Published May 5, 2004

Sounds in the dark

Who or what is in charge of quick flashes of memory, still in vivid detail after a long time? I know what triggered this one, and sent me in search of notes I had written at the time. It was a little child, in the hallway of the church, bursting into tears thinking she was separated from her mother.

It was eerie, that night years ago, the pitiful sound coming in waves through the bushes. Highs and lows of anguish! The moon, one day past full, rode low in the sky directly behind the moving sound, adding a ghoulish touch to the wailing.

It had not long been dark. In the last light, I had photographed a group of five deer passing within 10 steps of our campsite. We had seen no sign of the warning against bears, supposedly in the area. Anyway, I knew the anguished wailing was not from an animal, not any I had ever heard.

As the sound got to the first clearing, I saw what I had already decided it was. The frightened crying of a lost child! As carefully and gently as I could, I approached the little girl, whose name was Wendy, I later learned. I did not want to add to her fear.

It took some time for her frightened heavings to subside so she could speak. She, the little redhead, 8 years old, had come with her parents to the campground just at dark. While they set up their tent, she began to explore the camp area. Loft Mountain Campground, one mile off the Skyline Drive in the Shenandoah National Park, at an elevation of 3550 feet, is a sprawling area of trees, bushes, and open spaces, crisscrossed with trails and scattered campsites. The exploring youngster had quickly became confused and disoriented in the strange place. Within minutes she was lost, terrifyingly so.

I tried to let her know she was now in good hands and that shortly we would find her parents. It took a little searching, but we found them, they themselves now frightened. Anybody know a more joyful sight than that of a lost child and anxious parents being reunited? I do not.

What a warm feeling I carried for a long time, that I had had a part in the happy moment of reunion of that small redheaded youngster and her parents!

Dramatic moments like the one I have relived in its telling do not occur often. Yet, all around us are people of all ages, who are hurting from "lostness" and "separation" of some kind.

I talked just recently with a person who felt frustrated because he felt that he had no form of usefulness to others. Know what I suggested to him? I told him I knew about a greatly important ministry that he was well-qualified to do and one that would help many folk if he undertook it. Eagerly he asked what it was.

I said, simply, "It is a ministry of noticing." To his inquiry about what I meant, I spoke of the loneliness that many people experience. For example, newcomers to an area are separated from former friends, homes, lifestyles, churches, jobs, and other relationships. "If you are alert," I told him, "you just might have an encouraging word, a smile, an act of kindness, or an offer of assistance."

Furthermore, I told him, "You probably have friends and acquaintances that are going through a tough time. You do not have to be intrusive, nosey, or even curious. Just be friendly. Respect their feelings and do not intrude, but just be nice!"

Yes, "lostness" and "separation" are commonly experienced all around us. If we just notice, we perhaps can have a part in brightening somebody's life.

Written by Lloyd E. Batson
Published May 12, 2004

A birth announcement

We are happy at our house. We now are grandparents, with quadruplets!

For weeks we have spent time near the maternity ward out on the dam of our pond, eagerly waiting for birth to occur. Earlier this morning (the day this is written) new life appeared. The sitting goose is no longer sitting, but has set about the vigilant and demanding care of nurturing her offspring, four of them.

I went out, early, to check on the sitting Canada goose on the dam, and came hurriedly back to report to my lady that the goose was gone and only one fractured egg was left in the nest, with broken shells scattered around. I looked all over the area and could find no sign of the goose. Sadly, I reported that apparently some catastrophe had happened. The anticipated new family would not be coming!

After my sad report to my wife, I went back to search for the goose again. Nothing! Then up the pond, on the other side, and in the grass at the edge there, I saw movement and some flashes of yellow. Out of a shadow I saw appear the large and erect Canada goose with an extended chest, the one I had identified as the sitting goose's mate. Out of nowhere then came the strutting mother! When I made my way up the side, instead of the strong honking protests I had sometimes heard when I approached the sitting goose, I heard what sounded like soft and welcoming gentle honks from both the male and female geese. I think they were proudly telling me to "come and see your new grandchildren!"

Four, mostly yellow, brand-new goslings came out of the grass toward me. With a strange and warming sensation, I felt they recognized me and came to let me see them. The two adult geese came closer to me than they ever had. If Canada geese can smile, they were doing so to me. Back to the house I hurried to report to my own mate what I had seen, stopping only to tell the neighbor across the pond, who was working in her yard, what had happened. She, too, had been watching the sitting goose and now became excited. I went also next door to us to give those folk the news about the new family in our neighborhood. A visiting mother, there from Texas, had also been watching the long vigil of the sitting goose. Do you think a Texan can take back with her a bit of South Carolina euphoria relating to a sitting goose now a strutting mother?

Whether it is a normal thing for Canada geese so to do, I know not, but, later in the day, I saw the mother and father do a very human thing. They took the four goslings back to the now vacant nest on the dam. The four babies got in the nest and briefly huddled together. Do geese, like humans, have a need for a sense of identity with where they were born?

A natural response to new babies, human and in nature's world, is "Aren't they cute?" And they are! All babies will finally grow up, however, if they survive the rigors of birth and childhood. They will not always be in a "Aren't they cute?" stage.

There are certain "nuisance" stages in the growth process that call for the best in parents, in care and love. Humans, probably more than those in nature's world, may chafe, and even rebel, at the care and work in raising a family. If I am to be an "adopted" grandparent to the four new goslings, I will have to endure the "nuisance" stages of Canada geese and keep recalling how much I anticipated their birth. I will need to remember and rekindle the pleasure and joy I had awaiting their birth. I will need to discover in each stage of their development some newly recognized pleasure that will offset the "nuisance" factors.

From my own personal experience, I know that the rewards, blessings, and joys of human parenthood far outweigh the demands of parenthood. Inevitably, however, there comes the difficult "grown up" and "grown out" stage, and children and grandchildren leave for their own callings and purposes. But, do they ever really leave from the parents' lives? No! Relationships, changed for sure, and memories remain, still to be enjoyed and to give blessing!

Welcome, new family, to our lives and to our neighborhood!

Written by Lloyd E. Batson
Published May 19, 2004

From whom do you get directions?

I had gone only rarely to the town, and I had never been to the one funeral home there. Because I was to be a part of a memorial service there, I needed to get directions from somebody when I got to the town.

When I saw a nice looking elderly man standing in his yard, I stopped to inquire about the funeral home's whereabouts. I got out of my car, stood by the driver's side, spoke across the roof of the car to the man near the steps of his house.
"Can you tell me where the funeral home is?" I inquired.

The man, apparently thinking how best to give instructions to a stranger, walked around the back of my car to stand by me as he began his directions. Pointing to the right, he said, "It is over there." Then pointing to his left, he instructed, "It is over there."

Obviously, I showed a bit of confusion. Then, with a circling motion of his hand, he continued, "You go round and around and it is right there," pointing, as he spoke, to his feet.

Just then, a rather frantic lady burst through the screen door on the porch, shouting, "Ernie, Ernie, you get right back in here!"

Poor Ernie, and poor me! Of all the people in the town, I had picked for directions a person who needed some himself!

After the lady had hustled Ernie into the house, and speaking no disparagement of Ernie, I am grateful to say, she gave me simple directions to the funeral home and I got there in time to do what I had come to do. I was glad there was only one funeral home in the town because Ernie and I apparently had some things in common. He could not give directions and I could not remember the name of the funeral home.

In my lifetime of working with people, I have never known anybody who does not, at times, need advice, counsel, or "directions" from somebody else. One of the greatest strengths and blessings a person can have is to have somebody available, a friend or counselor of some sort, one who can be trusted to share, honestly and wisely, as needed and requested, in times of search or decision.

It makes a powerful difference from whom we get counsel and advice. Many times, as a minister and as a friend, I have shared in somebody's heartache, dilemma, tragedy, or confusion and have been told, "I got in with the wrong crowd," "I listened to the wrong people," "I got bad advice," or "I thought I was smart enough to do what I wanted without recognizing that somebody might be able to give me counsel or encouragement." Most decisions a person has to make, of course, are his or her own responsibility, but how wise is the person who knows when to seek sound advice from somebody proven and trusted.

There appears to be no a shortage of people who will eagerly tell others what to do and how to live their lives. There never seems to be a scarcity of folk who will give strong, and often unsolicited, opinions about anything, whether or not the opinions are intelligently or factually based. It is also true, that there are available many wise and considerate people with the capacity to be helpful and understanding, if we would be seek them out for "direction" with whatever is our need.

A person does have to be careful from whom he or she takes counsel or direction.

So important is a wise counselor or friend that Jesus himself told his followers that, after he left, he would send a dependable Counselor, always available. That one would be the Holy Spirit, the "Spirit of Truth."

It does make a difference from where we get our directions!

Written by Lloyd E. Batson
Published May 26, 2004

Scratcher times

Did you ever eat a scratcher? I have. Many times!

Occasionally I program a nostalgic return to some early moment in my life to attempt to feel it again and to compare it with my life now. It is a procedure I think can be meaningful for any person.

So, one day recently I ate scratchers again, not literally, of course, but in my imagination, trying to make it a current experience. I remember how good they could taste, particularly when I was hungry, and when it was the only thing left on the platter after the other boys had had their pick, or it was my turn to eat one.

Before I ate a scratcher, and if my parents did not interrupt, I made a toy out of it. If one could find the "string" (a tendon of some sort running down the leg), he could pull on it and make a scratcher do all kinds of funny things.

You do know what a scratcher is, do you not? It is the foot and "toes" of a chicken.

Early in my life, and particularly during the Great Depression of the 1930s, every part of a chicken was cooked and eaten, even the feet. Chewing on a crunchy, properly cooked scratcher ("properly," of course, meaning fried) offered certain gustatory delights, really.

Times were hard, I guess, but we thought scratchers were good as well as a necessity. Besides, you could make those chicken feet curl up and become a real scratcher under the table on the leg of a brother next to you, if a parent did not spot the surreptitious attack and cancel the action.

The day of the scratcher has gone, I guess, for most people anyway. The principle of the scratcher, however, is a perpetually valid understanding, that one should make the most of his or her resources and opportunities. Grumbling about what you do not have must not obscure what you do have.

I do not know whether the Apostle Paul, in the first century AD, ate scratchers, but I do know he called for people to make the most of every opportunity, a practice he called, in one of his letters in the Bible, "redeeming the time." While he used the term to encourage Christian folk to use every opportunity that presented itself to do the right thing, the principle of "redeeming the time" is a basic force in a life that is productive and one that makes an impact on others.

I now see that the "scratcher" period in my life had some subtle but important influences on me. Among them was that my parents and hard times let me understand, and appreciate, that one does not have to have, perpetually, the best of everything in order to have a good life. Scratchers, served with love, were infinitely better than choice parts provided with anger or resentment at having to provide for a family.

Additionally, in contrast to the diverse and sometime hectic patterns in some homes today, mealtimes were always made to be special times. In the "hurry, hurry, everybody has to go somewhere" time our culture seems to encourage, it is hard to have quality time for family togetherness around the table. Quality time for family togetherness, whatever makes such possible, is still one of the greatest needs, as I see it, of our present day.

One more carryover from a "scratcher feast," and taking turns eating it, is that I was made to feel I was an important member of the family, a need I had then and suspect every child needs now.

"Scratcher times!" They had a lot going for them!

Written by Lloyd E. Batson
Published June 2, 2004

Four Seasons Living

Since 1956, when I myself was a newcomer to Pickens County, I have had the privilege of meeting and conversing with many delightful people who have moved from other parts of the United States to make their home here.

In my conversation with these new folk, I have often asked, directly or indirectly, why they chose to move here to live. Any chamber of commerce would have been pleased to hear some of the things I have heard! Among the most repeated reasons, especially among those coming here to retire, has been, "We came here so we could experience and enjoy four seasons every year."

At a given time, a summer, for example, may be so hot and seem to last so long that it can seem like a one season place. Yet, fall, winter and spring will come, refreshingly so!

Pickens County really is a great place to live, isn't it?

On my mind, as I write about four seasons, is not the blessed cycle of nature we are fortunate to enjoy in Pickens County. It is the "same old, same old rut" some people allow themselves to get into personally and causes them to lose sight of the joy available in the life of just about everybody.

Monotony, or apparent monotony, in a person's life can take heavy toll upon young and old alike. Nothing to do, nothing to enjoy, nothing to be rewarding, nothing different from day to day, same old thing all the time (these expressions are heard by a lot of parents! But children often see nothing much of interest taking place with their parents!). I hear these terms at times from people with whom I talk.

I am convinced that monotony in one's life is largely self-imposed and comes mostly from indifference to, and from simple neglect of, the possible discovery of the many ways by which pleasure and satisfaction can be implemented.

I know, of course, that all kinds of things, like work conditions, inadequate income, health and family demands can limit certain resources for relieving monotony in living. Limiting, however, is not the same as eliminating them. For most people the mind is still capable of researching, and discovering, all manner of activities, relationships, community programs, recreational club activities, and church activities — and, believe it or not, reading which can take one on many kinds of monotony breaking journeys.

I strongly believe in the spiritual values of the Bible's teaching. I also find myself getting practical help there for my life. For example, in the context of the monotonous and unfulfilling living some settle for, there is offered some non-physical enhancements to a continually rewarding life.

Paul, the Apostle, in one of his letters in the Bible, in contrast to the unrewarding lifestyle of some he knew, offered some fabulous life-enhancing qualities as he says, "The fruit of the Spirit is love, joy, peace, patience, kindness, goodness, faithfulness, gentleness and self control." (Galatians 5:22).

Wow! A lot of things can be exciting and "monotony breaking," but if these things Paul names as available are brought into a person's life how could living ever be not interesting, rewarding, and, if you please, "four seasonal?"

Four seasons living! Sounds great to me!

Written by Lloyd E. Batson
Published June 9, 2004

A father's other children

Ever heard of Bemidji? Bemidji, Minnesota, that is? I have never been there and I have difficulty finding it on a map. It is way up yonder somewhere, in winter a bitter cold territory.

Bemidji is an important place to me. One of my "grand children" lives there! She was one year old just recently and sent me a beautiful picture of herself taken on her birthday. Her name is Caroline, if you have any interest in knowing. Her picture came in time for it to add pleasure to Father's Day next Sunday.

Father's Day, it seems to me, always walks in the shadow of Mother's Day, a fact, if indeed it is a fact, that to me is entirely appropriate. Fathers have a special place in a family, yes, but they are not mothers! I, personally, yield to the women any day.

On this Father's Day I will be rejoicing in all the "grand children" I have, and there are many. I really do not know how many. With joy I will take delight afresh in my blood grandchildren, three of the finest gifts given me in God's economy. My wife, my two sons, my daughter-in-law, and my three grandchildren! How grateful I am for my wonderful family that gives me such pleasure all year long, and I thank God for them.

On this Father's Day I will also be expressing thanks to the Father God for my "grand children." These are the vast numbers of children who across the years have touched my life in special ways.

Caroline, my "grand daughter," is the child of a couple for whom I performed their wedding ceremony. I have been privileged to be the minister in weddings for fifty-five years or so. I tell each bride and groom that their children will be my "grand children." In this case, Caroline went off to Bemidji to be born. I also ask couples for whom I do weddings to stay in touch with me and on their wedding anniversary to send me an anniversary card, or contact me in some way. I regularly get word about, and pictures of, my "grand children," some I did not know had arrived.

I am asking other fathers on this Father's Day to join me in celebrating the many children around us, children not related by blood but who put joy and happiness into our lives. Children in the neighborhood, children in the church, children in others' families, but children who smile at us, touch us in many ways, and do precious little things for us. As for me, there have not been many days in my life that I have not been blessed by a child.

On this Father's Day I ask all fathers to look beyond their own children and grandchildren to take note of the goodnesses of the love and joy given them from children all around them. Happy is the father who has other children, besides his own, who love him and to whom he can give love and attention. Impoverished is the father who has no identity with children other than his own.

Of course, no one can, or should try to, take the place of the real father in children's lives. On the other hand, I have never known a child who does not benefit from love from a wider "family" when it is properly and generously given.

Next Sunday will still be Father's Day, in the sense that real fathers will be honored (even if Mother's Day outshines us!). For this one Sunday, however, I hope there will be another dimension to the day, when all of us who are fathers will also take note of and be grateful for the "grand children" in our lives.

"Grand child" in Bemidji, I thank you for coming into my life!

Written by Lloyd E. Batson
Published June 16, 2004

Stinking Catfish and laughter

It calls attention to itself, too much so for me to use it often. It is the obviously expensive aftershave lotion I had gotten as a door prize, one provided by a department store for some gathering.

A few days ago I decided to try it one more time. What happened? I had a rushing, strong impression of a smell from 18 or so years ago, and I laughed again!

I had told a story to my congregation about my being out in my back yard, while dressed in my best suit, digging desperately through a black trash bag filled with papers and a lot of rank catfish heads, skins, and entrails I had not yet disposed of. I was frantically looking for a letter I could not find, one that supposedly had been sent to me and was urgently needed (turned out it had never been sent to me!). I was looking, in stinking stuff, for something that was not there, and was getting stinking myself.

That story took only a few days to get all the way to Summerville! I got a package from down there, with no name or return address. When I opened the box I found there a flask of pungent lotion, a bar of soap (the expensive kind on a string), a stick of fancy maximum strength deodorant, and a letter of great length, telling me that the winds had brought the smell of me all the way to Summerville and I should do something about it. Along with the absurdity of the mental picture I still have, of my digging in rotten fish remains for something that did not exist, I still laugh at the memory of such a friend who could respond as my Summerville one did.

What is important to me is the awareness of something I believe to be indispensable to good health — the capacity to laugh, and the joy of helping others to laugh. In my opinion, the person who sees no humor in life is in serious trouble. The person who cannot laugh occasionally, even regularly, carries an oppressive burden that does sad things to living.

No one should minimize the seriousness of life, and the heavy responsibilities that caring people must bear. Living seriously and responsibly is necessary and demanding! It is true, though, that many burdens have been made easier to handle by the touch of somebody's gentle humor or sparkling laughter.

I do not remember if the day I got that interesting package from a friend was a "down" day for me, but had it been, I think getting it could have been a lift to my spirits that no medicine could have brought. I still smile when I think about it. And what wonders a smile does for a person, even if nobody is around to see it!

Particularly do I think it is necessary for good mental, physical, and even spiritual health for a person to be able to laugh at one's own self. I think a person that has not learned how to laugh at himself draws a tight circle of misery around him. Such a person also is often a difficult person with whom to live or work.

Perpetual frivolity is not at all what I am writing about. On my mind is a healthy attitude engendered by the capacity to see the abundance of the humorous and the delightful in things and people all around (even stinking catfish remains, the odor of which hangs around!).

I think there is a precious ministry in wholesome laughter — ministry to others and ministry to one's self.

Think about it, and laugh, if you can. It will do you good!

Written by Lloyd E. Batson
Published June 23, 2004

Jugging up your batteries

I do not know how to spell the word "jug" or "jugg," as it is used here, for it is not in the dictionary. I never saw it written anywhere. I did, however, hear it spoken often in the lumber mill village of Alcolu where I grew up. It was an important word and term that communicated clearly.

It was used, for example, about rejuvenating a fire about to go out. One would say, "Better jug it up," meaning poke it or stir it to bring new life. The word "jugging" had nothing to do with storing in jugs certain by-products of corn as in earlier days in the mountains of Pickens County (which was also done in Alcolu!).

Alcolu had no psychiatrists, no psychologists, no resident doctors or nurses, but there were discerning and wise folk who often quickly could diagnose another's problems with "His batteries need jugging up" or "He better jug up his spirits or he'll weaken himself to death," and such like.

I "got my batteries jugged" up very recently. I am now officially an octogenarian, and started into my eighty-first year. To celebrate such, in conjunction with Father's Day, my two sons surreptitiously arranged with their mother to show up separately here in Easley (from New York and Kentucky) without my having the faintest idea they were coming. What a shock and surprise! How perfectly their actions fulfilled the ministry of "getting your batteries jugged up!"

On Wednesday I came in for lunch from the hospital, where I was on duty assisting the chaplain. There, in the middle of the living area, stood my son from New York. What a shock! His mother had picked him up from the airport (while manipulating the truth of her whereabouts!). The next day we were about to eat lunch and the phone rang. My eight-year-old grandson from Kentucky was calling to visit with me on the phone. Interesting and intriguing conversationalist that he is, he talked on and on about the pretty weather in Kentucky, about my column that he reads, asked about my well-being, et cetera. As I was talking with him, the doorbell rang, and, still visiting with him on the phone, I went to the door. There stood that eight-year-old character still talking on his cell phone! He and his father had come from Kentucky for the surprise visit.

My batteries are jugged up for a long time!

What a ministry pleasant surprises can be! My sons coming! The many cards I received, as surprises, beautiful and appreciated in their own right, moved beyond the delight of getting them to the precious recollections of the joys and goodnesses that the people who sent them had put into my life. With each card I relived my journey with the sender. My batteries got jugged up!

Gifts like flowers, pies, presents of varying natures, phone calls, celebratory meals, at home and away, came with their refreshing surprise, and with appreciation for the friendship and love thereby expressed! My batteries got jugged up!

All around us are people not necessarily becoming octogenarians, but who may need others' help to "jug up their batteries," using the countless ways that can be done. What a needed ministry!

The "jugging up batteries" ministry is one available to everyone!

Written by Lloyd E. Batson
Published June 30, 2004

What do you do after you have shot your firecrackers?

As I was walking across the large parking lot one day after a Fourth of July, I saw the thing lying on the pavement. I kicked at it as I passed, then turned back to pick it up. It was a thin, red stick, with something on the end that looked like a crayon casing with the crayon gone.

What I picked up was, I think, a bottle rocket, a kind of airborne firecracker, which had been fired. Reverting to my childhood, I twirled the thing like a baton as I did a little jig and picked up my walking pace. Then I made an arrow out of it and tossed it at the flagpole, nearby. The thing did not make a good arrow. Actually, it did not make a good any thing. I kept the thing for a time, thinking I might find something interesting to do with it.

A question was raised in my mind then, one that still shows up occasionally in some form. What good is a firecracker that has been shot, or a bottle rocket that has been fired? The question turned into, "What are you going to do after you have shot your firecrackers?"

Sound silly? I am not sure it is. In the case of whoever shot that bottle rocket, I am assuming he or she was celebrating the Fourth of July. It must have been fun. Did the celebration stop when the last firecracker or bottle rocket had been shot?

Yes, firecrackers are fun, and perhaps even important, but what happens after you have shot your firecrackers? Our country has just witnessed a stirring annual celebration of our nation's beginning. Exciting!

The feelings of patriotism, of expressed gratitude for our country, prayer for our nation must not now become like a shot firecracker. As a nation, we face unbelievably complex and difficult days ahead. With candor we must face a time and a world unlike any we have seen. There are no simple and easy answers to the turmoil in our world that impacts us all.

Certainly it is important to look at and celebrate what we and others have been! Yet, what we have been will not supplant the need for us to discover what we are now, and what our responsibilities are now. With firecrackers and bottle rockets we can celebrate the past, but unless we can now be wise, strong, understanding, committed, discerning and courageous there is vast trouble ahead!

The likelihood of doing, and being, the right things cannot be measured by what others have done, even our honored forebears. It will rest upon what our leaders and we, the citizenry, want now and will get constructively at doing. Celebrations of the past have an important and interpretive place, but there must be in the now common sense, fortitude, courage, intelligent thinking, and commitment to doing right things in the face of all manner of challenges and difficulties, present now and surely to increase in the days ahead.

No, it is not a silly question, "What are you going to do after you have shot your firecrackers?" As a nation, it might be the most important question facing us!

"Firecrackers" can be used for legitimate celebrations, but firecrackers do not make many contributions after they are shot!

May God help us, as people and a nation, to shore up our celebrations, our affirmations, our public stances with high goals, values, and commitment to right doing, necessary factors for the now and for the future!

What do we do after we have shot our firecrackers? It remains to be seen!

Written by Lloyd E. Batson
Published July 7, 2004

Living in South Carolina

There is a magazine that we get monthly at our house, one that we look forward to and enjoy reading. It is called *"Living in South Carolina,"* and is published by the electric cooperatives of the state.

While it has business and promotional purposes, I am sure, the magazine regularly sounds a theme that I endorse heartily. It is that South Carolina is a great place to live and that its citizenry could enhance the pleasures and quality of their lives by getting better acquainted not only with the local areas but also with the widely diverse attractions and experiences to be discovered all over the Palmetto State.

Regularly I have the delight of meeting "newcomers" to our area and talking with them about what interesting places and things await their discovery in South Carolina as they have, or make, opportunity to do so. By the way, I think we are fortunate to have so many wonderful folk come from other places to live among us!

Regrettably, I also regularly meet "old-timers" who have not learned and experienced much about the wide offerings of South Carolina to the pleasures of their living.

One would have to be a hermit not to be aware of the beaches, mountains, resorts, colleges and universities, lakes, cultural events, athletics, industries and such in our state. Beyond these, the magazine, *"Living in South Carolina,"* and other publications like it, offers a look at the less spectacular but rewarding features of living in our state.

The current issue of the magazine features an article on carnivorous plants that thrive under certain power lines in South Carolina. What an interesting and educational experience that could be for a person to pursue.

In a section focusing on agriculture, one can read the story of an award winning family farmer that could lead to an interest in the discovery of many working farms, still reminding "city" folks of South Carolina's bounty of the earth. Arranging a visit to one of the many productive farms in our state would make for an exciting and educational experience for adults and children alike.

One section is a listing, county by county, of roadside markets, presented as some of the Palmetto State's best kept secrets with their abundance of beneficial delights (including one of my favorites, new crop boiled peanuts). A great story of watermelon tasting adventures is included.

South Carolina is a state rich in festivals, workshops, museums, "singings," local arts and crafts shows, and you name it. The several page calendar in the magazine of such activities, with dates and phone numbers to call, offers a "discovering South Carolina" experiences with something for every taste.

A monthly feature offers a literal taste of South Carolina, right in one's own house, with savory recipes of favorite foods of some of its citizens.

I think a fresh look at South Carolina, by both "newcomers" and "old-timers," could identify many assets to make living here a continually good experience! The Palmetto State is waiting, ready to be enjoyed!

Written by Lloyd E. Batson
Published July 14, 2004

About tennis balls and church

Once, while I was an active pastor, I walked, as I often did, through the empty sanctuary, appreciating its beauty, reliving my experiences in worship, thanking God for my people who regularly attended church there and looking for anything that needed attention.

I spotted, lying under a seat, an attractive pocketbook or purse (or whatever else such a container is called). I retrieved it, opened it carefully, for those things mystify me, wanting to find some identification so it could be returned to its owner.

The total content was one tennis ball!

One tennis ball! Nothing else! It struck me as being funny. With my active imagination, I could react to that tennis ball in all kinds of ways.

I was, of course, curious about that purse with the tennis ball. Since no identification of any kind was in it, and nobody ever claimed it from the Lost and Found table, I never did have my curiosity satisfied.

I have some thoughts, important to me, about that tennis ball. To start with, a tennis ball can be a very important possession. Some simple things can give a lot of pleasure. I must be very careful how I sit in judgment on things meaningful to others. It is so easy to act as if only those things that are meaningful to me have value. A tennis ball might just be a precious possession to somebody, for many reasons! And, besides, if I should think it ludicrous for a tennis ball to be in somebody's purse at church, I should recognize that it just might be, for example, the exercise ball that a person who has had a stroke must use to get strength back in a hand.

Another thought persists. Just what is a person permitted to bring to church? Aside from the question of actual tennis balls, it should be understood that a person should be able to bring anything to church and expose it to the cleansing, renewing, healing, gentling power of worship.

Welcomed by God and the congregation, a person should be able to expose to the ministry of the church everything that matters to him or her, everything that affects, puzzles or confuses him, anything that hurts or helps, and have it touched by God's Spirit. A person needs to feel that life's best and worst can receive the scrutiny and influence of God without any thought of what others may think.

I confess I do not know what good a tennis ball itself could get out of church, but I do know that a person must be free to bring to church, and to a worship experience, the things that affect him or her, good or bad, and seek to have God's help with them. People can deprive themselves of needed help if they get the notion that God helps with only certain kinds of things and needs.

By the way, I think I was glad nobody ever claimed that tennis ball. I finally gave it to a delighted youngster. In my imagination I could see that youngster playing with the ball and bragging, "My tennis ball is the best there is. It went to church and got blessed!"

Written by Lloyd E. Batson
Published July 21, 2004

Watching a gift at work

Right here in our community it happened. A four-day basketball camp for youngsters, ages 7-13! No ordinary camp it was.

The camp was free, and was open to the entire community, all racial and ethnic backgrounds welcomed, and they were indeed in attendance.

One of the churches, in the middle of Easley, one with a family life center that includes facilities for basketball, hosted the camp, following the vision and leadership of one of its members, a former star basketball player at one of the Upstate universities. It had the full support and encouragement of the pastor and the church. The camp was planned and conducted in conjunction with an organization of committed students called Fellowship of Christian Athletes.

While it began as a ministry of a limited group, it quickly became an event with community dimensions. Many individuals and businesses provided support and assisting personnel.

I watched the camaraderie and enthusiasm beyond the youngsters themselves, and I confess I went into a private place and thanked the Heavenly Father for what I was observing.

The youngsters, 192 of them, had the benefit of skilled teachers of the game, with coaches from local schools and presently active and former players from at least three of our area universities giving full attention and instruction to manageable small groups.

Every day inspirational moments were provided and warmly received. The youngsters' eyes were on a basketball goal but they looked at higher goals, too. Better refreshments and lunches than some of us get at home were provided by various individuals, restaurants and food places. The providers were eager participants in a marvelous community experience. Hardworking volunteers served the meals.

I watched with fascination, and high respect, the "on the scene" visionary director of the camp, member of the host church, one who had been a gifted athlete and notable basketball player at one area university, as he quietly moved among the eager and active youngsters, giving instruction and information. I was amazed at the quick and disciplined responses to his quiet voice. The director has a demanding and painful physical disability and walks slowly with a cane. Nothing, however, impairs his spirit and commitment!

Among the many images in my mind, two will stand out of this amazing basketball camp. One is of the only unhappy camper I saw, and that unhappiness lasted only briefly. Apparently, the little girl had been hit on the nose by an errant ball and was hurting. Embarrassed by her tears and sniffling, she was trying to hide her discomfort. Another camper came quickly to her and gently put her arm around the embarrassed girl. The tears stopped and a smile appeared. The magic arm around the teary-eyed youngster was of another color than that of her own.

The second image is of a huge pile of blankets of varying sizes, colors and materials, alongside large boxes of canned and boxed foods. The inspirational speaker on the day before had been the director of a soup kitchen and homeless shelter in a nearby city. The blankets had been brought by the boys and girls in the camp to be given to help needy folk there. Do not ever discount the power of love and responsiveness of young folk to the needs around them!

What a gift was the basketball camp, in so many ways, to our community! Other wonderful and delightful things are regularly being done in our community for the good of others. I think all of us ought to go off in a corner somewhere and give thanks!

On a lighter note, was it possible this camp impacted me, too? The day before the camp ended, bags of gifts, provided by many people, were being prepared to give to each youngster at the end of camp. The gifts for each included, among many things, a beautiful New Testament. The bag of gifts for each camper also had a beanie bag Clemson Tiger.

As I left, one of the men helping with the packaging came bringing to me, a known Furman man, one of those beanie bag Clemson Tigers. It is now sitting on a shelf in my study, and I am proud to have it. The camp must have gotten to me, too!

Written by Lloyd E. Batson
Published July 28, 2004

Pretty things

I called my wife, asking her to look out the back window. "Do you see what I see?" excitedly I queried.

At the end of July, long past the blooming season, at the top of a huge azalea bush in our yard there was a large red blossom. A single bright flower in the midst of the greenery of rhododendron bushes, azaleas and an assortment of "take up" growth!

Aside from the surprise, and the beauty of the "out of time" azalea blossom, it seemed to me that the single colorful bloom was a stop sign of a sort. It was saying, "Hey, stop, look at the mosaic of beauty in all the varying shades of green right in your back yard for you to enjoy!"

For some strange reason, as I looked at that azalea blossom, I thought of an aunt of mine, long gone from a world she enjoyed. I never knew anybody who found joy in pretty things any more than she did.

My aunt's capacity to "ooh and ah" over things, important or inconsequential, big or little, that caught her eye had always delighted me. A tiny ceramic frog or a large painting, a piece of delicate hand stitching or a bright bedspread, a colorful butterfly or an unusual vine, anything pretty! It always evoked her admiration. In her home she surrounded herself with an amazing array of pretty things.

How important an awareness of pretty things is to the quality of one's life! How drab and dreary the life of the person that can see only the ugly and the evil in the world! How sad when pretty things cause no stirring of delight!

The world, of course, is not all pretty. Sometimes a person has to look for lovely things. And that is the point. Developing a love of and a search for pretty things means that one will see more of them than the person whose "pretty" sense is dulled. Looking for pretty things is a part of the discovery! An appreciation of "all things bright and beautiful" does not eliminate the ugly and the evil in the world but it helps immeasurably to keep them from being overwhelming and dominating.

Other things happen, too. In my aunt's case, she, in no way vain, always kept herself neat and attractive. Appreciation of pretty things helped keep her pretty. It works that way. People around her enjoyed the "pretty" in her.

The Creator God has made a wonderful world, with so much beauty and goodness to behold. People have messed up a lot of it, but it is not all gone! People need pretty things. Pretty things exist in abundance all around us, in things and in people.

Does your capacity to "ooh and ah" need developing? Your life will be immeasurably better if you notice and enjoy pretty things! And, somehow, I feel that the Creator God wants us to!

Written by Lloyd E. Batson
Published August 4, 2004

Chiggers

What a surprise! A shock! And an aggravation!

After eighty years of an "on again, off again" identity with them, I just recently had, by far, the largest collection of their claims for recognition I have ever experienced. I stopped counting the evidence of their individual attacks on me when I had passed three hundred and there were large areas still uncounted.

Had it been decent to show the evidence (which it would not have been because of some of the areas they picked for their invasion) I could have demonstrated, to anyone interested, the largest insect battleground, in amazing attack formation, I ever saw on me or anybody else.

Chiggers! That is the enemy's identity. They are also commonly called "red bugs." They are creatures so small they are rarely seen until it is too late!

One of the hazards of growing up in rural areas as I did, and being regularly in woods, fields, grass and weeds, was getting bit by a few chiggers or hordes of them. Chiggers will leave wherever their hiding places are and climb aboard unsuspecting ankles and legs and make their way down inside shoes and up to much of the human body. Individual chiggers will stop all along their journey, bite and stay there embedded in the skin. The result is a growing, itching inflammation from each new unwelcomed "house guest."

When I decided to use a weed eater on the grasses and weeds of a hard to negotiate, sloping area of the dam of the pond back of our house, it did not occur to me to do any of the few things that can be done to help ward off aggressive chigger attacks. One can tie a tight string around the bottom of the trouser legs, or spray shoes, ankles and elsewhere with "Off," or its equivalent, and hope for the best.

What can you do with chiggers after they have made themselves at home on your body? Not much! There are some ineffective "trial" things. One "old timey" effort is putting nail polish on each bite. In my case, there was not enough nail polish in our house to get half way up one leg! Hydrocortisone cream can help some with the itching. About the only thing one can do is the "grin and bear it" process, scratching and waiting out the demise of the embedded chiggers. My waiting for the death of hundreds and hundreds of chiggers was long and drawn out!

Now the question is whether I will "wade" in the weeds and grass again with some cutting tool (a lawn mower will not work on that part of the dam). My wife will raise strong objections again, as she has done before when there had not been chiggers lying in wait, but the next time she will buttress her objections with a "chigger flag!"

Prospective chiggers or not, I am guessing that, yes, if cutting those weeds has to be done again, I will do it.

If I, or others, refused to do something that needs doing just because there may be unpleasant factors related to it, many difficult problems or needs would not be tended to.

Chiggers, I will try to be better prepared for you the next time, but weeds do not stop growing, and I will come again!

Written by Lloyd E. Batson
Published August 11, 2004

Community

There are not many words more beautiful and meaningful than the word "community!"

Community is a place, a relationship or an experience. Sometimes it is all three. A few days ago, all three came together right here in a part of Easley. To a passerby, it may have seemed it was just a picnic for a large group of people who seemed to be having a good time in a lovely park area along a creek. It was that all right, but that was just a part of it.

The gathering was in Burdine Springs, one of the older subdivisions in Easley, and a very pleasant place to live. How many people are residents there I do not know, but I know that not everybody knows everybody else who lives there. In our fast-paced society the "old timey" sense of everybody knowing and appreciating all the neighbors rarely exists anymore.

With the desire that all the residents of Burdine Springs get to discover more of the wonderful people who live there than just the ones near them, plans were made to have a "community" picnic in the small park along the creek running along Burdine Road.

Some creative and talented folk took the lead in planning, organizing and doing a lot of the physical work involved. Some of the latest and the best models of outdoor grills left their home yards and garages and made their way to the park, accompanied by meats to be prepared for fabulous eating. Residents were invited, and assigned by alphabetic division, to bring salads and desserts.

The most important part of such an endeavor came — the residents of the neighborhood! In the words of those who sometimes try to describe such gatherings, "A good time was had by all."

Had a passerby taken time to stop nearby and watch for a while, many things could be seen. People of all ages, old folk like me, young couples. Small children, including some just a few weeks old. Happy groups sitting and eating together. Folk pitching horseshoes or playing badminton. Groups animatedly conversing with one another. What might not be recognized was also at work! People in the neighborhood already knowing some but meeting and enjoying other folk they had not known! The discovery of common interests! New friendships being started! A warm sense of belonging to a community where folk can enjoy being together!

It is likely that some other "communities" in our area are doing people things like what I have just described. However, would not it be great if perhaps some folk in all sections would undertake some similar or innovative way to get "neighbors" together as neighbors? No one activity would work everywhere, but any effort would be better than none to get people to feel an integral part of a community.

"Community" can be a place, a relationship or an experience.

Being all three at the same time can be great! And possible!

Written by Lloyd E. Batson
Published August 18, 2004

Nothing

It had to be the least prepared, most rambling, indefinite, confusing speech I ever made, and it lasted one hour! It also might have been one of the most effective I have done.

The speech was delivered more than 40 years ago and, surprisingly, I still occasionally am thanked for it, one person doing so a few days ago.

What was the speech about? Nothing!

One day the principal of the local high school, with whom I had frequently worked on varying projects, called me on the phone. His first words were, "I need you to come down here to the school and make a speech on nothing and you are the best qualified person I know."

The principal went on to explain that at the high school they were planning the first career day the school had ever had. They had passed out in the high school a list of various occupations and professions they thought the students might be interested in hearing about and were securing speakers for the day.

To give students opportunity to indicate interest in fields other than those listed, a place at the bottom of the list was left blank for indicating what such interests were. As a prank, more than a hundred students had collaborated among themselves and entered on the returned list their interest in "Nothing."

Gladly I accepted the invitation to participate.

On the planned Career Day the principal called over the loudspeaker system, one by one, each of the vocations prepared for and told the students to go to the room provided. I stood in an obscure place and waited for "Nothing" to be called.

"Those of you who chose "Nothing" will go to the auditorium," the principal solemnly announced.

I watched the crowd of students, mostly boys, as they gleefully made their way to the auditorium, clapping their hands and high-fiving, celebrating the prank they had pulled.

The principal came in, ordered the students to be seated, and announced that they would hear for one hour Dr. Lloyd Batson honor their request about "Nothing." He instructed them that they would face the discipline of the principal's office if they misbehaved or did not listen to what they had chosen.

For one hour, as eloquently as I could, I did indeed talk about "Nothing!"

While I cannot tell you what all I said about so profound a subject, I am sure it had to do with the folly of having no goals in life and no commitment to getting the best training and preparation for something important and constructive.

Surprisingly, over the years since, a large number of those students have sought me out to thank me for the shock of "Nothing," and for the emphasis that interest in "Nothing" as a life commitment would get them nowhere in their lives! Several have told me that in looking back on that day in the high school when their prank went awry they saw it as a turning point for good in their lives.

I have made many speeches and addresses in my life, on all manner of subjects, but it just might be that when I talked about nothing I, unknowingly, was at my best! For some wonderful folk it now seems so.

Commitment to nothing! It still invites an unrewarding life!

Written by Lloyd E. Batson
Published August 25, 2004

The Olive Leaf Crown

Hundreds of years before Christ an event was begun that has thrilled millions upon millions of people in the world, the Olympic Games. The first recorded Olympic race was held in 776 B.C., on the plains of Olympia, in Greece.

The Olympic Games, with many kinds of competition, would have been known to the Apostle Paul in the first century A.D., and he used athletic activities to illustrate great spiritual truths.

Suspended in A.D. 394 because of corruption that had developed in the games, they were renewed in 1896 with eight nations taking part. In 2004, the number of nations represented have been mind-boggling. What an exciting worldwide event the Olympic Games are now!

Others will choose different moments in the games to remember with special appreciation. I choose two, both in gymnastics. There was Paul Hamm of the United States competing for the all around championship and the medal and olive leaf crown that goes with winning. Leading all others at the time, Hamm fell in the vault event, tumbling into the judges' table. From leading all others, he dropped to fourteenth place. What an image of disappointment and crushed hopes! But Paul Hamm, against all odds of winning any medal, got up and in the final events performed superbly and, unbelievably, qualified for the awards ceremony. Apparently defeated, he got up, committed his heart and skills afresh, and was crowned with an olive leaf wreath and given his medal!

For the record, Paul Hamm was not responsible, in any way, for the controversy created by scoring mistakes not involving him but another competitor. What we saw was Paul Hamm come back from an apparently disastrous gymnastic mishap, one that seemed to destroy his chance of winning. His mishap did not defeat him as a person or as a competitor. What a winner!

The second image I will retain with pleasure is of the gymnast Carly Patterson, 16 years old, who since early in her life had committed herself to winning Olympic medals and had worked and trained with diligence and total commitment toward her goal. Then there she was, this beautiful, charming teenager being crowned with the olive leaf wreath and awarded the gold medal as the all around gymnastic champion, and blessing us all with her radiant spirit!

Long before there were medals of gold, silver or bronze, the crown of an olive leaf wreath, symbolizing victory, was the prized goal for athletes.

In receiving the olive leaf crown and his medal, Paul Hamm represented something vastly important across the scope of life for all. Errors, blunders, mistakes and mishaps do not necessarily have to mean defeat. It may be hard, and appear to be impossible, but life can be good after messing up!

That charming young lady, Carly Patterson, being crowned with an olive leaf wreath placed on her head and the gold medal being placed around her neck is a beautiful picture of determination and total commitment to achieving what was important to her. Probably not anybody I know will ever be crowned with an olive leaf wreath, symbolizing victory in an Olympic game, but the Apostle Paul wrote about the way that anybody can be crowned with victory in the most important race or event there is. Wrote he, near the end of his life, as recorded in II Timothy 4:7,8, "I have fought a good fight, I have finished my course, I have kept the faith. Henceforth there is laid up for me a crown of righteousness, which the Lord, the righteous judge shall give me at that day, and not to me only, but unto all them that also love his appearing."

Yes, it is possible to everybody at the end of his or her life to be crowned with the

Continued on page 188

The Olive Leaf Crown

Continued from page 187

highest and best of all symbols of victory, the "olive leaf" crown of righteousness awarded by the Great Judge himself.

I saw Paul Hamm and Carly Patterson crowned because of their victories in a demanding discipline. I will never be crowned with an olive leaf wreath, but I am committed to gaining the greatest award offered to anybody, the one Paul the Apostle described as the crown of righteousness, given by the Great Judge. It is available to anybody who will try for it with faithfulness!

In the athletic imagery of the Apostle, anyone who really wants to may receive heaven's "olive leaf" crown of victory!

Written by Lloyd E. Batson
Published September 1, 2004

Visiting the past and the future

Is it possible to visit the past and the future at the same time? I think so.

A busload of World War II veterans and interested older folk has just come back from a visit of several days to Washington, D.C. I qualified both as a veteran and as an interested older person, having served in the 87th Infantry Division in the European Theater and being now in my eighty-first year.

Some younger men in our church, wanting to do something special to honor the World War II veterans, arranged, and planned in detail, a trip to Washington to visit, especially, the new World War II Memorial.

How carefully and attentively these younger men shepherded 35 folk in varying degrees of foot traveling ability on a schedule of visits to the major memorials in Washington, Arlington Cemetery, several Smithsonian museums, the Holocaust Museum, the Spy Museum, the National Cathedral, the White House, the Capitol, and a smorgasbord of delightful eating places.

The primary objective was to visit the World War II Memorial. Awesome!

Breathtaking! Emotionally stirring! We visited the memorial three different times and saw it from a distance at other times.

The World War II Memorial, located on the mall in front of the Capitol, is not a building, but a series of granite pillars and sculptures linked together to portray the unity of the nation and its people at a grave crisis in world history.

Two 43-foot tall pavilions on the north and south end of the plaza, representing the Pacific and Atlantic theaters of war, commemorate the victory of democracy over tyranny. They serve as markers and entries to the plaza. Fifty-six 17-foot granite pillars embrace the memorial plaza in semicircular colonnades. Individually, the pillars represent the 48 states, seven territories and the District of Columbia that made up the United States during the war. Collectively, the pillars celebrate the unprecedented unity of the nation during the Second World War. The symbolism of "bonding" is accentuated by bronze intertwined ropes that appear on the balustrades between the pillars.

The foregoing is a partial and inadequate description of an incredibly impressive memorial to the millions who served in World War II and a tribute to the hundreds of thousands who died in the war.

One of our visits to the memorial was at night. For some reason the lighting system that night was not working and the area was dark. We had gone there to have a worship service for our group. With a flashlight, provided by a park attendant (the World War II Memorial is a part of our National Park System), our pastor, assisted by our minister of music, led in a moving time of worship. During the service, other visitors edged close to our group to share in it. A beautiful and emotional time! Some of the visitors expressed gratitude for the stirring moment.

I have titled this column "Visiting the past and the future." Much of what our group visited reflected the achievements and experiences of our nation in the past. Those are reflected in visible reminders in part to encourage us to be grateful for our heritage. It is also vastly important for our nation to learn from the past what can impact for good the future of our nation. In a sense, when we looked at, and contemplated the meaning of them, the monuments, museums and governmental institutions, we were visiting both the past and the future!

For me, the most telling moment of our wonderful visit to Washington was sitting in the darkness of the World War II Memorial, thinking about, and feeling deeply, all that the memorial represented. On this visit, we had come to worship God. We could faintly

Continued on page 190

Visiting the past and the future

Continued from page 189

see the memorial, reminder of a most difficult period in the past. Darkness bathed our awesome feelings. But, there was a single small light shining upon Words from God held in the pastor's hand. They were being read for us as information from and about the past. They were being, for us, light for guidance into the exciting and foreboding future.

We left the memorial feeling that we had been on holy ground there, yes, but also that no matter what lies ahead there will always be available for us holy ground if we will recognize it!

Written by Lloyd E. Batson
Published September 8, 2004

Blue and Green

Local fans were ecstatic. The event made huge headlines. A losing streak of 31 games was broken with a win by the Easley Green Wave football team over the Pickens Blue Flame, an archrival!

When I learned of that monumental happening, I relived a delightful experience in my life, while I was pastor for many years in Pickens.

For some reason I never fully understood, I was often responsible for enlisting ministers for the opening prayers at the high school football games. Such praying was, at that time, both expected and widely appreciated.

One year it dawned on me that there was a newly arrived minister in town whose denomination had never been represented in the invocations at the football games. I went to see him, both to welcome him to Pickens and to ask him to offer the prayer at Friday night's game. He graciously agreed so to do.

I explained to the new minister that there were some things he would need to remember as he prayed, including the fact that the prayer needed to be relatively brief, and that he should not try to catch up on his praying in the invocation. I also reminded him that there would be another team there besides the Blue Flame and his praying should be impartial. He assured me he understood and would handle everything properly and no partiality would be shown.

The night of the game, I was sitting in the stands. I heard, after the minister was announced, an articulate, well thought out prayer and I felt good I had asked him. Then came the last sentence of the prayer, "And may the flame of courage rise high tonight." I hope the Lord forgave me for laughing out loud!

When I kidded the new minister about his words, he said, "I didn't say 'Blue.'"

Then came the time when the Pickens Blue Flame and the Easley Green Wave were to resume playing after the unfortunate need to suspend playing each other because of bad crowd behavior on the part of the fans of both. I realized again there was another minister from a church whose religious expression had never been recognized in a prayer at a game, so I went to him and asked him to give the invocation.

I told the minister the same things I had told the other new minister. He, too, said he understood and would be glad to do the prayer. "Besides," he said, "I have members from both Pickens and Easley in my church."

The night of the game, I sat in the stands and waited to hear how this minister would handle the Blue Flame-Green Wave atmosphere. The minister prayed a beautiful and short prayer, and ended it with, "And may the flame of courage wave over us tonight!"

Well, I had to get forgiveness for laughing again! But Barney had been reasonably impartial! By the way, Barney became a good friend.

How glad I am that in our area we can still feel strongly about community identity, but can work with and respect one another. Healthy rivalry and competition can be constructive for all. Ugliness never can be!

To pick up on the words of a prayer at a football game years ago, and rephrasing it, "May the flame of courage wave over us all and make differing communities constructive contributors to the welfare of the larger community — all of us!"

May it ever be so!

Written by Lloyd E. Batson
Published September 15, 2004

Esprit De Corps

Not a child that went through elementary school in Alcolu, South Carolina when I did in the 1930's left without a strong impression of the fourth grade teacher. That teacher's trademark was what she stoutly proclaimed to any misbehaving or inattentive youngster. For all to hear, and cringe, she would declare, "I'll snatch you baldheaded!"

This "memorable" lady was actually a splendid and effective teacher. To my recollection, the first reference I ever heard to the relationship covered by the phrase "esprit de corps" came from her. She was trying to get the class to work together on some project and said we needed to get a big dose of esprit de corps!

I felt then that she was using something she had heard in her college days, for it certainly was not something anybody in the fourth grade of the lumber mill village of Alcolu ever had heard! We certainly did not know what it was we needed a big dose of! But we learned because I still have my hair!

The fact is that, then and now, a high level of "esprit de corps" is among the most valuable assets of any group working together, in schools, in businesses, in clubs, in churches, in athletic teams, in hospitals, in anything that depends on people working together.

Just for the record, this important phrase, esprit de corps, came into English usage from the French and is defined in the dictionary as "the common spirit existing in the members of a group and inspiring enthusiasm, devotion, and strong regard for the honor of the group."

A very recent happening at Palmetto Health Baptist Easley reflects the existence and value of esprit de corps in an organization (by the way, I attended the official opening of the new hospital in 1958 and have been grateful as an area minister for an ongoing and rewarding relationship with the hospital ever since).

On Tuesday night of the heavy rains that the Hurricane Frances brought our way, the water came in such volume near the hospital that a major storm drain clogged and the water level built up so high that much of the first floor of the hospital was flooded. Esprit de corps set in! Workers on duty called other employees at home. Husbands brought wives and wives brought husbands. They came as they were, in varying kinds of clothes, making for a kaleidoscope of color and activity.

For long hours they worked, pushing, pulling, and shoving water with all kinds of instruments. Dress shoes waded the water as freely and effectively as bare feet. Dress and casual clothes received the same soaking and splashing.

The employees, with varying responsibilities in the hospital, became one as they gave of themselves to taking care of the place where they not only work for a living, but where they are engaged in ministry to the lives of the folk who come to the hospital with all kinds of medical needs.

The large number of folk, both those already on duty and those who quickly showed up voluntarily to work without thought of pay, were exercising a precious relationship. They were family, working together for the good of the hospital so important to them, and so important to the folk of the entire area.

In the midst of the frightening invasion of potentially heavily damaging water, the men and women of the hospital family were showing the strength and goodness of an esprit de corps that did not come into being with the invading water. Esprit de corps is continually a major strength of the big "family" who work at the hospital, being for years an important plus in the effectiveness of the hospital's ministry to our area. I have

Continued on page 193

Esprit De Corps

Continued from page 192

watched it for years and been grateful.

A heavy "dose" of esprit de corps is a main factor now, and will continue to be in the ministry of the hospital.

In a family, every member is important to the whole. So it is in the esprit de corps at the hospital. How beautifully such was demonstrated in the heavy rains of a Tuesday night!

Esprit de corps! May it be multiplied everywhere!

Written by Lloyd E. Batson
Published September 22, 2004

Truth or fraud?

Most of my life I have heard reference to "calling your bluff." Am I, a minister, supposed to know what that means?

In Pickens County, up near Rocky Bottom, there is a premier boys' camp, the McCall Royal Ambassador Camp, in operation by the South Carolina Baptist Convention since 1960. The "McCall" in the name comes from the generous donor of the land, Mr. R. C. McCall of Easley. For 35 years, I spent one week there in the summer serving as camp pastor.

A recent acquisition of recordings of the camp staff of young men singing camp songs and hymns during some of the years I was there set loose a deluge of memories of my involvement with boys who were campers.

While at the camp, in addition to conducting worship services, I always tried to get to know as many boys as I could, and spend time with them, in their daily activities, wanting them to see me as a friend as well as a minister.

At the camp, I also enjoyed fishing in the lake. Except for my before breakfast excursions on the lake, nearly every time I went out in a canoe to fish, and the advanced swimmers got a chance to paddle a canoe or kayak, you can guess what happened. There I would be, out on the lake, fishing hard. Here the boys came, having recognized me.

Exuberantly, the campers in their canoes and kayaks, with their variously skilled paddling, descended upon me and surrounded me. Have you ever been fishing and were bumped on every side by canoes and kayaks? "Caught anything?" "Let me see what you have caught." "Hurry and catch one so I can see it." "I'll just wait here till you catch one." Exasperating? Yes. But, you see, I had worked hard to get them to believe I was their friend, as well as their pastor for the week, and they believed it! It was demanding, yes, the discipline to sit there in the canoe and to smile at the boys who had no idea they were breaking basic rules of fishing behavior. They simply came to see the one who had asked them to be his friend! Besides, I had to remember the lake was there for the boys and not for me.

What I am saying is that one should not pretend to want to be friendly and helpful to people unless he or she means it. One had better not profess to love and care for others unless he or she realizes that the cost of that love may be high in personal inconvenience and effort. A person had better not take a stance of being interested in others unless he or she is willing to carry it out. Somebody will find out if the person means it or is a fraud!

One cannot be caring in word only! Somebody will "call your bluff!"

On the other hand, is there not great joy in having an opportunity to prove the offered friendship, love, and interest is genuine, even if it becomes a demanding test? It is a simplistic observation, I know, but has not the world around us seen many words of caring, expressed interest and love fail under testing? In community stances, political pronouncements, "religious" declarations, many good things can be said and not lived out. Does not the old proverb say it well, that "the proof of the pudding is in the eating thereof?"

Do you think that the boys bumping me while I was fishing unknowingly were calling my bluff?

Would not it be great if all our public stances were exactly what we really mean and are?

Written by Lloyd E. Batson
Published September 29, 2004

Lost at home

If this column sounds like a sermon, I guess it is, but it is one for me, too!

My father-in-law, Dr. C. R. Barrick, a longtime and revered minister in New Mexico, had an older brother who many years ago was a sheriff in the panhandle of Oklahoma. Hiram, the sheriff, gave to Ransom, his brother, a .38 caliber Smith and Wesson revolver that had come into his possession during his "sheriffing." Dr. Barrick always was proud of that revolver.

Dr. Barrick died over 20 years ago. Recently, when I was looking for the date of his death, I found added to my record book that for his memorial service I had conducted the funeral, assisted by my older son, with my younger son playing the piano and my wife playing the organ. Precious and cherished memories!

Not long before Dr. Barrick exited this earth, he gave me his treasured revolver. I disassembled it, cleaned and oiled it, left it in a flat, white box on a shelf in our clothes closet. I decided, at one point, that a disassembled revolver had no proper place in the clothes closet so I put it somewhere for safekeeping. Sometime later, I wanted to show it to somebody and went to the closet to get it. It was not there. Then I remembered I had moved it, but where was another matter. For a long time I searched for that revolver. Effectively, it was lost — at home!

In the process of moving, after retirement, to our present home, I found that revolver and, remembering what had happened previously, I found the perfect place to put it so it would not get lost. You know what I am about to say. It is lost again — at home!

I hope sometime I can find it, but right now it is lost — at home — and I was responsible (by now you are diagnosing what is wrong with me — and you may be right)! I expect that revolver to turn up some day and it will be right where I put it.

The last time I was searching for the revolver I got to thinking about those things, sometimes valuable and treasured things, which get lost right at home. Just about anybody could name some of those that get lost right in his or her own home. Most of them, though, are not physical things, like that revolver.

Among the things that often seem to get lost, right at home, are common courtesy, manners, gentle talk, careful attention to one another's interest, and politeness. How about basic respect for one another? Or patience with the sometimes difficult moods of family members? Or expressed interest in one another? Or ongoing encouragement to family members!

What about expressions of love? Or reasoned and fair discipline? Cooperation with household chores? Or trust in one another?

Can simple joy in home life get lost right at home? Has the "spark" gone from marriage? I think that often the greater tragedy of losing some important things at home is not recognizing they are lost!

Perhaps the "sermon" part of this has to do with issuing a challenge, which I now confess to doing, to recognize what important things have gotten lost right at home, figuring out why they got lost, and, importantly, starting on a renewed search to find them again!

Perhaps for many folk a "treasure hunt" for precious possessions lost at home could be a rewarding endeavor!

Written by Lloyd E. Batson
Published October 6, 2004

Dealing with sorrow

A man, who apparently reads the columns I write, approached me somewhat hesitantly. Instinctively I knew he was carrying a heavy burden of some kind.

Without any preliminary words, he, speaking softly and slowly, said, "You do not know me, but I recognized you from your picture. I have had more sorrow than I know how to handle. If you have had to deal with sorrow in your own life, would you mind telling me how you handled it?"

To him, I, too, without preliminary words, said, "Let's go over here away from people and let me tell you an experience I once had."

What I told him I relate, in essence, here.

It was a most difficult time. The tragic death of a lovely and popular twenty-three year old had left everybody, the family and the host of friends, crushed.

I was not their pastor, but, because of a relationship of many years, I had been asked to share in the memorial service. The church was literally "wall to wall" with grieving folk. At the request of the family, the congregation was to sing "Amazing Grace" just before I was to speak.

From where I was, on the rostrum, I could see all the family and many of the supporting congregation. As we began to sing those great words, I watched the grieving family struggling to be a part of the singing. Suddenly, because of a gushing wellspring of tears, I could not see a word on the page of the hymnal I was holding.

When we finished those wonderfully expressive words of "Amazing Grace," I stepped forward to speak. "I have a confession to make," I began.

I went on to say, "I got where I couldn't see a word on the page, yet I knew I needed to sing. Not being able to see, I had to go by what I knew. And I guess that's what we've all got to do here today. None of us can see any way through this, or answer all the hurting questions that flood us. We just have to go by what we know."

I went on to read words from the Father whose presence was obviously real. Though we, blinded and confused by hurt and grief, could not explain it, we just knew our trouble was bathed by Holy Presence. It is not always what we "understand" that will see us through, but what we have come to "know."

A crisis hardly ever is handled with resources or understandings that come with the crisis. It will be the knowledge stored, the insights gathered, the strengths instilled, the values appreciated, and the beliefs established that will best come to bear when difficult times arise. In the face of the unbelievable and the unexplainable, it will be those things which one already knows that will rise up as towers of strength.

Death, while so natural and normal under so many levels of occurrence, is still a mystifying and shattering experience for those whose love is touched by it. The death of a young person, appearing to be so untimely, stretches the limits of my understanding and acceptance. I have no answer to the "Why?" — no easy one anyhow, that makes much sense. What I do know, however, is that, in the midst of a great hurt which boggles the mind and the spirit, the Father God's presence is real and he has strength and grace to give sufficient for the moment.

I do know, from faith and experience, that the Shepherd God brings his rod and staff to my rescue and deliverance.

I do know that a faith which is pleasant, enjoyable, and refreshing in good times becomes real stuff, made of substance and strength, in bad times.

Continued on page 197

Dealing with sorrow

Continued from page 196

I do know that words of comfort and assurance written in the Holy Book take on a reality that an unbeliever cannot possibly understand.

I do know that a peace, that not all can understand, finally steals into the deepest places of a hurting believer's heart and gives basic stability until the engulfing darkness is frightening no more.

Yes, many times in my life I have to go by what I know and not by what I am able to see.

When I finished my "testimony," we talked about some of the stored up resources that he had upon which he could draw. As he walked away, he said, still softly, "Thanks. Thanks. Thanks."

About twenty feet away he turned and smiled!

Written by Lloyd E. Batson
Published October 20, 2004

How are you feeling today?

One of my favorite places is a nursing home. I know, of course, that, in a nursing home, there may be unpleasant situations and folk with all kinds of difficult problems, but, still, the people in nursing homes are just that, people.

Folk in nursing homes, just like people anywhere else, come in all kinds of dispositions, personalities, peculiarities, happinesses and sadnesses. A constant discovery for me is the pleasure (and, yes, sometimes heartaches and frustrations!) I receive from people around me, no matter where, as I am privileged to be involved with them.

Once, in a nursing home in the community where I was pastor, I approached an elderly lady with the normal, if trite, question, "Well, how do you feel today?"

With deliberation and preciseness, she replied, "I am disappointed to have to tell you I am better."

In the same nursing center, another lady, when asked the same question, told me, "Well, I guess I feel all right today, but I know I am going to feel bad tomorrow."

In a nursing home, I find such reactions delightful, and the chucklings resulting there from refresh me for a long time. It gets sad, though, when this kind of outlook gets established in people, wherever they are, as a way of life. Some folk give me the distinct impression that not only do they not know how to be happy but that they really do not want to be.

I have known people who never seemed to be able to see any good in anybody or anything. It is almost as if they had programmed themselves not to allow any joy to get a foothold in their lives. Bad, for them, seemed to be more attractive than good. Do you suppose that some people really do keep reminding themselves not to let a good word about anybody slip out of their mouths? Or dare let themselves feel good?

Have you met anybody who wants to hear all the gruesome details about an accident, a broken marriage, a neighbor's misdeeds, or the latest salacious rumors? Do you know people (hopefully not yourself!) who appear to have a calling to pass on such revelations, usually with exaggeration and nearly always with judgmental opinion?

I have known some folk who never seem to feel good unless they are feeling bad. Have you met that person who, hearing something good about somebody, chomps at the bit until there is opportunity to inject, "But let me tell you what I know ...?"

Certainly, I know about pain, sorrow, disappointment, anxiety, illness and a thousand and one bad things abounding in the earth! Still, most people who are sour do not have to be sour. Folk with "impoverished happiness," if they are honest and want to, can identify some good things in themselves, in people around them and in their environment. It appears to me that unhappiness, as a way of life, is often by choice, or by default anyway. Perpetual pessimism, sourness, and their kindred attitudes are bad stuff. However, like most habits and addictions, they can be changed, if one really wants to and will work at it.

Well, how ARE you feeling today?

Written by Lloyd E. Batson
Published October 27, 2004

No "Fotching" here

One of the most important buildings in our area is the Pickens County Courthouse. Across the years I have advocated that all citizens, old and young alike, occasionally should visit the courthouse to observe, as a learning experience, a part of our legal system at work.

In the first years I was in Pickens County, beginning in 1956, it seemed that every time I went into the courthouse, and the court was in session, I would see a large man with some distinctive physical problems. He apparently was, at one time anyway, a bootlegger and a chicken fighter who made frequent appearances before the judge.

One of the first stories I heard about that man was that once, when the judge came out and the "interesting" man was presented before him again, he admonished the frequent "customer" that "You better not ever come back before this court again!"

The very next time the judge was back in Pickens there the man was before him again, charged as usual!

Bellowed the judge, "I thought I told you never to come before this court again!"

"But, your Honor," protested the man who had to adjust his eyes as he talked, "I didn't come. The sheriff fotch me."

There are some situations where a person can be made to do what he or she does not want to do, and can be "fotched." I can laugh at the memory of that "fotched" man but I can rejoice in something else I see happening every day somewhere.

All over our area there are amazingly large numbers of people who are not "fotched" but who voluntarily get involved in a great variety of activities helping make other people live better. Hardly a day passes that I do not see someone voluntarily doing something for the welfare of others.

A look, for example, at the organizations and projects represented in the umbrella "United Way," currently enlisting financial support, brings a picture that includes almost countless numbers of people volunteering in the work of the ministering groups and agencies.

It would be interesting, and amazing, if it were possible so to do, to see a compilation of all the efforts by organizations, clubs, groups, and individuals to help in the lives of people in Pickens County, efforts involving volunteers who gladly and faithfully give of themselves for the welfare of others. They are not "fotched" but act on their own will. Perhaps not many people think about it, but, almost certainly, the largest numbers of "volunteers" in action in our county are in the churches. Churches may have staff members as leaders, as many organizations also do, but no church could function without the "volunteers" who become involved in the various organizations and ministries of the church.

I know of one church that is currently trying to get some kind of listing of all the ministering things being done for people outside the church. The list is not nearly complete (and never will be because the very nature of volunteering to do helpful things for others discourages wanting to get credit for it) but it is already astounding what has been identified.

So, whatever the purpose of this column is it includes my personal gratitude for, and to, the many, many people, of all ages, who voluntarily show up, in so many varied ways and places, to do helpful and caring things for others. It also involves my desire to speak, vicariously, a thanksgiving on the part of all the people who are helped by volunteers who care about them!

By the way, have you ever been to the Pickens County Courthouse, voluntarily, to get a feel for what goes on there? I think you should!

Written by Lloyd E. Batson
Published November 3, 2004

November 11, 2004

I was in World War II and in combat in the European Theater against Adolph Hitler's German military forces. I have now for a long, long time been a veteran.

Nov. 11 is Veterans Day! Am I to be honored? For what? Am I to give honor? For what?

When I voluntarily enlisted in 1942 at the age of 18, did I have any concept of someday having a national day when I, and hordes of others like me, would be a part of a nation's honoring veterans with a calendar date and with some ceremonial activity?

When I did what I was convinced I should do, and enlisted to be a part of a war that was ugly, horrible, and deadly beyond comprehension, did it occur to me that, even if I thought I would survive the war, our nation on Nov. 11, 2004, would be honoring not only the World War II veterans but veterans from several other wars following mine? Would I have believed that in 2004 A.D. our nation, and other nations of the world, would still not have figured out how to settle differences without wars?

Veterans Day! Be it a token nod on the part of some, or a genuinely felt expression of gratitude by many for men and women who "put their lives on the line" in war, I am grateful that such a day is structured in our nation's calendar for recognition. For myself, as grateful as I am for the recognition, I did not consider then, nor do I now, that I did any more to earn honor than countless others who gave of themselves in the untold and varied roles of sacrificial effort and support of our nation and to military forces. I believed, at the time I enlisted and throughout my service as a soldier, I was doing what I could do, and should do, in a difficult time. Others, in many differing ways, were doing what they could.

It would be a cumbersome title, and a difficult celebration to carry out, but could there be a place for a "Veterans and Non-Veteran Veterans Day" honoring all sacrificial service for our nation?

There are not many veterans I know that, at the time they were serving, fully understood how they actually fitted into the larger picture of the war. For me, for example, in the 87th Infantry Division, in the artillery of that division, I had no clear picture of where we were fighting at a given moment, or how we were related to other troops in other units in combat, or even how successful were our efforts in terms of the larger war picture. I had to believe, though, that I and the ones I knew were not struggling alone but were a necessary part of a much larger effort to defeat the enemy and somehow to make possible a better world.

In terms of strategic objectives and efforts, I suppose that some veterans were at the time doing what some would consider more important than what some others were doing. I am aware that some heroic efforts were more spectacular than that of ordinary "G.I. Joe" assignments and activities that rarely got spotlighted. On Veterans Day we may hear stories of the truly brave and heroic military exploits many performed and were rightly honored for them. Believe you me, I am grateful for such people and I honor them!

The fact is, though, that in war, as it is in most worthwhile things, it takes a lot of folk carrying out their responsibilities, in the spotlight or behind the scenes, to get important things done.

The celebration of Veterans Day is an opportunity for a grateful nation and its citizenry to feel deeply an appreciation for all those who have, at a particular time, in the limelight or out of it, put their lives in jeopardy in war with the belief they were making a

Continued on page 201

November 11, 2004

Continued from page 200

contribution to a greater cause than may have been evident at every moment of struggle. Veterans Day uses Nov. 11, the day that "the war to end all wars" — World War I — ended, as an annual date to remember and give thanks for all veterans from all wars.

The end of wars did not come on Nov. 11, 1918, and such is not in sight now, nor likely ever will be, but there are many, many who have put their lives on the line, and many died, in an attempt to make it so.

Let us make Veterans Day, this Nov. 11, a genuine expression of gratitude and honor!

Here is a personal prayer of mine, "I thank you, God, for all veterans who have served their nation honorably and courageously, but please, God, help our nation and the nations of the world to find a way to keep from having to make so many other veterans."

Written by Lloyd E. Batson
Published November 10, 2004

A contest where everybody loses

I still can hardly believe it happened. But it did! I remember it nearly every time I pass a certain spot on a street leaving Greenville. It happened at a traffic light, while the red light stayed on for what seemed an interminably long time.

We stopped at the same time, alongside each other. He, a young man, in a shiny new sports car, I in my faithful old chariot. His windows were down, mine partly so. His radio was going at what I thought surely must be full blast, getting into my car with the jumping sounds of rock and roll, or whatever kind it was besides loud. My radio was turned to the soothing sounds of a favorite "good music" station. I looked at him, rather pleasantly, I thought, and reached to turn up my radio.

Well, I was wrong about his radio being at full blast, for he looked at me and reached to turn up his sound.

Ouch! Again, I looked at him and turned up my station louder than I think it wanted to be. Want to guess the next step? He looked at me, laughed, reached and really let me have it! I smiled, I hope, and turned my "soothing" music to full blast (admittedly only a fraction of his multi-powered, multi-speakered system).

The light changed, and I was glad. I was out of ammunition. I doubt that he was. At first, I was a bit annoyed, but then I guess I enjoyed the whole rather childish episode. Here we were, with two distinct and clashing musical preferences. Each was interfering with the other's preference. He had a right to his taste and I to mine, but we were not very tolerant of one other (does it reveal something to say that I apparently did feel he had no right to impose his loud "noise" on my good music?).

In retrospect, I have had many laughs about the whole episode. However, do you not think that both he and I could have resolved that little episode better than we did? For one thing, he and I both could have closed the car windows and that would have let the differences be less noticeable. He and I both, out of consideration for each other, could have turned down the volume instead of getting into that ridiculous contest. If he and I had been sufficiently aware of, and sensitive about it, the "hair raising" we were causing on the other, we could have done the unthinkable but easy thing of turning off the radio, or at least turned it down, while we were alongside one another.

We could have done several things to minimize the confrontation, but we did not. Instead, insisting on each other's right, we made matters worse. Nobody "won" (though his radio was much louder than I could get mine!). Perhaps, though, each of us felt a bit "self-righteous" about not yielding to the other.

I have a feeling, if I had space, that this ridiculous little encounter could be shown to speak to many human relationships.

How can young people, with all their enthusiasm, differing ideas, and life-styles, and older, more settled, more traditional folk get along? Could not somehow both extremes work together, perhaps each giving a bit, and find strengths of both for the good of all rather than letting the perceived "wrongs" and differences of the other alienate?

In the multiple confrontations between people on many levels, is tolerance from all, properly understood and acted upon, not still a virtue? Is sensitivity, in love and respect, to others not still desirable? Is not it possible that people of varying understandings and interpretations can find a higher relationship of some kind and not only get along but benefit from one another?

In so many of the confrontations that occur, are not there some things we can do to get along and benefit from one another rather than keep trying to "blast" one another (and do so even if we think we are right)?

I am not sure many victories are finally won by taking the "blasting" route!

Written by Lloyd E. Batson
Published November 17, 2004

An honest Thanksgiving

Thanksgiving is a word. It is a national holiday. It is a celebration related to the earliest days of American history. It is a family gathering time. It is a day to eat turkey. It is a public activity. It is a personal experience. It is religious. It is secular, in that gratitude can be in the mind and heart of anybody, whether one is religious or not. It is many things.

During one Thanksgiving season, my family was about to eat breakfast. My four-year-old son expressed some disapproval of the food before him. It was his turn to say the blessing. As he prayed, he thanked God for many things, including family members, refrigerators, spoons and trees. When he finished, my older son said to his brother, "You didn't thank God for the food."

"I didn't want to," was the quick reply.

Be it to his credit my younger son was honest. It is not right to be hypocritical about things one does not believe. Prayer about anything should be completely honest. Heaven knows our pretensions or pretenses! Expressions about any matter should not be a mouthing of things we think we are expected to say. Goodness knows there is too much of that going on, in political life, in leadership positions, in religious expressions, and you name it!

Thanksgiving! While it is many things, with many wonderful experiences related to it, it still is what the first Thanksgiving was for, a time and an experience for thanking God for his blessings.

For one to thank God when he or she is not thankful is not right. One should be honest enough not to be hypocritical. There is, however, something that everyone could do frequently. The same honesty of not being hypocritical should cause a person to examine closely the "thanking process."

It is possible that, in the "non-thankful" position, the powers of observation are getting dull, or sensitivity has soured, or, worse, self-centeredness has increased. While one should not manufacture thanksgiving to God, he or she probably could discover many fresh reasons which should prompt thanksgiving. It might be that the very things for which we are not thankful should be looked at again. Perhaps we did not see them rightly the first time. Perhaps preconceived notions have blinded the eyes of appreciation.

This Thanksgiving there are many things existing and happening that I, honestly, cannot be thankful for. It would be hypocritical for me to pretend to be, but honestly, though, Thanksgiving is a time for me to be truly thankful for so many blessings I have received, and they are indeed many.

Thanksgiving is a great time for me, and for all of us, in the spirit of the earliest Thanksgiving, to identify and to express thanksgiving, honestly, for many, many experiences, relationships, material and spiritual blessings, and to do it to God.

Thanksgiving, 2004! Could it be, honestly, a day of thanksgiving?

Written by Lloyd E. Batson
Published November 24, 2004

Re-pearling pearls

It is still a laughing matter at our house.

Years ago my wife walked into the room where I was intensely involved in the paper I was reading. She spoke to me, asking a question. What she asked made me respond with, "Say that again." I wanted to be sure I had heard what I thought I heard. Before she replied, I looked up. She was holding in her hand a string of discolored beads. Said she again, "Do you know where I can get these re-pearled?"

"What are they? Where did you get those things?" I queried.

"This is the pearl necklace you gave me when we married. They need to be re-pearled," she informed me.

I looked at them, a sad looking pearl necklace, that string was! The beads were indeed peeling and in varying shades of discoloration and the clasps had turned green. Worse than anything, I guess, was that I had forgotten I had given her a string of pearls as a wedding gift.

When we married, in 1950, in Albuquerque, N. M., I was a seminary student in Louisville, Ky., with very limited income. Buying the engagement ring and the wedding band had severely challenged my resources. I had shopped around in downtown Louisville for a suitable wedding gift and had found a beautiful, affordable string of pearls. I was proud of my wedding gift to her.

My, that string of pearls was pretty when I bought them and my new bride was proud of them. How gorgeous she looked wearing them when we were married!

After many years, I discovered why they were affordable! I had been had by some shyster! I had bought those beautiful "pearls" in good faith, as a gift of love, and that was the way they were received. I guess, after all, that was what really mattered.

While one cannot get a pearl that is not a pearl made into a pearl, I do think that most people would do well to look at what things in their lives, and for married folk in their marriage, need "re-pearling."

If "re-pearling" means renewing or making as good as new, then there probably are many things that could benefit from "re-pearling." So big, and so fundamental, a matter as commitment, not only to the person but also to marriage, may need renewing.

What about the custom in courting and early marriage days of planning pleasant little surprises for one another? Or the careful attention to grooming to make oneself as attractive as possible? What about the excitement of living and sharing together? And a hundred and one other things. Any "re-pearling" needed?

How about the "re-pearling" of values, standards of morality and religious faith, of the sense of personal worth and well-being, of the quality of community involvement and assistance to the less fortunate people in abundance around us? The need for "re-pearling" may be unlimited!

There is not much I can do about that original string of "pearls" which need re-pearling, but I surely can try a bit harder to let my wife know I love her. I can do my own "re-pearling" of many things that could brighten every day, even common ordinary days with her and with people and events in general

By the way, a few years ago I did strain my budget about as much, relatively, as I did 54 years ago, and bought my lady a real pearl necklace. A great investment!

Honest now, what do you need to get re-pearled?

Written by Lloyd E. Batson
Published December 1, 2004

A penny post card

Every time I have to make the laborious effort to put something my wife wants up into the attic, or out in the space above the garage, something she thinks she cannot do without and must keep, I tell her the same thing. "You know what you are doing, don't you? You are putting away stuff so our boys can have a yard sale when we die," I say, as pleasantly as I can manage.

Sometimes my lady reminds me I have a lot of old stuff stuck around the house, too. The difference, though, as I see it, is that mine are "treasures."

Recently I came across one of those treasures, an unused penny post card I have. I held it in my hand a long time, remembering and reminiscing.

A penny post card was widely used in the Great Depression days of the 1930s. The "penny post card" now costs 23 or 24 cents, I think. I remembered seeing people, my grandmother included, write long "letters," usually in pencil, on the back of a penny post card, she never used an envelope which cost two cents to mail. The post office people and the mail carrier often read the post cards, thus becoming well-informed about families' affairs.

A card with an affixed one-cent stamp, usually simply called a "post card"! Once again, I took a nostalgic trip to years long gone, remembering people, events and relationships from the era of the one cent card, it being a means of communication between family members and friends, and even a means of doing business.

A penny post card!

For a moment I guess I also wished things did not cost so much now. I do, however, sometimes point out to folk, complaining about the high cost of things now, that as late as 1940 a loaf of bread, if you could afford to buy one, cost 10 cents in the store, and a gallon of gas cost 19.9 cents. In the sawmill of the village where I lived, an unskilled laborer made 10 cents an hour, meaning he worked one hour for a loaf of bread and two hours for a gallon of gas! Good old days?

From that penny post card, I went on a pilgrimage to review many things as I used to know them. Shortly I stopped that. Certainly one can benefit from reviewing the past, but it is the present that one has to live in, and with which to come to grips.

Times have changed, and will continue to change. Living conditions rapidly change. Public morals are in flux. Governmental confusions continue to cause anxiety. Is it possible to find some "constants" in the midst of escalating changes? Yes! And it is important so to do.

Nostalgic longing for things as they used to be is generally a waste of time.

My "treasures" from the past must not obscure my responsibility and opportunity to identify and draw pleasure and strength from my "treasures" in the present.

As I held that penny post card in my hand, reminiscing, I moved to a survey of the things of value in my life now. Wow! I was overwhelmed! Yes, of course, I wished that some things were like they used to be, but there are so many things that are "treasures," strengths, and blessings in the now!

Looking at a penny post card was good for me. I thanked God for my memories and blessings of the past, but I moved to thanking God for my many "treasures" of the moment.

I gazed at that penny post card from the past, appreciating that my life now has a lot of good in it! It is up to me to use the present well.

Written by Lloyd E. Batson
Published December 8, 2004

A treasured testament

While I have preached in hundreds of churches, for a great variety of occasions, before and since my ordination in 1947 as a minister, I was pastor in only three churches. In the last of the three, I served as pastor for thirty-three years.

Recently a person I was with was reminiscing about some of the unusual things that happened during the 33 years I was his pastor. Chuckling, he recalled, that for one entire year, in the church service every Sunday morning, Sunday evening, and Wednesday night, I held in my hands a different one of my Bibles, read and preached or taught from it. I also told the circumstances of my acquiring the particular Bible or portion of the Bible I was using.

I have no count of the total number of Bibles I have, in English, Greek, Hebrew and various languages of the world (Bibles in various languages have been given me by missionaries and friends. I cannot read most of the foreign languages). I regularly read and profit from many translations, versions, and paraphrases of the Bible.

The message from God is the same in any Bible, no matter what the language. If, however, I should attempt to identity the one Bible I have that I treasure most of all, it likely would be the New Testament my Sunday School teacher gave me when I left Alcolu, my home village, to go away, in 1941, to college.

It was that Testament which I carried on my person all through my military services in World War II, including combat in Europe. The Testament was a part of me, one that I read everyday, often by flickering candlelight. Because of its now fragile condition, I keep it in a small zippered plastic bag, only occasionally taking it out to hold and to read again from it.

The words from God in that New Testament are, of course, what is most important. Along the way, though, I had entered in abbreviated form on the blank pages in the front and back a rough itinerary of our military movements and combat areas.

The full Bible that I had taken overseas, perhaps the finest edition in leather and paper I have ever had, I had to leave in a duffel bag at the beginning of combat. The bag was stored somewhere, I know not where, and retrieved, remarkably, at the end of the War from somewhere in France. That Bible, costing me, in 1942, six dollars and thirty-three cents, I ordered from a catalogue and paid for from wages of 15 cents per hour. I still have that Bible on my shelf.

The stories related to the ministry of that New Testament, not only to me but also to the ones with whom I shared its contents, are many. I intend to write some of them among the stories I am writing for my grandchildren. I will include the story about my first sergeant, a professed agnostic, who, when I was filling in for the chaplain, as I sometimes did, always came to hear me read from my Testament. He said it was not because he believed it, but because he believed in me and knew I believed what I read. Somehow, I feel that the word of the Testament did find a way into that crusty old sergeant's heart.

It is not important how much a Bible costs, what the binding and paper are like, or what language in which it is written. What is important is that it be read and received as a word from beyond one's self. I do not profess to be a great student of the Bible, or to understand all it says, even if I do often study the New Testament from the Greek, the original language of the New Testament, and sometimes the Old Testament from Hebrew, the original language in which it was written. I do believe that God has something to say in his book, the Bible, for every person, no matter what his or her situation, that can be helpful and even life changing.

Yes, I have many Bibles, some in storage and perhaps as many as two hundred on my several shelves. I treasure every one of them. But, a book, even a Bible, on a shelf does not communicate its worth unless it is read.

World War II New Testament, I treasure you for what it meant to me in specific and difficult times, but I still need your words!

Binding and paper may deteriorate but words from God never do!

Written by Lloyd E. Batson
Published December 15, 2004

Where is God? The Christmas answer

I had been on a deer hunt with him. He was not yet strong enough to do much walking in the woods, so he mostly sat under a tree, reading and listening to the sounds of the hunt.

That night, in the farmhouse where we were spending the night, after a great meal and sitting by a roaring fire, I listened as this one of the ablest ministers I have ever known talked. A man of intelligence, with a rare gift of keen perception and a quick wit, he shared some of his insights on a variety of difficult matters.

Breaking away from the subject under discussion, that outstanding preacher of many years began to tell something obviously deeply felt by him. He recounted the moment not long before when he was suddenly stricken and it was discovered that the main artery to his heart was almost totally closed. Emergency surgery would have to be early in the morning. If the artery totally closed before morning then that would be the end.

He could not sleep. He prayed. He agonized. He desperately needed assurance. He kept crying in his soul, "God, where are you?" Over and over he repeated Scriptures, like the Twenty-third Psalm. Songs and hymns from his childhood kept coming to him and in desperation he sang them over and over. "God, where are you?" every part of him wanted to know.

About 4 a.m., he said, something strange and wonderful happened. A consummate peace came over him. Every anxiety quieted and disappeared. Peace! He no longer needed to cry, "God, where are you?" He no long needed assurance. Peace! God was with him.

In three days we will celebrate Christmas. Whatever else Christmas is, it answers the desperate cry, "God, where are you?" That was the meaning of the first Christmas. The very name Immanuel featured in Christmas carols means "God with us." The heavenly host declared to the shepherds,"... on earth peace...!" John wrote, "And the word became flesh and dwelt among us ...."

"God, where are you?" How many times and in how many ways that has been the plaintive cry of us all! Great need and knifing hurt has a way of accentuating the cry. God is not one to stand aloof from his people. He wants every child of his not only to want his presence but also to discover, in terms understandable and intensely meaningful for whatever are the needs, the "with us" ness of God. When, easily or with great difficulty, that awareness comes, there is peace!

Christmas points to a little baby, a long time ago, but that little baby says forever that not a single person who knows who the baby is need ever wonder again where God is. Whoever has ever discovered that baby, though the burden of hurt and need and sin may for a moment have obscured his brightness, may hear again, often through hymns, songs, and Scriptures, the declaration of who he is and experience afresh the presence of a God who is not out yonder somewhere but here!

The "here" ness of God! That is peace, Christmas peace!

That is Christmas!

Written by Lloyd E. Batson
Published December 22, 2004

Thank you, and a Happy New Year

It started several years ago with an occasional article about some current happening or one for some special project the paper was working on. Then it drifted into a regular weekly column for *The Easley Progress*.

While I am not a professional writer, I have been given the privilege of visiting with the people of our area through the freedom given me by *The Easley Progress* to express whatever was on my mind at the time a column was due.

What pleasure has come to me through the many new friends I have met as an outcome of my written observations! How appreciated have been the encouraging responses made to me about what various writings seemed to have meant to individuals! Frankly, I have been surprised at how many people apparently have read my written talking.

Because of several projects I need to complete before my earthly journey is finished (I am now in the eighty-first year of my journey!), this column will be the last of my regular ones.

One of my uncompleted projects underway for some time is the writing of stories for my grandchildren. These are not autobiographical, as such, but they are true stories about people, experiences, events and relationships that have played important roles in my life. They are not in any chronological order. They are anecdotal stories, each separately entitled, going back as far as my earliest memories. They are stories I hope will reflect to my grandchildren and their children and grandchildren the good life I have been privileged to enjoy.

As this year comes to a close, and the regular appearance of this weekly column with it, I want to thank *The Easley Progress* and the people of the area who are readers of the paper for the gracious reception given me.

The year 2005 AD is at hand. I wish for all of you a wonderful year in your own journey.

It will mean much to me if some of you will continue to speak to me once in a while!

Because of its personal meaning to me, in letters I write to people I often conclude with the same benediction. I use it here, now, for all who have been readers of my newspaper "letters."

May Holy Presence bless and keep you!

Thank you, friends!

Written by Lloyd E. Batson
Published December 29, 2004